The Voices of Hockey

The Voices of Hockey

Broadcasters Reflect on the Fastest Game on Earth

Kirk McKnight

ROWMAN & LITTLEFIELD
Lanham • Boulder • New York • London

Published by Rowman & Littlefield
A wholly owned subsidiary of The Rowman & Littlefield Publishing Group, Inc.
4501 Forbes Boulevard, Suite 200, Lanham, Maryland 20706
www.rowman.com

Unit A, Whitacre Mews, 26-34 Stannary Street, London SE11 4AB

Distributred by NATIONAL BOOK NETWORK

British Library Cataloguing in Publication Information Available

Library of Congress Cataloging-in-Publication Data

Names: McKnight, Kirk.
Title: The voices of hockey : broadcasters reflect on the fastest game on earth / Kirk
McKnight.
Description: Lanham : ROWMAN & LITTLEFIELD, [2016] | Includes bibliographical
references and index.
Identifiers: LCCN 2016011744 (print) | LCCN 2016031007 (ebook) | ISBN
9781442262805 (cloth : alk. paper) | ISBN 9781538107560 (pbk. : alk. paper) | ISBN
9781442262812 (electronic)
Subjects: LCSH: Hockey—History. | Hockey teams—History. | Sportscasters. | Radio
broadcasting of sports—History. | Television broadcasting of sports—History.
Classification: LCC GV846.5 .M44 2016 (print) | LCC GV846.5 (ebook) | DDC
796.62—dc23
LC record available at https://lccn.loc.gov/2016011744

Printed in the United States of America

To my lovely little daughter Adaira, who let me take her to her first sporting event ever, a hockey game. She couldn't tell you the final score, but, to tell the truth, neither could I. As long as she's cheering—even if my team is the one on the losing side—I'm cheering, too.

Whether it's hockey, basketball, or baseball, there's a major difference if you're doing radio or television, particularly in hockey. Doing play by play on radio, in effect, you are the game. That probably holds true for all sports. It's very descriptive. It's nonstop. The terminology is important in hockey as to where the puck is and to just paint the picture. In television, obviously, you see it and there's time to breathe a little bit. Hockey is just nonstop on radio. It's more difficult on radio for the analyst to get in. It has to be a quick in and out of the commercial break. On television, I feel play by play is a little more pulled back. The analyst has a little more time to get it in, but they still have to be very careful because things happen so "bang bang." It's a completely different venue when you're doing radio and TV.

—Marv Albert, former New York Rangers
radio play-by-play broadcaster

I say this very often. I am extremely honored to be a part of the hockey broadcasting fraternity. One of the biggest thrills I have is to be able to do every game and to be able to visit and talk with my fellow broadcasters. There are young ones and there are old ones, but I especially get a thrill out of talking with guys who have been around for a long time. Not only the Bob Coles, but also the Rick Jeannerets in Buffalo, the Mike Langes in Pittsburgh, the Kenny Alberts of the Rangers, the L.A. Kings guys out there, and the list goes on and on and on. Mike Emrick is such a class act. It's really something to be able to be around him for a couple of games a year. We run into one another and are able to soak in some of the knowledge and the experiences we've had. That's what really motivates me and makes me so proud to be a part of this fraternity.

—Randy Moller, Florida Panthers
radio play-by-play broadcaster

Contents

Foreword

Breaking the Ice . . . of Fandom

I was only a year and a half old when Herb Brooks coached the U.S. Men's Hockey Team to their victory over the seemingly invincible Russian team in Lake Placid during the 1980 Winter Olympics. Being a resident of Las Vegas practically my entire life, I'm not sure the game and Al Michaels's call were even on the TV inside my house. The McKnight family, growing up, was "baseball first," and that included a six-year-old Kirk. At about the age of 10, what I will refer to throughout this book as "arguably the biggest trade in sports history" took place. Wayne Gretzky, the biggest star the game of hockey had ever seen up to that point (and perhaps ever), was packing his bags for Southern California to play for the Los Angeles Kings. Still, even in 1988, hockey was a distant third or fourth to baseball, football, and college basketball. As a Las Vegan in the late 1980s and early 1990s, there was nothing going on in the sports world outside of UNLV men's basketball. Larry Johnson, Stacey Augmon, Greg Anthony, George Ackles, and Anderson Hunt—four of whom would be drafted by the NBA a year later—were dominating the hardwood floor at the Thomas & Mack Center, all the way to a national championship in 1990. In the meantime, Gretzky's former team was winning their fifth Stanley Cup championship title in seven years in Edmonton, but who knew in "Sin City"?

A couple of years later, I started taking a liking to the game of hockey. Wayne Gretzky and "Super" Mario Lemieux, arguably the two most exciting players the sport has ever seen, were exhibiting their craft on opposite sides of the country, Gretzky in the West and Lemieux in the East. I've been a Pittsburgh Steelers fan since Bill Cowher became their coach, and, following the Steelers, I couldn't help but notice the Pittsburgh teams with their black and gold color schemes. My becoming a fan of hockey just so happened to coincide with the discovery of Hodgkin's disease inside Lemieux. When Mario came back to the game after his treatments, I, and everyone else watching, was amazed by his resilience; I couldn't help but cheer him on. There's no question my two favorite players to watch were the two best ones on the ice. How could you not enjoy watching such prolific goal scoring between these two Canadian-born players? Living in the West, I couldn't get Penguin broadcasts like I could for the Kings, so anything related to Lemieux was reserved for the nightly edition of ESPN's *SportsCenter*. Gretzky, on the other hand, I could watch on Fox Sports, and, believe me, I watched any game I could. Being a baseball fanatic, the transition to hockey was allowable, because the seasons oppose one another. While baseball's offseason was taking place, I was watching Lemieux and Gretzky, and, while those two were on their "summer leave," I would go back to Frank Thomas, Cecil Fielder, and MLB.

Speaking of "America's pastime," the year before MLB decided to leave its millions of fans high and dry, and forego the last six weeks of the regular season—as well as the postseason—Las Vegas was introduced to the minor-league world of hockey. The Las Vegas Thunder were the biggest thing to hit the city since Johnson, Augmon, and Anthony had raised a championship banner into the rafters at the Thomas & Mack Center. I was in the arena on opening night for the Las Vegas Thunder, watching live hockey and taking in the cool breaths of air, which I was not accustomed to after attending UNLV basketball games for all those years. There really is something about going to see a hockey game live. Whether it be the IHL, ECHL, WHA, AHL, EHL, or NHL, the feel of a professional hockey game is unimitated—the acoustics produced by the glass boards, creating that puck "right on the tape" sound that precedes a 110-mile-an-hour slap shot, the chill of the arena making you feel like you're walking past a five-acre dairy section in the supermarket, and, let us not forget, the one thing that is to be expected in a hockey contest: fighting.

I had seen scraps on TV and the occasional "spin cycle" fight in some of the first Thunder games I went to watch during the team's inaugural year, but I will never forget the first all-out line brawl I witnessed live with (who else but) my mother during the team's second year in Vegas. Thunder goalie Clint Malarchuk, whom I would learn had his own throat cut by a skate playing in the NHL, was our guy in the crease, and boy was he tough. The fight had already broken out on the other end of the ice, but Houston Aero goaltender Troy Gamble was getting into it with one of our players. It was in this moment that I learned of another hockey "no-no." Malarchuk, who was on the side of the rink just below our seats, skated the length of the ice to a rousing cheer from the Thomas & Mack Center crowd and cleaned Gamble's clock in his own team's zone. My mom wasn't as entertained as I was, but this was what hockey meant back then. It wasn't about stats. In fact, it wasn't in your best interest to watch a minor-league hockey game if you were skittish about blood and violence, because there was going to be a scrap, if not a brawl, before the night was over. If you were a player, what else were you going to do? The NHL already had its Gretzkys, Lemieuxs, Selännes, Bures, and Fedorovs. Who was going to compete with that?

Unfortunately (depending on which side of the check your signature fell on), fighting and line brawls have become heavily regulated and all but abolished in the NHL. Sure, the occasional fight breaks out and the participants quickly exit the ice and the game, but this doesn't happen nearly as often as it once had. There are far fewer "gruesome" modern-day stories like those to which you're about to become privy in this book, but the game hasn't lost its appeal. The Gretzkys, Lemieuxs, and Fedorovs have hung up their skates, but their superstar torches have been passed to the next generation of offensive juggernauts. Lemieux's went to current Pittsburgh Penguin team captain Sidney Crosby and Fedorov's to fellow Russian (and my and my daughter's favorite player) Pavel Datsyuk in Detroit, and later, in Washington, to another Russian teammate, Alexander Ovechkin. Whether you prefer yesterday's hockey to today's—or vice versa—this book addresses both eras from perhaps the only perspective truly capable of doing so, that of the broadcasters.

With larynxes better reserved for the lead role in a Gilbert and Sullivan musical, today's NHL broadcasters capture the "fastest game on Earth" in arguably the most difficult capacity in the world of major sports. With no shot clock or TV timeouts, and the pause for station identification being their only shot at a swig of water, the NHL's play-by-play broadcasters, both on TV and radio, give fans a guide to the action that no one else could possibly provide for more than two and a half hours practically every other night for six to eight months of the year. Featuring 42 TV/radio broadcasters, including 10 Hall of Famers, *The Voices of Hockey: Broadcasters Reflect on the Fastest Game on Earth* brings to you the bloodied ice surfaces, five overtime marathons, the raising of the Stanley Cup, and record-setting individual performances of yesterday and today in the words of those who have called the game for decades. From "Jiggs" McDonald to "Doc" Emrick, it is my hope that the experiences of those who have been the voices of hockey will rejuvenate—if not bring out of its state of dormancy—your love for the game that, in my opinion, is the most exciting the world of sports has to offer. As Wayne (Campbell, not Gretzky) so famously puts it, "Game on!"

Introduction

The Other *Miracle on Ice*

$\mathcal{S}$omewhere between Minnesotan Herb Brooks leading the U.S. Men's Hockey Team to victory in the semifinal round over Russia in Lake Placid in the Winter Olympics and Wayne Gretzky coming to the Los Angeles Kings in arguably the biggest trade in sports history, one of the greatest NHL dynasties of all time budded and blossomed, winning four of their five Stanley Cup titles in a space of five seasons. The Edmonton Oilers, led by the greatest scorer in history, Wayne Gretzky, went from imported WHA franchise to NHL dynasty in less than nine years. Although the New York Islanders were sporting their own dynasty at the time, thanks to players like Bill Smith, Mike Bossy, Bryan Trottier, and team-builder Al Arbour, the Oilers were piecing together a team that would break NHL offensive records left and right.

Led by a captain who would win a record eight straight Hart Memorial trophies, the Oilers hit a stumbling block early in their building process against a team who would claim their beloved superstar by decade's end. The biggest blow to this maturing yet overconfident team from Alberta took place on April 10, 1982, in game three of the NHL's Division Semifinals at the Los Angeles Forum—some 1,750 miles south of their home—in what is commonly known in reminiscent hockey circles as the "Miracle on Manchester." Los Angeles Kings Hall of Fame TV play-by-play broadcaster Bob Miller discusses, in his own words, the small detour Edmonton would have to take through southern California before claiming their dynasty status:

> The most exciting game I ever did at the Forum was called the "Miracle on Manchester," because Manchester Avenue ran past the Forum. It was a playoff game against the Edmonton Oilers in April of 1982, when the Oilers had Gretzky, Mark Messier, Grant Fuhr, Glenn Anderson, Paul Coffey, and all those great players. They finished so far ahead of the Kings

in the regular season and then got into a best-of-five playoff round against them. The Kings opened in Edmonton with two games and split those games. Everybody likes to say, "Playoff hockey is so tight and so defensive minded." Well, the first game ended 10–8 in favor of the Kings. Here's a playoff game and it's 10–8. Then the Oilers won the next game to even the series. It came back to Los Angeles and most everybody figured there's no way the Kings are going to beat the Oilers. In game three in Los Angeles, the Oilers led 5–0 at the end of two periods. It was so disappointing because everybody was so excited about the Kings splitting up in Edmonton and anxious to see them back at the Forum. It was so disappointing, the owner, Jerry Buss, left the game.

With goals by the Oilers' Mark Messier, Lee Fogolin, and Risto Siltanen, and two by the "Great One," Wayne Gretzky, the probability of Edmonton going into game four with a commanding 2–1 series lead would have best been displayed by a percentage sign at the end of the "99" on Gretzky's back; however, with 20 minutes remaining in the game, the Kings began their 22 minutes and 35 seconds march into the record books, starting with goals by Jay Wells and Doug Smith.

Not witness to this improbable comeback was team owner Jerry Buss. Miller adds,

> The story goes he was in a limousine headed to Palm Springs in the third period. The Kings started to score goals and the chauffeur turned around and asked, "Should we go back?" Jerry said, "No. The farther we go, the better they seem to play, so keep going." He missed what is still the greatest single-game comeback in NHL playoff history. The Kings got five goals in the third period, the final one to tie the game with five seconds remaining. Then it went into overtime, and the Kings won in overtime to take the lead in the series. They won the game, 6–5.

With the "Miracle on Manchester" having transpired, the only true fairy-tale ending to this story would be a series victory, and the Kings still needed one more win to accomplish that. Miller continues,

> The next night, the Oilers won, and so it was tied 2–2 with one game left. That game was in Edmonton. After game four in the Forum—and this very rarely happens—both teams flew on the same charter plane back to Edmonton. They couldn't find another plane to charter, so they both got on the same plane and had to get special waivers from the insurance companies. The Oilers got on first and sat in the back. I was told the referees sat in between the two teams, and the Kings sat in front. We didn't leave Los Angeles until it was about one in the morning in Edmonton, and we didn't land there until about 4:30 a.m., with the deciding game to be played

that night. The Kings got to the hotel at 5:30 in the morning, and there was a cleaning lady vacuuming in the hotel lobby. She was shaking her fists at the Kings players, saying, "You didn't treat my boys very well in Los Angeles." Mark Hardy, a defenseman for the Kings, said, "Lady, it's 5:30 in the morning. Go home and get some sleep." The Kings, that night, in the deciding game in Edmonton, won the game 7–4, to eliminate the Oilers, who had such a spectacular team. That was the most memorable game and probably one of the most memorable series that I ever did at the Forum.

Although the Kings would beat them once more in the postseason in 1989—this time with Gretzky on the other side of the face-off circle—the Oilers, amid their five Stanley Cup titles between 1984 and 1990, would exact their revenge on Los Angeles during the 1985, 1987, and 1990 playoff seasons, sweeping two of three series. While Los Angeles wouldn't win their own Stanley Cup title for another three decades, no other team in NHL history has been able to lay claim to such an insurmountable comeback in a postseason game, and, thanks to the fiercely competitive and more evenly matched nature of the game, it's highly unlikely one ever will.

Anaheim Ducks

$\mathscr{It}$'s difficult to tell whether Walt Disney, when he envisioned a recreational place where parents could take their children, foresaw—40 years down the road—a hockey rink, bloodied knuckles, and bruised faces moving in next door and bearing his company name. In 1993, thanks to the prior year's success of its film *The Mighty Ducks*, the Disney corporation tried its hand at professional team ownership, and the Mighty Ducks of Anaheim would become the NHL's 26th team, giving the Los Angeles Kings the neighbor they had been waiting for since 1967. On October 7, 1993, it didn't take long for the fans inside (then-named) Arrowhead Pond to realize whose signature was on the company checks, as an ice skating Lumière from Disney's *Beauty and the Beast* kicked off the pregame festivities with a Mighty Duck-specific rendition of "Be Our Guest." The "Beast" was apparently suiting up in the opposing locker room, as the Detroit Red Wings would trounce their hosts, 7–2, in front of a sold-out crowd. The results on the scoreboard on opening night would prove to be the low point of the season, as the team would win an impressive 19 road games, the most ever by an NHL expansion team. While their eventual 33 regular-season wins wouldn't suffice for playoff qualification, the Mighty Ducks of Anaheim had established their NHL presence in Southern California.

FROM DUCKLINGS TO DRAKES

After their inaugural year, the Ducks would prove to be not so "mighty" in the next eight seasons, qualifying for the playoffs only twice and making it past the first round just once. The shakeup was as bad behind the bench as it was in the team seamstress' office, as Anaheim would burn through five coaches during that time and have just as many players brandish the letter "C" on their chest. One of these captains, Paul Kariya proved to be an offensive machine, scoring 108 points in just his second year and adding 10 game-winning goals in his third. With Winnipeg import and Calder Trophy winner Teemu Selänne completing the tandem, Kariya and his new teammate would lead the Ducks to a second-place finish in the division and first playoff series win against the Phoenix Coyotes before being swept by eventual cup winner Detroit.

After the 1996–1997 season, the "high-flying" Ducks would quickly be grounded, as the team would finish higher than fifth in their division only once in the next five seasons. Making matters worse, the top brass traded Selänne to the San Jose Sharks in the middle of an abysmal 2000–2001 season. Despite losing Selänne, the Ducks would make an impressive run late the next year but miss the playoffs; however, there was improvement and the Ducks would once again gain their "might" in what would become the team's most successful season to date.

2002–2003: JEAN-SÉBASTIEN GIGUÈRE. ENOUGH SAID.

With Mike Babcock behind the bench as the new head coach, the Ducks added experience in 2002, signing Adam Oates and Petr Sýkora in the offseason and Sandis Ozolinsh at midseason. Throwing imports Steve Thomas and Rob Niedermayer into the mix, Anaheim would finish second in their division and, after a three-year absence, return to the playoffs to face the defending Stanley Cup champion Detroit Red Wings.

Despite the frantic atmosphere inside the office of the team's general manager, Bryan Murray, during the previous 10 months, it would be an earlier import who would turn the Western Conference on its head during the Ducks' 2002–2003 playoff run. Facing a defending Stanley Cup champion to open a playoff run is one thing, but doing so against a dynasty is another. Future Hall of Famers Sergei Fedorov, Brett Hull, Brendan Shanahan, Nicklas Lidström, Igor Larionov, Chris Chelios, and Luc Robitaille would prove to have a lot of fuel left in their tanks against the Mighty Ducks of Anaheim, but it would be for naught once across the blue line and into goaltender Jean-Sébastien Giguère's zone.

In the series opener, Giguère faced an overwhelming 64 shots, allowing only one past, and Paul Kariya's goal in overtime left the defending champs stymied, a feeling the Ducks would not allow them time to get over. Anaheim radio play-by-play broadcaster Steve Carroll describes Giguère's presence in the 2002–2003 playoffs, saying,

One word: *Unbelievable*, especially the series against Detroit because he single-handedly won a couple of those games. Detroit was a better team than we were with personnel, but when you get goaltending like that? We were fortunate to get off to a good start, but I guarantee you if it wasn't for him and some of the saves that he made, we wouldn't have won that series. I thought there were what you could actually term "miraculous" saves in those games where there's no way he had any business coming up with a glove or a kick save—whatever it might be—because there were times Detroit, with that team they had back then, would just be dominating in your zone for a minute at a time and this guy would be kicking everything out. I think it got to the point around games three or four, they were getting so frustrated, maybe they just thought, "There's no way we're going to beat this guy." It was scintillating. It was unbelievable. It was one of the greatest goaltending performances I've seen as a fan or in person as a broadcaster. Especially in the first-round series. He was a huge part in getting us to where we were going. That performance there probably is the greatest goaltending work I have seen or even heard of since Anaheim has had a franchise.

Even after sweeping Detroit, Giguère still wasn't getting a reprieve in the Conference Semifinals opener against Dallas, as he would face 63 shots, stopping all but three of them in a game won in overtime on a goal by Petr Sýkora. Although not sweeping Dallas, the Ducks would ride another 134 saves by Giguère in the next five games to the Conference Finals against the Minnesota Wild. While neither team had made a Conference Finals appearance in their brief history, Giguère and the Ducks seemed like proven veterans against Minnesota, as the increasingly reputable goaltender would allow only one goal in 123 shots.

Anaheim would once again sweep a playoff series and arrive at the Stanley Cup Final to face yet another dynasty. Reaching the finals for the third time in four years, the New Jersey Devils and veteran goaltender Martin Brodeur would capitalize on every ounce of their home-ice advantage and end up beating the Ducks in seven games to capture their third Stanley Cup in nine seasons. Although on the losing side, Giguère, with his 659 playoff saves and .945 save percentage, would be awarded the Conn Smythe Trophy.

Looking back on the Ducks' remarkable run in 2002–2003, Steve Carroll comments,

If you look, that was our first run ever to the Stanley Cup Final. I don't know if that year in particular we were a team that people considered a threat to win the Stanley Cup. I don't know if we were on their radar. Playing Detroit in the first round was a big draw that got the building filled right away. We eventually swept them in four games. That really got the interest going here. The fact that we were able to defeat a legendary-type team. They had played Detroit in two previous series, and I don't think they had won a game, so to come in and not only win a game, but sweep them, I think that elevated some more interest into the hockey club. In that particular year, we beat Dallas in six games. Then we swept Minnesota. When we got to the final, I don't think anybody gave us a chance, looking at New Jersey and guys they had, like Martin Brodeur, Scott Stevens, Scott Niedermayer. The biggest game of the series was game six, when Paul Kariya was flattened at center ice by Scott Stevens. I thought he was done. He went down and never moved; yet, he came back later in the game from the hit, scored a goal, and we won that game 2–1. At that point, I thought, "You know what? We're destined to win this." You win a game six like that—with all the emotion of that hit—and Kariya scoring one of the goals. New Jersey eventually won that series—I think—based on experience. When you look at the two teams, we didn't have much playoff experience to that point on our hockey club. New Jersey did, and I think they were just too much. We gave it a shot. That certainly put hockey on the map here. From that point on, people knew who we were. I think that particular series and playoff run really catapulted the interest in hockey here with the Ducks to an all new level because of that season's playoff success.

Four years later, the Ducks would complete their legitimacy with a new name, a new logo, and one more playoff win, en route to the team's first-ever Stanley Cup championship.

DROPPING THE "MIGHTY" ON PAPER, NOT ON THE ICE

The following couple of years would prove quite busy both inside and outside general manager Bryan Murray's office, as team captain and restricted free agent Paul Kariya would leave the team to rejoin former teammate Teemu Selänne in Colorado. Following the 2004–2005 lockout, Murray would leave Anaheim for Ottawa and another Brian (Burke) would take the reins as general manager. Interestingly, that same year, Disney would sell the team to billionaire Henry Samueli and his wife Susan. One of the first actions taken by the team's new ownership and management following the season-long lockout was reacquiring Selänne from the Colorado Avalanche. Although Kariya wouldn't be reuniting a third time with teammate Selänne, Rob Niedermayer would have an on-ice family reunion with brother and new team captain Scott. Tossing in promising draft picks Ryan Getzlaf and Corey Perry, the Ducks would go to the Conference Finals before losing in five games to Edmonton. The following year, in 2006, Anaheim would spare sportscasters, color commentators, and hockey writers their voices and wrists by officially changing their name to one they'd been called for more than a decade—the

Anaheim Ducks—and shedding their cartoon-riddled uniform for a simple, winged "D."

Statistically, the biggest difference for the team came in imported defenseman Chris Pronger. Mentally, especially for players on the opposing side, the difference came with imports Shawn Thornton, George Parros, and reputable veteran Brad May. Carroll notes,

> The one thing people will forget sometimes is that we had a team that intimidated people. If you were a visiting team coming in here, you had to deal with Shawn Thornton, Travis Moen, Brad May, George Parros, and those are just a few. If some guy got in a fight and we lost him for the night, we still had three or four guys that nobody wanted to mess with. Think about this group of tough guys: One of the biggest heavyweights in the NHL, George Parros. Tough as nails. A veteran intimidator in the lineup, which gave Ducks players room to operate. Shawn Thornton knew how to pick his spots and maximize his impact on every shift. He was a real team guy, sticking up for teammates. Travis Moen, who could handle himself, scored the game-winning goal in game five of the Stanley Cup Final versus Ottawa in 2007. He was also a member of arguably the most influential forward line, a checking line for the Ducks with teammates Samuel Påhlsson and Rob Niedermayer. Then there was Brad May, one of my all-time favorites. There were five Brad May fights with Krys Barch over the course of three seasons. Left-hand haymakers from May in every fight and Barch returning punches as well. Good clean fights. Nothing dirty. Just two tough guys going at it. That series of bouts have stayed with me to this day.
>
> The Ducks won with some intimidating, physical players in their lineup. The Ducks were the most penalized team in the league during the 2006–2007 NHL regular season. We were a tough team. I remember then-Ducks general manager Brian Burke saying despite risks, his team would not back away from its physical style. The team played a certain way, and Burke said the style was successful for his team. "We are not a dirty team, we are a physical team. There's a big difference," he said. That 2007 cup team in Anaheim also had a guy by the name of Scott Niedermayer, who actually played with Chris Pronger on the power play. Niedermayer and Chris Pronger on the same blue line? How many times has that happened during the course of history of a hockey team? They were two number-one defensemen on the same team. We had Teemu Selänne. We had the Perry/Getzlaf kids coming up in their early years. You knew early in the year that was going to be a special team come playoff time. Great goaltending, four good forward lines, solid defensive pairs, depth players contributing, top-notch coaching. This team was destined to win.

Advancing beyond game five only once in their playoff run, the Anaheim Ducks rolled to their first Stanley Cup title in team history.

Looking back, Carroll relishes this milestone from his broadcasting perspective, saying,

> There's nothing better than having a ring from a professional team. I've got a Stanley Cup ring. I've had it out of my house three times since 2007. Wouldn't want to lose it. I guard that with my life. The night we won the Stanley Cup in 2007—game five against Ottawa—I recall the goal scorers and everything quite well. I knew we had a good chance to win after we beat Detroit. Selänne gets the big goal in game five at Detroit in overtime. We go on to win that Western Conference Finals series. Once we got by Detroit, you knew we had a good chance to beat Ottawa. Game five of the Stanley Cup Final series, coming back from Ottawa, you felt like this was the opportunity to wrap up the series. The Ducks weren't going to let the opportunity go by, and that arena just went nuts.
>
> I've got pictures on the wall in my house. We won that game. It was probably the best broadcast I ever did, because I prepared thoroughly for it. I was on. There's going to be some highlights played some day about those moments in Anaheim Ducks history, and I wanted to make sure I didn't make a mistake. I was with a championship team. First one ever. You sit up in the booth, and you call the game, and you start getting emotional about it. All the work you put in in your career, you feel like you're a part of something very special. That was three hours I will never forget, and nothing will ever take the place of it. Everything you did and everything you worked for, it all came in one night in three hours. That made everything I've ever done in broadcasting worthwhile.

THE ANAHEIM DUCKS TODAY

With the town painted the team color orange at times, the Ducks, now with the Getzlaf "kid" turned captain, have reached the playoffs in all but two of their last nine seasons. Having finished first in their division the last four years (2012–2016), Anaheim returned to the Conference Finals in 2015, only to be bested by the eventual Stanley Cup champion Chicago Blackhawks in seven games. With Vancouver import Ryan Kesler manning the second line, Ryan Getzlaf leading the scoring, and goaltender John Gibson guarding the pipes, Lord Stanley's Cup may yet again find itself in the back seat of an Anaheim Ducks player's convertible racing down U.S. Highway 101, taking in the cool coastal breeze and watching the sun dip into the Pacific Ocean on its way to being displayed at the next fish taco stand along the beach.

• *2* •

Arizona Coyotes

*M*uch like its central Floridian counterpart Tampa Bay, the city of Phoenix, Arizona, having hosted preseason professional baseball since 1929, couldn't put a major professional sports team on the crushed clay and Bermuda grass in the Sonoran Desert before putting one on the ice. With the city of "Winterpeg" playing the role of "Go on. Leave. You'll be back in 15 years anyway," the Jets shifted climates, leaving the Manitoban snow in 1996, for the "Valley of the Sun," where they would be known as the Phoenix Coyotes. With the move, southern teams like the Los Angeles Kings, Mighty Ducks of Anaheim, and Dallas Stars, although not racking up as many frequent flyer miles on road trips, had a much closer dance partner and, with it, an easier travel schedule for intraconference matchups.

Having come from a place where white clothing would seem more like camouflage than pre-Labor Day fashion, the Coyotes carried with them over the U.S.–Canadian border and Rocky Mountains a tradition that, considering the dust storms and flash floods common to the area, could have used a more stain-resistant color, like, perhaps, brown? Coyotes TV play-by-play broadcaster Matt McConnell, who came to Phoenix years after the team had already settled in, discusses the fans' Winnipeg-adopted playoff apparel, saying,

> A tradition they carried over from Winnipeg when they moved in 1996 was Winnipeg used to have the "whiteout" for the playoffs, where everybody would wear white. They carried that over here as well, so anytime there's a playoff season in downtown Phoenix or here in Glendale, fans are encouraged to wear white. In terms of playoff atmosphere, it's as loud and crazy as anything I've ever experienced, whether it's actually at the game itself or watching it on television. It's an unbelievable scene.

A tradition more specific to both the area and the mascot has surfaced since the team's move in 1996. McConnell continues, "You hear a lot of howling. The fans have their own routine. They pick certain times of the period where they try to get a collective howl going in the stands, which I always thought was pretty cool and unique." Of course, Coyotes aren't the only creature common to the warm Southwest climate of Arizona. McConnell adds,

> Arizona has a lot of transplants. We get a lot of fans who are snowbirds. They come out here and love hockey. You get a lot of western Canadians, so, whenever we're playing Edmonton, Vancouver, or Calgary, we will have a lot of their fans in our building as well. It's a great atmosphere. It's electric. It's a real good fan experience, and it doesn't hurt when you can walk out of the arena and it's 75 to 80 degrees outside. That's kind of nice, too.

With the thermometer dial rising the longer the team plays past game number 82, fans would probably prefer the uncomfortable three-digit temperatures known to inhabit the Phoenix area during the NHL's postseason.

Being a relocated rather than an expansion team, the Coyotes didn't take long to bring the playoff atmosphere in Winnipeg to Phoenix. Their first year in the Southwest, the Coyotes finished third in the Central Division, earning themselves the fifth seed in the Western Conference playoff bracket. Much like they had done for nine of their 11 playoff appearances in Winnipeg, the team's first four seasons in Phoenix, although playoff-qualifying ones, still resulted in first-round playoff exits. Much to the surprise of both the team and the rest of the hockey world, the Coyotes, after the 1999–2000 season, were about to get help in the front office, and eventually behind the bench, from the greatest hockey player to ever take the ice: Wayne Gretzky.

THE NOT SO GREAT YEARS UNDER THE "GREAT ONE"

A year removed from his retirement, Wayne Gretzky, a player so legendary his number "99" was retired by all of professional hockey, would go in with local Phoenix developer Steve Ellman and purchase the Coyotes from Richard Burke. Unfortunately, Gretzky's nine Hart MVP trophies and four Stanley Cup titles as a player didn't translate into nearly as much success behind the desk. The Coyotes, suffering both financially and statistically, lost their top two offensive weapons, as team captain Keith Tkachuk was traded away mid-season and Jeremy Roenick, a free agent, signed with the Philadelphia Flyers. With attendance dwindling more and more each year, the Coyotes shifted venues from downtown Phoenix to neighboring suburb Glendale for the 2003–2004 season. Although the number of onlookers passing through the turnstiles improved with the quarter loop around AZ 101, the Coyotes' position in the Western Conference's Pacific Division fell from fourth to fifth. After the season, the league took a year off, giving the "Great One" the opportunity to come back and "suit up" in a different way.

In his four seasons as team-builder, Gretzky failed to lead his team into the postseason, finishing with a winning record only once—and barely at that (38–37–7). Eventually, Gretzky would resign as head coach, and the team would be purchased by the NHL in an attempt to keep the franchise in the valley. In the team's first year post-Gretzky, the Coyotes, after a six-year absence, once again qualified for the playoffs. Much like the previous nine trips by both the Coyotes and the Jets, Phoenix failed to make it past the first round, losing in seven games to the Detroit Red Wings. A year and a second-place finish in the Pacific Division later, the Coyotes found themselves in back-to-back playoff appearances and facing the Red Wings yet again. This time, Phoenix wouldn't win a game, let alone the series, as Detroit swept them in four. With seven "one-and-done" playoff appearances in 14 seasons in the desert, the Phoenix Coyotes headed into the 2011–2012 season with something to prove, not only to their diminishing fan base, but also to the rest of the Western Conference.

WELCOME TO UNCHARTED TERRITORY, PHOENIX FANS

With a slight change of personnel, namely signing goaltender Mike Smith from the Tampa Bay Lightning, as well as the mid-season addition of Columbus Blue Jacket center Antoine Vermette, the 2011–2012 Coyotes, although finishing with two fewer points than the previous season, finished first in the Pacific Division and were slated to take on the Chicago Blackhawks in their playoff opener. With the teams splitting the opening two games in Phoenix, both in overtime, the series shifted back to Chicago for a notorious game three. McConnell, having called the series, looks back on the game that would shift the momentum for the Coyotes, saying,

> I could tell you so many things about that series. That was the series of the infamous Raffi Torres hit on Marian Hossa that warranted a 25-game suspension. My partner Tyson Nash originally called it a clean hit on the air, and he got death threats. The fans were all over him. As he would like to say, he was getting "chirped" on Twitter. The game after the Torres hit, which would have been game four in Chicago, we're on a commercial break, and one of the vendors in the upper deck of the United Center is carrying a tray of beers. He looks up in the booth and he's screaming,

"Tyson Nash, Tyson Nash" and is all upset. Tyson can't hear him because he's got his headset on, so I turn to him and say, "Tyson, the beer vendor down there is trying to get your attention." So Tyson looks down. The beer vendor again says, "Tyson Nash," and Tyson says, "What?" The beer vendor looks up at him holding his tray of beers and he's screaming at Tyson, saying, "Clean hit my ass!" At this point, everybody in the section is looking at the beer vendor and looking up in the booth. Tyson looks down at all 250 pounds of him and yells, "Mix in a salad," and the whole section just starts laughing. It was pure comedy right in the middle of a hockey game during a commercial break.

While job etiquette was not being displayed in the stands or on the ice, the Coyotes went on to win game four in overtime to take a commanding 3–1 series lead over Chicago. Going back to Phoenix to close out the series at (then-named) Jobing.com Arena, the team lost the fifth straight game of the series decided by overtime, forcing them to fly back to the Windy City for game six at the United Center, with its unruly vendors. Undoubtedly his most memorable game in the team booth, McConnell describes game six:

We had a lead on Chicago of three games to one. We came back to Arizona looking to wrap it up, and the Blackhawks won game five, which meant we had to go back to Chicago. I think a lot of people were thinking, "You've got to go back to the United Center. That's going to be really tough to win. Let's face it. This thing's going seven games." They got into game six, and Mike Smith, the goaltender for the Coyotes, played the best game I have ever seen live in my life. At one point, the shots were something along the lines of 24 to 2 in favor of the Blackhawks. The game got into the third period, and we found our offense. We scored a couple of goals and got the lead. At one point, Shane Doan stripped the puck from Johnny Oduya and scored. Mikkel Boedker, who's another one of our young players, had a huge series. It was Mike Smith's performance, not only in that game, but the whole series. That game in particular he was unbelievable. He was the reason we were able to shut them out in six.

Apparently, the vendors weren't the only ones employed by the Blackhawks with sour grapes. McConnell continues,

We were doing our postgame show, and all of a sudden we lose our lights in the booth and we lose the power to our microphones. I guess when the game ended, they just started pulling cables downstairs and accidentally knocked us off the air. We were trying to put a bow on arguably the biggest win in franchise history. It was the first time the team had ever won a series in the playoffs. I just remember us being in that booth at the very end basically having to shut the show down because they were pulling cables. It was the most bizarre thing in the world.

After 15 years in the desert—still 25 shy of Moses and his people—the Coyotes had their first playoff series win, and the fans were quick to show their support. McConnell adds,

> They came back the next day, and when the plane landed at the charter terminal, there had to have been a thousand fans on the other side of the fence from where the players park. That kind of became a tradition during the playoffs. They eliminate Chicago and there's 1,000 fans lining the way out for the players as they're driving their cars. There's this line all fired up. I had a copy of the *Chicago Tribune* with the headline of the Hawks getting eliminated, and I gave it through the fence to a fan and said, "Have this for your scrapbook." We were all excited. Then they beat Nashville in the next round, and as the series went on, the crowds at the airport for the greeting got bigger and bigger. It was a great experience.

There would be no airport scene at the conclusion of the 2012 Conference Finals, as the Coyotes fell at home in game five, against the eventual champion Los Angeles Kings, ending the deepest playoff run the team had seen in both Phoenix and Winnipeg.

SAME GAME, NEW NAME

The Coyotes, while not having returned to the playoffs in the four seasons since their magical Conference Finals run, continue to redefine themselves, starting with their identity. Having played in Glendale at (now-named) Gila River Arena since 2003, the Coyotes, prior to the 2014–2015 season, finally dropped Phoenix from their name and simply became known as the Arizona Coyotes. McConnell notes, "A big part of why they changed their name is they wanted to create more of an appeal statewide than just in the valley. I think the name change was very important to the team and also to the city of Glendale."

While the team has finished in the bottom three for average attendance the past eight seasons, Arizona continues its efforts to once again put a competitor on the ice and bring more fans to Glendale's Westgate complex and on into Gila River Arena. With Raffi Torres serving lengthy suspensions elsewhere in San Jose, today's Coyotes, still with Doan and Smith, as well as recent import Brad Richardson, mix speed with experience in the hopes of revisiting that warm terminal greeting of 2012, only this time with Lord Stanley's Cup joining the motorcade.

• 3 •

Boston Bruins

On November 1, 1924, the boys from Canada glanced at New England and gave a group of skaters the proverbial "wave over," introducing the Boston Bruins to their sporting fraternity and commencing NHL hockey in the United States. While it's hard to imagine the Bruins playing in a venue other than the famed Boston Garden, where they had taken up residence for 67 seasons, during their first four years in the league the team "competed" at Boston Arena, now home to college hockey's Northeastern Huskies. While the growing pains manifested themselves in the team's inaugural year, when it finished 6–24, the Bruins quickly rebounded by qualifying for the playoffs in two of the following three seasons. The 1928–1929 season was the team's first ever inside Boston Garden and proved commemorative in more ways than one, as the Bruins won their first Stanley Cup, against the New York Rangers, in the league's first "All-American" Cup Final, giving Canada second thoughts about their border-crossing invitation five years prior.

Before the "original six" were officially established in 1942, the Bruins won two more Stanley Cups, in 1939 and 1941, thanks to such future Hall of Famers as Milt Schmidt, Eddie Shore, Bill Cowley, Frank Brimsek, Bobby Bauer, Roy Conacher, Dit Clapper, and a half-dozen other names reserved for the $2,000 slot on Sports Jeopardy. While there were only six teams in the league for another 25-plus years, it would be hard to "snake" a title from the likes of the Toronto Maple Leaf and Montreal Canadien dynasties. The league would eventually expand to 12 teams in 1967, a year after one of the most explosive players in NHL history arrived in "Beantown" and put the sport on its head.

BOBBY ORR "FLIES" ONTO THE SCENE

Entering the league at the ripe age of 18, Bobby Orr made a quick splash, winning the Calder Memorial Trophy for rookie of the year as a defenseman. In the next seven seasons, Orr would take home the James Norris Trophy for top defenseman and, along the way, pick up the Art Ross Trophy for the league's top scorer, three straight league MVP honors, and two Conn Smythe Trophies during the team's Stanley Cup championship runs. In some circles, mainly outside of Edmonton, Detroit, and Pittsburgh, Orr is thought of as the greatest to have ever played the game. His "flying" goal past the St. Louis Blues' Glenn Hall in 1970 is one of the most recognizable images in professional hockey history.

Although labeled a defenseman, Orr boasted six straight seasons in which he scored more than 100 points, leading the league in offense on two different occasions. Unfortunately for the defenseman, Orr's vulnerable knees required surgery, reducing his role to the point that he was traded to the Chicago Blackhawks, where he would play 26 games in his final two seasons before hanging up his skates for good after the 1978–1979 campaign. Not forgotten by his Boston fans, Orr's number "4" was retired and raised to the Garden rafters almost immediately after his retirement. Ignoring tradition, the league decided to enshrine Orr into the Hockey Hall of Fame that same year, perhaps hoping the image of a flying number "4" might spruce the place up a little.

While Orr and his acrobatics were getting all the attention, his teammate and scoring partner Phil Esposito was surely not to be kept from the spotlight. Also playing on Boston's two championship teams, Esposito, the team center, won the Ross Trophy for top scorer on five occasions and took home two Hart MVP awards. During a seven-year span, Esposito scored more than 100 points six times, with the lone two-digit effort landing him at 99 during the 1969–1970 season. A year before his defenseman—bad knees and all—had been shipped to Chicago, Esposito was traded to the New York Rangers for defense-minded players who would hopefully fill the void left by Orr's injury. Jean Ratelle, the gauntlet runner of this replacement scenario, led the team to the Stanley Cup Final in his first full season with the Bruins, but the Montreal Canadiens and their date with hockey immortality stopped them short of the finish line, setting the league record for most regular-season points en route to the second of their eventual four straight Stanley Cups. Ratelle would retire a Bruin four years later, but his number would not ascend to the Garden rafters alongside the man he "replaced."

A *BAH*-STON TRADITION

The city of Boston is no stranger to championship droughts. The Red Sox went 86 "cursed" seasons between World Series titles, and the Celtics, although minuscule in comparison to their Yawkey Street compatriots, went 22 seasons without brandishing a championship banner in the Garden. Having suffered a drought double the length of one and half the span of the other, the Bruins found themselves in a near-four-decade spell of playoff futility. Amid that cup-less drought, the Bruins were still capable of qualifying for the postseason 29 straight times, a record that holds to this day. While the parades weren't filing past the "dirty waters" of the Charles River like their curse-ridding intersport brothers come mid-June for nearly 40 years, fans still gathered in the Garden, as well as at its successor, the TD Waterhouse Garden, making their New England sports fandom known. Bruins radio play-by-play broadcaster Dave Goucher describes the fanaticism of Boston, saying,

> It's the passion fans have in Boston and throughout New England for the game. Being an original-six team and having been in the NHL for 92 years, I think what's always struck me the most is how much people care. They take it personally, whether the team wins or loses, or wins the Stanley Cup or misses the playoffs. That's the part that always has impressed me the most. I grew up a Bruins fan and watched and listened to the Bruins my whole life. I don't really remember a time when I didn't care about how the Bruins were doing. They've sold out every game for over six years. They let the team know if they're doing well, and they let them hear it if they're doing poorly. I'd much rather have that any day of the week than apathy. That's the worst thing for a fan base. The undeniable passion Bruins fans have is what I loved the most as a kid and what I still love after calling the games for the last 16 years.

FROM NEW ENGLAND PONDS TO PROFESSIONAL RINKS

Aside from the intense fanaticism, one thing that distinguishes the New England era from most others of the NHL is the local farming of talent. Having spent a great deal of his broadcasting career around Boston on both a collegiate and a professional level, Dave Goucher describes New England's presence come NHL draft day:

> Because it's such a deep-rooted tradition here in Boston and throughout New England, you see, at a young age, from youth hockey right through high school and college, how many kids come out of New England—more

specifically Massachusetts—that have gone on to play in the NHL. I went to Boston University, and my second year of school, they had a line of Tony Amonte, Keith Tkachuk, and Shawn McEachern, and they all went on to play in the NHL. I think you see it throughout different levels of hockey. Excellent prep school programs, excellent high school programs, some of the best college programs in the country. We just had a Frozen Four championship game between Providence College and Boston University (2015), two campuses separated by about 45 miles. I think that's where you see it the most. It's pretty far-reaching throughout New England. Sometimes I feel for the college programs up here because Boston is a pro sports town. It's Bruins, Red Sox, Patriots, Celtics. Whatever the sport—but more specifically hockey—college teams, to a certain degree, are forced into the background because there's so much attention given to pro sports. But that doesn't diminish the deep tradition schools have here, whether at BU, Boston College, Harvard, Northeastern or Providence College. They've had successful and elite programs at a national level for a long time.

With Boston springing up so much NHL-caliber talent through local universities, it's interesting to note that one of the team's most explosive players and eventual Hall of Famers came via a route different from that of the textbook-toting, dorm-thrashing, fraternity-pledging college crowd.

A PLAYER FOR THE "SOUTHIES"

In the 2013 census, Boston came in first in American cities with respect to concentration of Irish population, with a whopping 20.4 percent of people having Irish ancestors. Having won two of the last three Stanley Cups, the Bruins, in the fall of 1972, were about to introduce to the rest of the NHL *their* representing Irish population in the form of 6-foot-1 right winger Terry O'Reilly. With his highest accolade being finishing eighth in league MVP honors during the 1977–1978 season, O'Reilly had a much different role on the ice than the Bobby Orrs and Phil Espositos.

Playing in 13 full seasons—all as a Bruin—O'Reilly chalked up 2,095 penalty infraction minutes (PIM), crossing the 200-PIM threshold in five straight seasons. Having accumulated 228 career fighting majors, O'Reilly scrapped with the league's toughest, including "Broad Street Bully" Dave Schultz and, on December 23, 1979, Madison Square Garden patron John Kaptain, whom O'Reilly suspected of hitting teammate Stan Jonathan with a rolled-up magazine. Noticing Kaptain holding Jonathan's stick up in the stands, O'Reilly was the first of what would become virtually the entire Bruins team to climb over the glass and enforce Kaptain's display of fan interference. One lost shoe, a litigious mother, and a month later, O'Reilly was dealt an eight-game suspension by the league, along with a $500 fine. The cost of Kaptain's lost shoe would be included in the $500 penalty levied on O'Reilly's teammate, Mike Milbury, who literally took the fight "one step too far" in removing Kaptain's shoe and subsequently beating him with it. While such a display of "fan interaction" might shock the sports spectating world outside of Boston, it wasn't so surprising to those inside it, especially Dave Goucher, who notes,

> What I remember most about those teams of the late '70s and maybe even into the early '80s was they could beat you a lot of different ways, but physically, they had punishing teams. Terry O'Reilly and John Wensink and Stan Jonathan and even Wayne Cashman, they led the way there. O'Reilly, just the rage and fury he played with, I never saw anyone else play like that again until Cam Neely. He never got enough credit for the amount of skill he had, too. In addition to being able to beat you up, he also put up some real good numbers. The Bruins had 11 players with 20 goals or more in 1977–1978, and he was one of them. He just led with the passion he played with. Wensink was physically imposing and intimidating. I vividly remember that Minnesota North Stars game when he challenged the whole bench and nobody moved.
>
> Stan Jonathan was a little bit different, a smaller guy who had an incredible toughness to his game. The fight that he had with Pierre Bouchard in the Finals in 1978, where he broke Bouchard's nose, goes down in Boston lore. It was a big point in the series for the Bruins. They ended up losing in six games. They ran into that Montreal dynasty of the late '70s, losing in the Finals in 1977 and '78, and the Semifinals in '79, with the "too many men on the ice game." That was the end of that run for both the Bruins and Canadiens. But those three guys, O'Reilly, Wensink, and Jonathan, remarkable toughness and remarkable passion.

Although O'Reilly missed the Stanley Cup boat by a season when he entered the league, he retired with plenty of proverbial hardware from being one of the NHL's toughest players for more than a decade.

JOINING THE PARADE CROWD ONCE AGAIN

By the time the Bruins began their Stanley Cup run of 2011, there was plenty of motivation on the streets of Boston. The city's three other professional teams, the Red Sox, Patriots, and Celtics, had, during the previous 10 years, won a total of six championships for their respective sports. In the year prior to 2010–2011, the Bruins became the fourth team in major sports history to have a 3–0 series lead and lose four straight, falling to the Philadelphia Flyers and extending their cup-less drought to 38 years. The following fall and winter, the Bruins, thanks to a balanced scoring effort by players like Milan Lucic, David Krejci, Patrice Bergeron, Nathan Horton, and Mark Recchi, as well as the defensive presence of Zdeno Chára, Dennis Seidenberg, and goaltender Tim Thomas, would tally 103 regular-season points, good enough for first in the Northeast Division and the number-three seed in the Eastern Conference. Going the distance in all but one of their playoff series, the Bruins hoisted Lord Stanley's Cup once again in front of a stunned crowd inside Vancouver's Rogers Arena and a soon-to-be riotous crowd outside. Having the good fortune of being a radio broadcaster and not ceding the playoff experience to the national networks, Goucher describes his experience calling the Bruins' return to hockey's summit:

> When the Bruins won the Stanley Cup in 2011, in game seven in Vancouver, that's at the top of the list. You get into this business as a young person, and you don't know where it's going to lead. You hope maybe—by luck or circumstance or both—someday you'll have a chance to call your team winning a Stanley Cup. In that year, the Bruins won three game sevens on the road to winning the Stanley Cup. Just the opportunity to be a part of that was unbelievable. To be in the booth calling it, going down to the locker room and witnessing the whole scene after the Bruins won. It was complete chaos. The parade a few days later through the streets of Boston with over a million people yelling and screaming. I'll never forget that roar. You hope it's not a once in a lifetime thing. It actually makes you hungrier to be part of something like that again. If you do what I do for a living, that's the pinnacle, having a chance to call your team winning a championship.

Winning their sixth Stanley Cup, the Bruins had their membership privileges to the "Boston Champions Club" reinstated, buying themselves some time with the fans. Goucher explains,

> In Boston, the other teams—the Patriots, Red Sox, and Celtics—had all won championships in that last decade before the Bruins won it. So considering they hadn't won a cup since the Nixon administration, it was an enormous monkey off their back, and it bought them some time, not much, but some. They were right back to the Final two years later and lost to Chicago in six games. In 2013–2014, they had the best record in the league and got knocked out in the second round. Last season, they missed the playoffs, and fans were enormously disappointed—as was the team. Winning it in 2011 takes some of the heat off, but not for long.

AFTER THE CUP

Two years following their Stanley Cup run, the Bruins played in what Goucher refers to as the "1a" to his 2011 game seven Stanley Cup–clinching broadcast, beating the Toronto Maple Leafs in seven games in the postseason's opening round. Goucher comments,

> The Bruins had a big comeback in the playoffs against Toronto in 2013 in game seven. They were down 4–1 at home with 11 minutes left, came back and tied the game with under a minute left, and Patrice Bergeron scored in overtime to win it. I went nuts, the fans went nuts, and I think the whole city went nuts. It was the biggest comeback ever in a game seven. There were probably 4,000 or 5,000 people that left when they were down three goals with 11 minutes left who were making U-turns in their cars and trying to get back in the building. Fortunately, the Bruins were able to stage a comeback for the ages.

The Bruins went on to beat the New York Rangers and Pittsburgh Penguins, en route to their six-game showdown with the Chicago Blackhawks, but the team fell to the budding dynasty in six games, bringing the "next year" mantra back off the closet shelf and spilling it down Legends Way and past TD Waterhouse Garden. While the "next year" RSVP has yet to be tendered in the five seasons following their cup championship, the Bruins, with familiar faces Chára, Bergeron, Krejci, and Brad Marchand, as well as new bloods Torey Krug and David Pastrnak, are looking to buy some more time with their beloved New England fan base and ensure that the next banner to be draped inside TD Waterhouse isn't another 39 years in the making.

· 4 ·

Buffalo Sabres

$\mathcal{A}$long the west end of the "Empire State," tucked deep in the northeast corner of Lake Erie, is Buffalo, New York. Coming in ninth in the category of "Coldest Major U.S. Cities," Buffalo has fittingly been host to professional hockey since 1928. After a stint in the IHL and a brief departure from the AHL, the Buffalo Bisons began a 30-year history inside what would become a landmark for the sport of hockey, Memorial Auditorium, better known as the "Aud."

When the city was awarded both NFL and NHL franchises in 1970, the Aud expanded its seating capacity by almost 50 percent, welcoming their new team, the Sabres, into the community and sending the Bison out the door and "over the falls." During the team's 45-year existence, the Sabres have appeared in the postseason a considerable 29 times but have made it to the Stanley Cup Final only twice. Although not the half-century championship drought of Cleveland, its Lake Erie counterpart, Buffalo has yet to parade a Vince Lombardi Trophy or Stanley Cup up the Niagara River, lending to one of its nicknames, the "City of *No* Illusions"; however, it's with another of the city's nicknames that Sabre fans likely prefer to associate themselves.

THE CITY OF GOOD NEIGHBORS

While Philadelphia's "City of Brotherly Love" title may come into question at times, especially during a sporting event, Buffalo's "City of Good Neighbors" manifests itself in all areas. Sabres TV play-by-play broadcaster Dan Dunleavy describes what one can expect from a Buffalo fan:

19

One thing I've noticed about people in Buffalo that's big out here, and it's not to say that people in Southern Ontario are not this, but people in Buffalo are very much "they are who they are." There's no trying to figure out who or what a Buffalo Sabres fan is. They're very kind people. Vocal. Passionate. You'll know the first 10 seconds of meeting a Sabres fan what type of person they are because they're just so genuine. There's no facade about them. I've come to very much fall in love with the people and fans of Buffalo just because of that. I think anyone who's ever come here has realized very quickly it's a caring community and a fan base that sticks together. They're there for one another, as well as their team. I think a lot of that has to do with the weather. We're getting more snow out on Lake Erie, which is just 10 minutes from the rink. People are out there after every game helping others start their cars with jumper cables or are digging each other out from a snowstorm before they get to the game. I know you see that almost anywhere, but you're seeing that in a city where the team right now (2015) is last in the NHL. It's the coldest place you could be, and people still come out to the games. They easily could stay away, but they're not because they love this team. It's a very true and loyal fan base.

Confirming Dunleavy's words, Los Angeles Kings Hall of Fame radio voice Nick Nickson describes how Buffalo's weather sometimes brings fans together a little more than they had originally planned:

> In the early '80s, the Kings were playing in Buffalo. We get to the rink about two and a half hours before the game starts and we notice, as it gets closer to game time, there's not a lot of people coming to this game tonight. As it turns out, there had been a snowstorm that had come in off of Lake Erie, which happens all the time in Buffalo, and when the storm started that was about the time people would consider getting to the rink for the Buffalo game. We played the game. The teams were there. The referees were there, but there were only about 2,000 people in the old Aud. They played the game, and then afterwards, Bob Miller and I walked back to our hotel. I remember that walk from the Aud to our hotel. It's only a three- or four-block walk. It's not far, but it was the coldest walk either one of us had ever taken anywhere, anytime, as kids or adults. Bob grew up in Chicago. I grew up in Rochester, so we knew what cold winters were like. We had frostbite on our ears for about three days. We found out the next day some people actually slept in the Aud—they slept in the penalty box—because they couldn't go home after the game. Nobody could drive. The city was shut down.

With weather as harsh as that in Buffalo, it's only natural for the town to garner yet another nickname: "B Lo."

FROM THE "FRENCH CONNECTION" TO "MAY DAY"

Even though the Sabres haven't won a Stanley Cup in their 46-year history, that doesn't mean they haven't been an exciting team for fans to watch, especially in the franchise's early days, with the "French Connection" of Gilbert Perreault, René Robert, and Richard Martin. With French Canadian roots, Perreault, Robert, and Martin accumulated 2,573 points, 1,116 goals, and 6 playoff appearances during their tenure with the team, leading the Sabres to their first Stanley Cup Final in 1975. Even without the famed trio there for half of it, the Sabres went to the playoffs 11 straight times between 1974 and 1985. During the next several years, players like Dave Andreychuk, Mike Ramsey, and Craig Ramsay proved themselves offensive forces and secured their places among Buffalo's all-time scoring leaders. But it would be a goal from a Sabre better known for his other hockey talents that would forever be remembered in the hearts of Buffalo fans.

In April 1993, with the Boston Bruins all but buried by an 0–3 series deficit to Buffalo, left winger Brad May sealed the coffin in overtime with his famous "May Day" goal to beat Andy Moog and Boston in a four-game sweep. Already part of his bag of signature phrases, Hall of Fame Sabres broadcaster Rick Jeanneret's call of "May Day" resounds in the Buffalo community some 23 years later as if it were yesterday.

Although only part of the team for the first six and a half campaigns of his 18-season career, May left his mark, along with one of the most intimidating groups the sport had seen during the mid- to late 1990s. Former Buffalo Sabres radio broadcaster and current Nashville Predators voice Pete Weber looks back on May's cohorts of 1996, saying,

> I was with the Sabres, and that was a club that came together. Let's just consider Rob Ray, Brad May, Matt Barnaby, and then Bob Boughner, who came and joined the club. There's a memorable night there at the Aud in Buffalo against the Flyers. Matt Barnaby was face down in the face-off circle after a huge collision, and Garth Snow, the goaltender on the ice, came out and jabbed Matt Barnaby with a stick, and you wouldn't believe what ensued after that. Matt Barnaby jumped up, pulled Snow's mask off, and started pummeling him. Then Derek Plante, who was a known pacifist, was on the ice. He got tied up with Rod Brind'Amour there trying to pull Barnaby off his goaltender. It was really a three-ring circus; maybe one of the most memorable in the last season of hockey in the Aud.

During the next couple of seasons, the bad blood between the Flyers and Sabres began to spill over on the fresh ice of (then-named) HSBC Arena and

Core States Center, as a brawl ensued seemingly every time the two teams played one another. It's safe to say that a large portion of Rob Ray's 3,207 penalty infraction minutes (PIM)—good for sixth most all time—were issued when Philadelphia was on the other end of the ice. May was no stranger to the box either, accumulating 2,248 PIMs himself, landing him 37th on the all-time list.

Once, Ray's punches were reserved for someone *not* from the other team, at least not one wearing their uniform. Former NHL defenseman and current Florida Panthers radio voice Randy Moller, who played both against and with Ray, recalls the night "Rayzor" gave a Quebec Nordique fan a literal "center ice" package, saying,

> With the Buffalo Sabres, Rob Ray and I were involved in the game in Quebec City where the fan jumped into the players' bench and Rob Ray hit him with 75 rights in about 12 seconds. The fan climbs the glass and says he's going to jump over. Of course, we're all over there egging him on and were surprised when he jumped into the box. Boy did he get it from Robby Ray.

While a team of Ray, May, Boughner, and Barnaby would be exciting for any hockey market, Dunleavy explains why they were a perfect fit in Buffalo:

> In Buffalo, when Brad May and Rob Ray were skating around, defending their teammates and letting the talented players know what they do, this place was going nuts for those two. They love blue-collar, hard-working hockey players. They appreciate finesse. They know it's necessary, but because of this community the way it is, Brad May could sign with the hockey club, play the last 20 games of the season, and the city would go crazy right now. That's the kind of fans that are here in Buffalo. They just want hard-working guys that care.

Among the hardest-working, most caring faces for the Sabres, especially on April 29, 1997, was Pete Weber, who shares,

> Buffalo has been a great hockey market. I still have many friends there, but I have been privileged, at least on the radio side. I called the only game seven victory in Buffalo Sabres history. All the drama around that was incredible. Dominik Hašek effectively had quit on the team earlier in the series because of a spat with head coach Ted Nolan, so Steve Shields came in. The Sabres were playing the Ottawa Senators in '97, and Ottawa had a three games to two lead. Steve Shields, the backup goaltender, had to start the last two games. Shields came up with a shutout in Ottawa to force game seven on a Sunday afternoon in Buffalo, and then Derek Plante comes up in overtime with the game-winning goal. Just glanced off the glove of Ron

Tugnutt. I don't know if I've ever felt more adrenaline surge through my body than I did on that day, at least to that point in time.

Buffalo would go on to lose to (who else but) the Flyers in the Conference Semifinals but would make it all the way to the Conference Finals in 1998, before falling to the Washington Capitals. The 1998–1999 season would start as one to remember but end as one to forget for Sabre fans.

THERE'S A *HULL* LOT OF DEBATE ON THIS ONE

In the fall of 1998, with Brad May a half-season removed from his trade to Vancouver and Bob Boughner accompanying Pete Weber to the expansion Nashville Predators, Rob Ray, Derek Plante, and Matt Barnaby were still in Buffalo's picture. Adding team captain Michael Peca, leading scorer Miroslav Šatan, and a now-happier-that-Nolan's-gone Dominik Hašek, the Sabres won a trifling 37 regular-season games; however, they added nearly half that in their improbable playoff run to the Stanley Cup Final. Although the seventh seed, Buffalo mowed through Ottawa, Boston, and Toronto in their Eastern Conference matchups, en route to facing a considerably favored Dallas Stars team. With the series tied 2–2, Dallas capitalized on their home-ice advantage in game five and returned to Buffalo with a chance to clinch the first Stanley Cup in team history.

While a much longer tenured Sabres team had the same design in mind, Dallas made theirs a reality first by winning game six, 2–1, in triple overtime, on a goal by future Hall of Famer Brett Hull. After 11 seasons of playoff futility playing for the seemingly cursed St. Louis Blues, Hull was finally able to raise the cup, but the "Monday morning quarterbacks," replay enthusiasts, and virtually every Sabre fan on the planet, to this day, contest the validity of Hull's goal, as his skate was over the goal's crease, a hockey "no-no." Hašek moved on to both closure and redemption in Detroit, hoisting two Stanley Cups to close out what would eventually be recognized as a hall of fame–worthy career.

HOCKEY IN THE "NICKEL CITY" TODAY

Since their Stanley Cup Final run in 1998–1999, the city of Buffalo has been featured more on CNN's *National Weather Report* and less on ESPN's *SportsCenter*, as the Sabres' only real postseason noise since then has been two straight trips to the Eastern Conference Finals; however, in February 2011,

Buffalo businessman Terry Pegula purchased the team, an act he had dreamed of for almost 30 years, and started making Sabre fans a number-one priority. Not long after taking the reins of the organization, Pegula announced the construction of HARBORCENTER, a multiuse facility across from (now-named) First Niagara Center in the city's Canalside District. Although finishing last in 2013–2014 and 2014–2015, season tickets are selling at a premium in Buffalo, as even the number of people on the waiting list (3,000) proves impressive throughout the league. Dunleavy comments, "Sabre fans continue to wait patiently for their team to rebuild similar to the way they waited patiently for their city to be rebuilt; something the Pegulas have undertaken themselves. Terry and Kim have done a wonderful job of that so far."

With Ted Nolan once again departed from the organization—this time *not* at the request of Dominik Hašek—the Sabres are looking to Stanley Cup champion builder Dan Bylsma to lead their team back to the game's biggest stage. With the help of Evander Kane, Zach Bogosian, and established scoring leaders Tyler Ennis and Matt Moulson, who knows? Maybe Buffalo can finally drop their professional sports curse *and* "City of No Illusions" nickname, and float Lord Stanley's Cup up to (but not over) Niagara Falls, joining that "Empire State Champions Club" that has eluded them for almost half a century.

Calgary Flames

*W*hile the city of Atlanta has served as the final destination for a Braves organization that has been playing Major League Baseball since 1876, it has been more of a transportable boarding school for the NHL. In 1972, with yet another wave of expansion increasing the league's size from 6 to 12 teams and then 14 to 16 teams, the Atlanta Flames accompanied the New York Islanders into the Eastern Conference and awaited further instructions. Eight seasons and six first-round playoff losses later, the Flames made the move from the "Deep South" to the "Great White North" and took their seat at the center of focus for hockey-starved Calgary fans everywhere. One lesson the Flames quickly learned is that the proverbial "red carpet" isn't rolled out the same way everywhere.

After playing in the Omni Coliseum in Atlanta, a venue capable of seating more than 15,000 hockey fans, the Flames found themselves in Calgary's Stampede Corral, an arena that could hold only a little more than half the number of onlookers as the team's former home. Original voice of the Calgary Flames and Hall of Fame broadcaster Peter Maher discusses the team's first Albertan home, saying,

> One unique thing about the Corral—and I bring this up often when talking to people about Flames history—is in those first three years, the capacity was just under 7,000 people. They charged $25 per seat for a game, and if you wanted to stand and watch the game, the cost was $15. The significance of that is it was the highest ticket price in the entire NHL in that day. When you look at today and what the ticket prices are just to go watch an NHL game, they're nowhere close to that number unless you're 100 miles from the ice. The reason the Flames ownership had to charge such a high price was the fact that their building was half the size of the other

ones around the NHL. Some of the other ones were even larger than twice the size of the Corral, so in order to pay the bills, that's what they had to do. There was such an excitement about the Flames coming to town they had no difficulty selling out every one of those games while the Scotiabank Saddledome was being built. Of course, when the Saddledome opened, it was a huge novelty for fans there, and they just moved across the street. The Corral, as it still stands, is right across the street from the Saddledome.

Given the immediate success of the Flames, albeit in a venue less than half the size of virtually every other facility in the NHL, it would take a building with a saddle-shaped roof to hold the rodeo that quickly became the Calgary Flames–Edmonton Oilers rivalry.

NEVER PUT OIL ON A FLAME

Having to wait only one year after its NHL introduction to receive an in-province rival, the Edmonton Oilers wasted no time making their Albertan neighbors feel unwelcome. Between 1983 and 1990, either the Flames or the Oilers represented the Clarence Campbell Conference in the Stanley Cup Final each year, with Calgary taking home one cup to Edmonton's five. The Oilers and Flames faced off against one another in four of those eight post-seasons, and while the playoff tally would read Oilers 3, Flames 1 by the time Edmonton would hoist its fifth cup in seven years, it was Calgary's lone series win that prevented a possible five-peat by Edmonton, an act that has taken place only once, by the 1955–1960 Montreal Canadiens. With anywhere from 16 to 21 teams in the league during that time—not to mention only 10 in the Clarence Campbell Conference—the Flames and Oilers played one another eight times in 80 regular-season games during the 1980s and early 1990s. Coupled with an almost inevitable matchup in the playoffs each year, the two teams weren't exactly lobbying for opportunities to see one another in the offseason. Maher notes,

> It was a very heated rivalry. Today, when the Flames and Oilers play, the night before a game, there's players going out to dinner with each other on opposing teams. You find on the morning of the games (rival) players having little chats with themselves in the hallway near the dressing rooms. That never even came close to happening back in the '80s and early part of the '90s, during the battle of Alberta. These guys didn't even say, "Hello" to each other anywhere.
>
> Each summer back in those days, the motor dealers association in Alberta put on a charity golf tournament in Red Deer, which is about halfway be-

tween Calgary and Edmonton. Each year, the Flames and the Oilers would send four or five players to the event, which constituted a dinner the night before and then a golf tournament the next day. I was on the organizing committee, so I know all the details the organizers had to make. For the dinner the night before, they strategically made sure the Oilers players were on one side of the room and the Flames players were on the other side so they didn't interact. After the dinner was over, they'd go out to separate bars. They didn't want anything to do with each other, even during the summertime. At the golf tournament itself, they'd make sure the players were well separated. There was no having of any camaraderie. You could tell just by the way they responded to one another.

While brawling during a charity golf tournament may not be the best way to raise money for the Special Olympics, there was always a place for it in the Saddledome or Edmonton's Rexall Place during the 1980s.

Of course, with a heated rivalry came the players. On the Edmonton side were Wayne Gretzky, Mark Messier, and Jari Kurri handling the puck, and Steve Smith, Kevin McClelland, Jeff Beukeboom, and Marty McSorley handling the opponents. Calgary had Joe Mullen, Doug Gilmour, Joe Nieuwendyk, and Håkan Loob leading the scoring, and one of three team captains, Tim Hunter handled the "business" side. Maher comments,

> The one who was the enforcer for the Flames longer than anybody else was Tim Hunter. He's a Calgarian who joined the Flames during that third year in Calgary after the team came over from Atlanta. Tim stayed here until 1992. He was, to me, a big factor in those Flames games in the late '80s and early part of the '90s when the Flames had a lot of success. He was the premier enforcer, if you will, and in the battle of Alberta took on all the heavyweights that Edmonton had to offer in those days. He made a big, positive impact on the Flames over a long period of time at a time when the rivalry was hugely popular and fierce. He started out basically as a guy who would be an enforcer, could handle himself well in fights, but he worked really hard, especially with Bob Johnson when Bob was the Flames coach for five years in the '80s. He then improved his game tremendously to a point where you could put him out on a shift on a fairly regular basis and he would make other contributions.
>
> In those days, there were bench-clearing brawls and then there were line brawls. Tim was always in the middle of those things and asserted himself really well. His overall presence being in the Flames lineup was a huge factor in making sure the star players on the team in that era—guys like Lanny McDonald, Theoren Fleury, Doug Gilmour, Joe Nieuwendyk, and Gary Roberts—were guys players from other teams didn't take liberties with, be it against the Oilers or the Canucks, or any other team in the league.

The role of the enforcer would prove quite impactful during the Flames' first run to the Stanley Cup in 1986. Maher explains,

> In the Flames' run to the Stanley Cup Final in '86, Tim Hunter was part of that team, but two other guys on the Flames that played some pretty big enforcer roles were Neil Sheehy and Nick Fotiu. Sheehy joined the Flames and came out of Harvard. He told everyone he was the heavyweight champion of the Harvard boxing team. For the first while that he played against the Oilers, that word got around, and he got himself some room. Some guys were leery of wanting to fight with him. Later they found out there wasn't even a boxing team at Harvard. He was pretty good with the BS, if you will, and created a bit of a reputation that way. I wouldn't have considered him the heavyweight champion of fighters at that era or anytime in the NHL, but he certainly did have that intimidation factor given the fact that he let everyone know, allegedly, that he was the heavyweight boxing champion at Harvard.
>
> Nick Fotiu joined the Flames at the trade deadline of the '85–'86 season. Prior to Nick coming to the Flames, they could never beat the Oilers. If they did, it was pretty rare. After Nick came, the Flames won a couple of regular-season games there and then won the playoff series, upsetting the Oilers. Nick played a pretty big role in that, and then he stayed with the Flames for a couple of years after that. He was always a focal point when the Flames and Oilers played. The Flames were winning more games than they were losing to the Oilers. I saw him two years after he left the Flames, and he said, "You couldn't beat the Oilers before I came. I left, and you can't beat them again," so he felt he was a pretty significant factor in changing the outcomes of those games.

While denying the Oilers their third straight championship, the Flames lost the 1986 Stanley Cup Final in five games to the Montreal Canadiens, beginning the Flames' three-year journey back to gaining some sweet revenge on their Quebec counterpart.

A CUP FOR THE SOUTH ALBERTANS THIS TIME

In 1989, after their 14th straight trip to the playoffs (including five seasons in Atlanta), Calgary finally hoisted the cup its neighbor to the north had won four times prior. With a seasoned Joe Mullen leading the team in scoring and making up for the departure of Dan Quinn, the Flames won an impressive 54 regular-season games and finished with a league-best 117 points. The post-season was no different, as the team's closest series was the first, the Division Semifinals against Vancouver, which went the distance and then some when Joel Otto sent the Canucks home with his game-winning goal.

Playing a familiar face wearing new team colors, the Flames swept Wayne Gretzky and the Los Angeles Kings and then took care of the Blackhawks in five before their Stanley Cup Final rematch with Montreal. After a heartbreaking loss in double overtime put them in a 1–2 series hole, the Flames won three straight, including two in Montreal's famed Forum, to take home the team's first-ever title. Calling the Flames' arrival at hockey's summit, Maher reflects,

> The team has only won one Stanley Cup. May 25, 1989, the night the Flames won the Stanley Cup, is without doubt the game that stands out as the most significant in my broadcast career in the NHL. Even though it was 26 years ago, I can remember it almost as clear as if it happened last night. It was on a Friday night. It was in Montreal. It was the Forum. The Flames led the series three games to two. I can still remember and see in my mind Colin Patterson opening the scoring for the game. McDonald's goal in the second period that broke a 1–1 tie. The Flames never trailed after that. The big saves of Mike Vernon and then the two goals in the third period from Doug Gilmour to clinch the victory. There's no doubt in my mind that game is the one that will stand out forever from my broadcasting career as the game of the team's history. Hopefully there's going to be more Stanley Cup championships in the future, but having had the honor and pleasure of being in the broadcast booth and calling that Stanley Cup win in 1989 certainly stands out as a highlight.

There would be room for plenty more highlights by the time Maher retired from broadcasting some 25 years later.

"C OF RED"

Following their Stanley Cup championship, the postseason would prove a short one for the Flames in all six of their playoff appearances. Then, beginning with the 1996–1997 season, the team would take a postseason sabbatical, casting an invisible cloud over the city for seven straight years. Maher notes,

> The pulse of the Flames is the pulse of the city of Calgary. When the Flames are doing well, the mood is very upbeat in the area. When the team is floundering or not having success, it's a down mood. I've talked to people in all various walks of life here, and they tell me when the Flames are doing well, it increases the positive attitude in the workplace, and when it's not going so well, it's going in the other direction. This is something that's been prevalent right from day one with the arrival of the Flames in 1980. The team has totally embraced the city, and it affects the mood of the people.

After a seven-year absence from the postseason, Calgary's 84 points during the 2003–2004 season were good enough for third in their division and a first-round matchup with the first-place Vancouver Canucks. Stunning a different community of Canadian hockey fans, the Flames outlasted Vancouver in the seven-game series, after an overtime goal by left winger Martin Gélinas completed the upset and had the team packing its bags for Detroit.

Prolonging their magical season, the Flames would clinch yet another series via Gélinas and his overtime magic, ousting the Detroit Red Wings in six games. Maher recalls,

> The Flames were definitely underdogs. They had upset Vancouver in the first round and were going up against a very powerful Detroit team. The series came to a game six, but this one was in the Saddledome. It went to overtime, with Martin Gélinas scoring the goal for the Flames that would give them the win and clinch that series. That goal is another one that stands out in my mind as if it happened last night. Sometimes when I go to speaking engagements, especially if Marty's there, I'll say, "Marty Gélinas put me in the Hockey Hall of Fame with that goal," because that goal, with the excitement that was built up in that building and the fabulous roar from the crowd with the call, gained all kinds of recognition and play, not only here in Canada, but also in the United States.

The Flames would gun down yet another first-place team en route to the Stanley Cup Final, beating the San Jose Sharks in six games. Although the magic would finally run out in game seven of the final by way of a Tampa Bay Lightning victory, a red mark was put on the city, but in a good way. Maher comments,

> It wasn't until that run in 2004 that the "C of Red" became prominent. Prior to that, there were very few people watching games wearing Flames jerseys or T-shirts with a flame on it, but when that run got going and the city got so caught up in the excitement, the "C of Red" became paramount in the Saddledome and is still there to this day. In the Saddledome, one of the unique features is the saddle-shaped roof. For many years in there, you wondered about the crowd noise. Even though some nights there were 20,000 people in there, it never seemed to be a real loud crowd. Many of us felt maybe it had something to do with the construction of the roof. That would prove incorrect.
>
> When the Flames got into that playoff run in '04, that was as noisy of a building as you could find in the NHL. It was deafening. So the conclusion reached by myself and a number of people who were involved around the team in the earlier years is that when the Flames had those big crowds in the '80s and early '90s, it basically was a corporate crowd. The seats were sold to corporate people, and, to a lot of them, it was a social night

out. The noise level was never really high, but when the team fell on hard times—not being in the playoffs from 1997 through to 2004—attendance really decreased by a significant amount. The fans that then got caught up in the wave of the tremendous run the team had were more the mums and pops, the kids, and that type of thing, so they were a much louder crowd.

Following the Flames' magical run, the team, along with the rest of the league, took the year off. In the 10 seasons since the league's return, the Flames have only qualified for the playoffs half the time, making it to the second round only once; however, the "C of Red" still fills the Scotiabank Saddledome seats, as the Flames have finished seventh or better in average attendance since the players lockout of 2004–2005. With such offense-minded players as Johnny Gaudreau, Sean Monahan, and Mikael Backlund, as well as defensive standouts Dennis Wideman and Mark Giordano, not to mention goaltending import Brian Elliott tending to on-ice affairs, the Flames are looking to keep Calgary's pulse "upbeat" for many years to come.

· *6* ·

Carolina Hurricanes

*I*n the fall of 1979—and against the wishes of some NHL teams—the World Hockey Association (WHA) and its four teams joined the NHL to bring the league's total membership to 21. The only non-Canadian squad of these four teams, the Hartford Whalers, brought with them a familiar face who most assumed had played his NHL swan song almost a decade earlier: "Mr. Hockey," Gordie Howe. Having played professional hockey since the age of 18, the 51-year-old Howe suited up for all 80 regular-season games for the Whalers, adding 15 goals to bring his career NHL total to 801. With an AARP membership lurking around the corner, Howe ended his 32-year career at the hands of the Montreal Canadiens in the postseason's preliminary round.

During the next 17 seasons, the Whalers had two five-year playoff droughts sandwiched between seven straight postseason appearances. With their deepest playoff run being the Division Finals in 1985–1986, the Whalers left the hockey-friendly confines of New England and traveled southward to the "Tar Heel State," North Carolina, where the team was renamed the Hurricanes. With its future home, PNC Arena, still under construction, the team made a pit stop in Greensboro on the journey to its ultimate destination in Raleigh. Hall of Fame radio broadcaster Chuck Kaiton, who has been with the team since their first year in Hartford, describes the marketing and PR nightmare created by this Whalers–Hurricanes transition:

> When we announced we were moving here in May of '97, in lieu of Minnesota or Columbus, I thought to myself, "What the heck's going on here? We're moving to Raleigh, North Carolina?" Little did I know places like Nashville and Atlanta would come in later and there would be a move to the south with other franchises. It turned out to be a pretty good move. When you talk about the impact of the area, we had to play the first two years in

32

Greensboro after the move from Hartford because there wasn't an arena finished yet here in Raleigh. In those two years, that's when you really had to do the leg work to ensure hockey would be popular in the area. It was tough because you're trying to get people coming an hour and 20 minutes to buy season tickets for something they had never seen before. You're not just trying to get season ticket-holders from people—the transplanted northerners who are already exposed to the game—but you're also trying to recruit and expose the native North Carolinians to the game of hockey.

Apparently, two years of season tickets weren't in the cards for fans who knew their city held interim status for the franchise, as the Hurricanes finished last in average league attendance by more than 3,000 tickets for the 1997–1998 and 1998–1999 seasons. Hurricanes owner Peter Karmanos Jr., probably feeling like Howard Hughes just before the "Spruce Goose" lifted above the waters in Los Angeles Harbor in November 1947, was likely having his own reservations about being a season ticket-holder. Nevertheless, the team arrived in Raleigh for the 1999–2000 season and, with 4,200 more in average attendance, crawled out of the league cellar—not exactly "flying high" but at least not treading water.

MAKING TOBACCO ROAD AN ICY ONE AS WELL

While professional hockey came a little bit late to the party, which is the sports tradition of North Carolina, it doesn't mean the door wouldn't be opened—or, in this case, the gate wouldn't be dropped—for them. Chuck Kaiton explains,

> One of the nice things about being down here in Raleigh is people have a football mentality when they come to a game. Whether it's on the weekend or during the week, they tailgate like they do coming to a football game, which I think is really unique. It's found a lot of fans—especially Canadians—taken aback by it because of the way our arena is configured. We have a parking lot around the entire arena, which is adjacent to the football stadium, so they share the same parking lot with North Carolina State University. One of the neat traditions here is people tailgate no matter what. It came to light back in '02, when the Hurricanes played the Toronto Maple Leafs in the Eastern Conference Finals. Because they couldn't get tickets at their place, Toronto fans made the pilgrimage down to Raleigh for a couple of games in that series and got caught up in it. Now, I noticed in Toronto, they try to do their own version of tailgating. They go out and have a good time before the game, especially when the weather gets better in Toronto, so it's kind of stuck there, too.

In the spring of 2002, Hurricane fans, with the team advancing past the first round for the first time since coming from Hartford, probably had the best tailgating weather one could ask for.

2001–2002: GETTING A HEAD START ON HURRICANE SEASON

Under the direction of team-builder Paul Maurice and led by captain, two-time Stanley Cup champion, and future Hall of Famer Ron Francis, the 2001–2002 Hurricanes finished first in the Eastern Conference's Southeast Division for the second time since moving to Carolina. Facing the scrappy defending Eastern Conference champion New Jersey Devils in the opening round, the Hurricanes advanced in six games and went on to face half of the NHL's original six during the next month and a half. With another six-game series win—this time over Doug Gilmour and the Montreal Canadiens—the Hurricanes, in just their fifth year in their new surroundings, had advanced deeper into the playoffs than during their more than 18 years in Hartford.

Facing a Toronto Maple Leafs team that hadn't won or been to a Stanley Cup Final since 1967, the Hurricanes once again closed out a team in six games, thanks to an overtime goal by Martin Gélinas that sailed past legendary goaltender Curtis Joseph. Gélinas would have two more series-clinching goals further down the road in a Calgary uniform, but, in 2002, his feat set a date with the team's third "original six" opponent, the Detroit Red Wings.

Facing a roster chock-full of future Hall of Famers, the Hurricanes won the opening game of the Stanley Cup final, 3–2, in overtime, but it would be the team's final victory of the season. With Detroit's end of the scoring reading "3" in the next four games, Carolina's would read "<3," and the Red Wings, finally achieving dynasty status, went on to win their third Stanley Cup in six seasons. As the traditional handshakes were taking place between the teams at center ice, Ron Francis was the first to receive the news from his former coach and nine-time Stanley Cup champion Scotty Bowman that the legendary builder was calling it a career. Bowman would lace up his skates one final time and parade the cup on the ice, creating one of hockey's most memorable images of the last 20 years. Francis himself would call it a career two seasons later, just in time for the 2004–2005 NHL lockout.

SECOND TIME'S THE CHARM

The two seasons following the franchise's first-ever trip to the Stanley Cup Final, the Hurricanes failed to qualify for the playoffs. Luckily, in 2004–2005, the NHL hit the reset button and suspended the season for the entire league, giving Carolina ample time to gear up for what would become an even more magical season than in 2001–2002. With the signings of veteran Ray Whitney and the defensive František Kaberle and Oleg Tverdovsky, it didn't take long for the Hurricanes to shake the rust off their blades, finishing first in the Southeast Division with 112 regular-season points. Eric Staal, having waited patiently during the lockout just a year after his rookie campaign, posted 100 points to lead the team's scoring at the tender age of 21. With mid-season imports Matt Cullen and Doug Weight "learning their lines" just in time for the postseason, the 'Canes were slated to face the Montreal Canadiens to open the 2006 postseason.

While Martin Gélinas wasn't there to clinch yet another series with an overtime goal, Carolina had Cory Stillman, who, on a pass from future Hall of Famer Rod Brind'Amour, slipped one past Canadiens goalie Cristobal Huet and helped his team move on to face the New Jersey Devils. While the shortest series his team would play during their 2006 playoff run, Brind'Amour again assisted an overtime game winner, this time to Niclas Wallin. The Hurricanes preserved their energy for the final two series, as both went the full seven games. The Hurricanes prevailed in the series decider against a championship-hungry Buffalo Sabres team led by Chris Drury and Maxim Afinogenov to move on to the Stanley Cup Final for the second time in four seasons.

Having reached a commanding 3–1 series lead after stealing one in Edmonton, Carolina lost two straight to Chris Pronger and the Oilers, setting up a game-seven showdown at PNC Arena. As the 'Canes broadcaster, Kaiton describes the game that finally brought a Stanley Cup down tobacco road:

> Obviously game seven of the Stanley Cup Final in '06 against Edmonton takes the cake as the most memorable. The thing I'll never forget is we had close to 19,000 fans in the building and none of them sat down for the entire 60 minutes of the game. They stood. People were that captivated, and it was such an exciting game. Another thing that stood out in that game was until Justin Williams scored an empty-net goal to make it 3–1 to really solidify they were going to win the Stanley Cup, the Hurricanes had two goals scored by two defensemen who had never scored a goal in their life. With all the star power we had, two defensemen, František Kaberle and Aaron Ward, scored the first two Hurricane goals. Peter Laviolette was our coach. We had a very aggressive team; great offensive players like Eric Staal, Rod Brind'Amour, Ray Whitney, Eric Cole, and Justin Williams, who has won a couple of cups with L.A. now. With all those guys, two defensemen scored, and both scored from the point. They hit slap shots from the point and beat the goaltender, Jussi Markkanen.

Another thing I remember from that game is with 3:24 left in the third period, we get a power play. We're up 2–1 in the game, and the puck gets stolen by a player named Fernando Pisani. He goes in on Cam Ward, and Ward makes a spectacular kick save to keep the game 2–1 Carolina. That's indelibly etched in my mind. They even have a picture of that save in our arena for fans to see all the time. That save preserved the lead. Otherwise, who knows what would have happened? The game could have gone to overtime, and anybody could have won it. Three minutes later, Justin Williams scored in the empty net to make it 3–1, and the Hurricanes won the cup.

Aside from defenseman becoming "offense-men," perhaps the biggest story of the Hurricanes championship run is that of goaltender Cam Ward, winner of the Conn Smythe Trophy, who, as a backup, took over for Martin Gerber and won 15 postseason games, joining Ken Dryden and Patrick Roy in an elite class of rookie goaltenders.

THE CAROLINA HURRICANES TODAY

Three seasons after joining Duke, North Carolina, and North Carolina State in the "Tobacco Road Champions Club," Carolina made another deep playoff run but fell short to the eventual Stanley Cup champion Pittsburgh Penguins. Since 2008–2009, the 'Canes have failed to qualify for the postseason. In hopes of changing this negative trend, the team brought on former captain Ron Francis as the new general manager after the 2013–2014 season. Working with such young draft picks as Victor Rask, Noah Hanifin, and Elias Lindholm, Francis is piecing together a Hurricanes team he hopes will bring the NHL playoffs back to the Tar Heel State. With veteran imports Jay Mc-Clement and Lee Stempniak, as well as now veteran Cam Ward (and only remaining player from 2005–2006 championship squad), the Hurricanes hope to once again let their fans tailgate so long into the summer that they pass early bird North Carolina State fans on the way out of the parking lot with a Stanley Cup championship parade procession leading the way.

· 7 ·

Chicago Blackhawks

$\mathcal{T}$he "Windy City" is notorious for its superfandom, so much so that *Saturday Night Live* created a sketch titled "Bill Swerski's Superfans" to showcase the city's two most popular teams at the time, "da Bulls" and "da Bears." More than a decade since Michael Jordan's third and final retirement, and more than 30 years removed from the Vince McMahon-choreographed "Super Bowl Shuffle," the skit could easily be reaired to feature the second most recent installment of Chicago's success in the world of sports, "da Blackhawks." One of the NHL's "original six," the Blackhawks came into the NHL when their former identity, the Portland Rosebuds, went by the wayside, along with the Western Hockey League, in which they played. The Blackhawks, unlike their "Second City" compatriot Bulls, Bears, Cubs, and White Sox, would not have to wait decades for their first league championship, taking home their first Stanley Cup title in 1934, thanks to such future Hall of Famers as Doug Bentley, Arthur Coulter, and goaltender Chuck Gardiner.

Despite tragically losing Gardiner to a brain tumor, the Blackhawks would regroup four seasons later with goaltender Mike Karakas, one of a record eight American-born players on a Stanley Cup–winning team. Although not the near-century or century-plus droughts of the White Sox and Cubs, respectively, the Blackhawks would go almost two decades before the arrival of two of the team's all-time superstars, Bobby Hull and Stanislav "Stan" Mikita, would eventually bring Stanley Cup title number three to "Sweet Home Chicago."

Hall of Fame TV play-by-play broadcaster Pat Foley, who, having been with the team since 1980 and growing up in Chicago during the days of

"Stan" and the "Golden Jet," describes the team's impact on its city's noted superfans:

> I grew up here and I remember as a kid when Bobby and Stan showed up in 1959, the Blackhawks, for a decade and a half, were the hottest ticket in town. I don't know the story of other cities, but, certainly in Chicago, I don't think anybody would question the fact that currently and maybe forever, the Bears have been the biggest sports story in town. Chicago is a Bears town. I think that has to be stated, but if they're "1," the Blackhawks are "1a." This franchise is right there with them. Through the '60s, the Blackhawks were—I'd say—a hotter ticket than the Chicago Bears were.

During their respective careers with the Blackhawks, Hull and Mikita scored a combined 1,145 goals and 2,620 points. Aside from their 1961 Stanley Cup, the two superstars won a collective seven Art Ross Trophies and four Hart Memorial Trophies during their time with the team. While Hull was accumulating the most goals in team history, a record that still stands, Mikita, along with wingers Ken Wharram, Ab McDonald, and Doug Mohns, headed the famous "Scooter Line," which dominated the league offensively during the 1960s. Hull played most of his twilight years in the WHA with Winnipeg. With the WHA–NHL merger to start the 1979–1980 season, he was once again padding his NHL career stats and would end his career in Hartford alongside his longtime rival, Gordie Howe. Mikita played his entire career with the Blackhawks and, although second to Hull on the team's all-time goal list, holds the top spot in assists and points scored.

A BETTER SEAT TO WATCH A BLACKHAWKS GAME

Going from watching the games at home, or, at best, from the cheap seats inside the team's old home at Chicago Stadium, Pat Foley, after calling games for the International Hockey League's Grand Rapid Owls, got the job behind the microphone for Chicago and took the seat once graced by legendary Blackhawk voice Lloyd Pettit. In his first broadcast, Foley likely had to check his press credentials to make sure he wasn't back in the IHL. Foley explains:

> I got the job with the Blackhawks at 26 years old. I'm thrilled and out of my mind, and the first game I ever did was in the old stadium. A couple of crazy things happened. The Blackhawks actually scored a goal

from about 180 feet away. They were killing a penalty. They just flipped the puck down the ice, and Mike Palmeteer came out of the net and nonchalantly—one-handed—tried to play it. It hits his stick and goes into the net. They scored a goal on a dump out. That was weird. The same night, there's a brawl on the ice. It's a five on five. Everybody's paired up and chucking 'em. I'm trying to call all these battles, and things settled down. In the meantime, some drunk fan climbs over the boards and gets on the ice. He's walking around out there waving a pennant, so the security guys get on the ice. They try to haul him off, and he's fighting with them, trying to stay on the ice. They finally get him down and grab him by the ankles, and are hauling him through the penalty box door and, because he wants to stay on the ice, he grabs the door. This security guy in an orange jacket sees him grabbing at the door so he just shuts the door. He didn't grab the door much longer. I thought I had seen it all in the minor leagues, here's my first NHL game and I'm going, "Really? This is how it works up here?"

Foley would see many more nights reminiscent of his IHL broadcasting days.

COWS AREN'T THE ONLY MEAT
FOR SALE IN THE WINDY CITY

Even though players like Stan Mikita were finishing out their guaranteed Hall of Fame careers in Chicago, the "meatpacking" the city had unfortunately become famous for wasn't taking place in Chicago Stadium. Says Foley,

> They really had a number of off years. In 1980, in a 17,000-seat arena, it was a big deal to get 11,000 to 12,000 people in there. That's how far it had fallen off. Denis Savard, an electrifying, bring-you-out-of-your-seat type of player, showed up, and the team started getting good really quickly. In the early '80s, the Blackhawks were good. You think about some of the great players that were there. Al Secord was a 50-goal scorer. Steve Larmer was—*I believe*—a Hall of Fame player and the best two-way winger I've ever seen come through here. Doug Wilson, a perennial NHL All-Star, was—*I believe*—a Hall of Fame defenseman. There were teams here that were good enough to win the Stanley Cup. Unfortunately, then you get to the semifinals and you run into Gretzky and the Oilers, and play a team with six Hall of Famers. The Blackhawks had really good teams for quite a long time but could never quite get over the hump with the Oilers. That's a major hump. Not many other teams got by them either.

One of Foley's most memorable games, which took place on December 11, 1985, was a testament to just how major the Edmonton "hump" was. Foley recalls,

> The Blackhawks played the Edmonton Oilers back when it was a different league. Edmonton was scoring 400 goals a year. The Blackhawks once played a home game, scored nine goals, and they were never in the game. They lost, 12–9. At one point, it was 4–0, but with nine goals, we were never in the game.

The contest between the Blackhawks and Oilers tied the NHL record for most combined goals in a game, set by the Montreal Canadiens and the (then-named) Toronto St. Patrick's in 1920.

Sadly, by the time Gretzky shipped out of Edmonton for Los Angeles and Mark Messier and Jari Kurri landed in New York, Chicago players, too, had become a flight risk. Foley continues,

> As time went on, you get into the mid-'90s, and there was sort of a consistent pattern that had developed. Year after year, people's favorite players would leave town. It was almost always over money. As time went on, the team could not stay at the same level because all of their best players kept leaving. They weren't replaced adequately, and the team fell off. There were some dark times here in the late '90s/early 2000s. There were nights of 5,000 people in a 20,000-seat arena, and it was not great. You could sit in the upper reaches of the United Center and hear the puck hit the stick when a pass was made. It was not good.

Among the departed Blackhawks during this period of playoff futility were Hall of Famers Ed Belfour and Chris Chelios, and longtime fan favorite Jeremy Roenick. Chelios, while already having won a cup with Montreal prior to his eight and a half years with Chicago, would go on to win two more cups with the team's longtime rival, the Detroit Red Wings. Belfour would win his sole championship in a Dallas Stars uniform in 1999. Roenick, one of hockey's most familiar faces both on and off for the past two decades, never drank from Lord Stanley's Cup as a player.

During this period of time, when Chicago's role in the NHL was prepping the game's most promising stars for championship glory elsewhere, the team went through a 10-year span in which their only playoff appearance was a five-game series loss to St. Louis in 2002. In the meantime, in Chicago, Michael Jordan and the Bulls had polished off another three-peat, the Bears had appeared in their second Super Bowl in team history, the White Sox had won their first World Series in 88 seasons, and Steve Bartman had become "public enemy number one."

On the Blackhawk side of things, Bill Wirtz, who had been the team owner for more than 40 years, passed away in 2007. Taking over ownership of the team was Bill's son, Rocky, who, unlike so many heirs to nine-figure companies, opted to go in a different direction than that of his father. Rather than selling his fruitful crops (players) to the highest bidder, Rocky chose to cultivate them, starting with the team's number-one overall draft pick in 2007, a 19-year-old right winger by the name of Patrick Kane. A season after winning the Calder Trophy in 2008, Kane, along with fellow youngster Jonathan Toews, would not only return the Blackhawks to the playoffs for the first time in seven years, but also lead them all the way to the Conference Finals before losing in five games to the eventual league runner-up Detroit Red Wings.

Keeping this promising core of players rather than "taking them to market," Rocky, with the help of players the likes of Patrick Kane, Jonathan Toews, Kris Versteeg, Patrick Sharp, Brent Seabrook, Duncan Keith, and Niklas Hjalmarsson, as well the leadership of team-builder Joel Quenneville, has overseen five Conference Finals appearances and three Stanley Cup championships in seven years (2008–2015), making the Chicago Blackhawks the latest NHL dynasty. Foley, behind the mic during this fruitful period, relates how calling a game to a crowd of 5,000 onlookers in the United Center has become a distant memory:

> When Rocky Wirtz took over and brought in John McDonough and Jay Blunk, the transformation of this franchise in the last eight or nine years has been nothing short of remarkable, unlike anything in the history of pro sports. I would make the case that they're an even bigger story now than they were in the '60s, when they were the hottest ticket in town. There's obviously some marquee stars here. The Blackhawks have marketing geniuses. It obviously helps to have great players. Nothing helps more than winning. They've hosted three parades and have a lot of great stars here. In addition to that, the genius of the organizational approach regarding marketing and the way things are now, it's been a complete transformation from the way things used to be.
>
> John McDonough created a midsummer sold-out convention, the first in hockey. The fans feel more connected than they ever have. I've been around long enough and have seen a lot of ups and a lot of downs. When I first showed up here, this franchise had fallen off a long way from where they were when Bobby and Stan's teams were really good until the early '70s. They basically fell off the radar to the point of irrelevance in the early 2000s. Then Rocky took over and there was a complete change in approach to how the Blackhawks do business, and I believe they're bigger here now than they ever have been, and if you look at the makeup of the crowds, there is a high percentage of young people. The younger

generation has attached themselves to and been included in this franchise. These are not your father's Blackhawks.

With three Stanley Cup titles in six years, it is safe to say that the Chicago Blackhawks are the hottest ticket in *other* towns as well. Foley continues,

This team travels well. There is not a road game we go to anywhere that we don't see hundreds, if not thousands, of Blackhawk sweaters throughout the arena. It happens religiously. It doesn't matter where we are. It's easy for our camera crew to get crowd shots with Blackhawks people in there. It happens nightly no matter where we are. You can be in Western Canada, on the East Coast, anywhere. Hawk fans are everywhere. There's a passion around this franchise now I don't believe ever existed. There's always been passionate fans here, but I think the connection with the Chicago sports fan—certainly the hockey fan—to this team, franchise, and these players feels stronger than it's ever been. It's certainly stronger than most franchises in Chicago.

GOODBYE, OLD "FRIEND"?

While a Blackhawks game certainly makes for the "hottest ticket in town" no matter who the team is playing, the attraction doubles when the other "five" of the "original six" NHL teams stop by. Unfortunately, in the past 16 years, the Blackhawks have seen the original six representation in the Western Conference fall off, first with the Toronto Maple Leafs in 1998–1999, and then with the team's arch nemesis, the Red Wings, in 2013–2014, a season after the two met in the Conference Semifinals. With the Eastern Conference stacked with five of the original six, the Blackhawks, while proving themselves as the most dominant of the group, still find themselves stranded at the train station when the season schedules are released. Foley, who could easily be labeled a hockey "purist," states his case against the league's current alignment:

I understand you have to have divisional play emphasized. I get that geography has to be a factor in how you schedule. We're the only original six team in the west. That's fine. We belong in the west. We don't belong in the Eastern Conference, but there should be a provision that these original six teams play each other at least four times. We only play each other twice. Rest assured, whenever any of those teams comes in here, it's a bigger ticket than it is even against some of the divisional opponents we have rivalries with. Any time the Boston Bruins or the New York Rangers show up, it's a big deal, and it should be. I think that's been a scheduling mistake as far as the NHL is concerned. I think that original six holds significant meaning, and I don't think it should be overlooked to the point that it is right now. Red Wing games are still a big rivalry, but, as time goes on, it's going to lessen, if not go away. Certainly the networks understand how big a game it is. It always has been, but is it going to be that way 12 years from now when you play each other only twice a year and you're not going to play in the playoffs unless it's the finals?

On the bright side, should the Wings and Blackhawks renew their playoff rivalry and play for the 17th time in the postseason, this time the winner truly will "take all."

A HALL OF FAME SIGN OFF ON A HALL OF FAME TEAM

Having grown up in Chicago, Pat Foley was audience to some of the most legendary voices in sports, including Harry Caray and former Blackhawks play-by-play icon Lloyd Pettit. Although his TV play-by-play duties were turned over to the national networks for the team's three Stanley Cup championships, Foley has been witness to many keystone moments for the Chicago squad. From calling former "Bruise Brother" Bob Probert's on-ice bouts with the toughest players in the NHL to being the voice behind the greatest figures outside of Bobby Hull and Stan Mikita the city has ever known, he was an obvious choice for induction into the Hockey Hall of Fame in 2014. Looking back on a career that is likely far from over, Foley describes his unlikely journey thus far as follows:

> I'm a Chicago kid. I grew up here. In my little corner of the world, the whole thing's been remarkable. I've gotten to work at home all these years. When I first wanted to become a broadcaster, I wanted to do a big-league team in a big-league town. The fact that it's worked out for me at home, it's not a million to one long shot. It's infinity to one. I can make the statement I've broadcast over a third of the games ever played in the history of an original six franchise. That's a special thought. An original six team means something. I'm proud of that.

Considering Joe Maddon and the Chicago Cubs winning the team's first title in 108 years will trump any and all Chicago sports stories for the next decade plus, the Blackhawks may have to maintain that "1a" status—at least until Patrick Kane and company parade another cup or two down West Addison and out onto the shores of Lake Michigan.

• 8 •

Colorado Avalanche

*M*ajor League Baseball's Colorado Rockies, while having a name suitable for their surroundings, aren't the first franchise of that nomenclature in the Mile High City. On October 6, 1976, the NHL's Colorado Rockies took the ice at McNichols Arena, beating the Toronto Maple Leafs, 4–2. That inaugural win, however, may be the only memorable one to this day, as the Rockies, having only appeared in the playoffs once in their six-year history, were moved by new team owner John McMullen to New Jersey, where they would become the Devils.

Two seasons before the Rockies were on their way out of Denver, an NHL franchise was on its way to Quebec, as the Nordiques began their first of 16 seasons in the Gibraltar of North America. Although finishing first in a strike-shortened 1994–1995 season, the Quebec Nordiques would relocate their budding team and bring NHL hockey back to Denver, where it would take little time for the newly renamed Colorado Avalanche to make their presence felt in the Western Conference.

A ROCKY MOUNTAIN *HIGH*

In 1994, while Quebec was bringing up exportable fruit in the form of such players as Joe Sakic, Peter Forsberg, and Owen Nolan, Denver was unknowingly preparing its sports fans for championships, the likes of which they had not seen. Colorado Avalanche TV play-by-play broadcaster Michael Haynes, who has been with the team since day one, describes the welcoming party, which lasted two years:

I was here the year before the Avalanche came in. I arrived in Denver in the summer of '94, for a minor-league team called the Denver Grizzlies. That was their first year. The town was very excited about hockey that year. We drew great. The team was phenomenal, and they won the whole championship. I believe that because of the success of the Grizzlies, the ownership of the Denver Nuggets saw how much the fans loved the game. I think that went a long way to convincing the ownership of the Nuggets that they should purchase the Quebec Nordiques and bring them in. I was part of that and saw all that happening, so I had a pretty good perspective that it was a great hockey town before the Avalanche arrived.

While plenty can be said about the haul brought to Denver via Quebec, it was another Canadian import that truly made the difference needed to raise Lord Stanley's Cup atop the Colorado "Rockies." By the time he was stocking up on Dramamine and inhalers in his new mile-high home, goaltender Patrick Roy had already accumulated 289 regular-season wins, 70 playoff wins, and two Stanley Cup engravings for the Montreal Canadiens, one of which took place at the age of 20. In his eight seasons between the pipes for the Avalanche, Roy won another 262 regular-season games and 81 playoff games, and had his name etched twice more onto the Stanley Cup. Roy's 551 career regular-season wins are second only to Martin Brodeur, but "Saint Patrick's" 151 playoff victories (most all time) best Brodeur's 113 (second most all time). Roy being the key variable in the equation, Haynes describes the Avalanche's penchant for success:

It certainly goes a long way when you have a team that comes in, and, very quickly, you make a trade for Patrick Roy and then the team just takes off. Huge success. Young players like Joe Sakic. You had Peter Forsberg. They traded for Claude Lemieux. They traded for Sandis Ozolinsh. That team was flying. It was very exciting to watch. They didn't just win. It was the way they won because they had a great skating team that was fun to watch. They scored goals. They had the best goalie in the league, and it just was the perfect formula. There really weren't any sort of growing pains at all with the team. If you're any kind of hockey fan, you wanted to see them. If you weren't a hockey fan, you got caught up in all of the excitement because the team was winning and the way they were winning. You have a lot of those expansion teams that come in and it takes years for them to put together a decent team. Even teams that move, a lot of times, do so because they're not doing well. They're not drawing, and it's not initially a good team, but that wasn't the case. When it arrived, it was a great team that was ready to take that next step and take the town by storm.

In its first seven seasons in Colorado, the Avalanche failed to reach, at the very least, the Conference Finals only once. For their first eight seasons out West, the team won its division every year, always posing a threat come late April and into mid-June. Haynes adds,

> You could make a case the first nine seasons of the Avalanche, they were a team that could have won the Stanley Cup in any of those nine years. That adds so much to it. This has always been a Broncos town. The Broncos won the Super Bowl twice in the '97 and '98 seasons, but the Avalanche, during those nine years, were right behind the Broncos—a couple of years maybe right there with them—in terms of popularity. Every year, the team was good, and it seemed like the ownership and GM/president Pierre Lacroix made a big trade to get Ray Borque or Rob Blake. They got the Patrick Roy deal done. It seemed like every year there was a big splash.

One could argue that the biggest splash came at the hands of team left winger Chris Simon during the second round of the team's first playoff run in Colorado. Although part of the "package deal" Nordiques team that came from Montreal, Chris Simon got the Avalanche going in a way Patrick Roy couldn't against the Chicago Blackhawks. Haynes notes,

> I don't think there's any doubt the toughest guy the Avalanche ever had was a guy named Chris Simon. He was about as tough as anybody at that time in the NHL. Their first year in '96, in the second round against the Chicago Blackhawks, they were looking for something to give them some momentum to win that series. You talk to most people, and they'll tell you there was a fight between Chris Simon and Bob Probert, who, at that time, anybody would have considered the toughest and maybe all-time toughest. You could take a survey, asking, "Who is the best enforcer or somebody who contributed offensively as well as being the enforcer?" I would think 99 out of 100 people are going to say Bob Probert is the all-time best. Chris Simon beat him up pretty good and won the fight, and it really gave the Avalanche some momentum in that series. They went on to win that series and the Stanley Cup. You always hear about fights changing what's happening throughout the course of a game, trying to swing the momentum. It didn't always happen that way. That one was clearly a case where it did happen, and it worked to the Avalanche's advantage.

While one season is hardly enough time to do much of anything with a franchise—let alone put together a championship-caliber team—the Avalanche managed to do just that *and* pick up a new rival along the way.

ALI VERSUS FRAZIER . . . ON ICE

Between the 1995–1996 and 2001–2002 seasons, the Colorado Avalanche and their instant rival, the Detroit Red Wings, won a total of five Stanley Cups between them, facing one another five times in the postseason for a total of 30 games. In their first playoff series, the Red Wings came in having accumulated the most regular-season wins (62) and second most regular-season points (131) in NHL history (1976–1977 Canadiens, 132); however, with Patrick Roy on the other side of the ice, Colorado bested the Wings in six games. In the clincher for the Avalanche, the "Blood Feud" between the two clubs began with Avalanche right winger Claude Lemieux. Former Colorado Avalanche and current St. Louis Blues TV play-by-play broadcaster John Kelly describes just how deep into the ice the bad blood between these two clubs seeps:

> Certainly one of the most memorable nights I've had would be when the Avalanche played in Detroit in March of '97. You'd have to understand the rivalry that had built up in just a year. The Avalanche had won the cup the year before and had beaten Detroit in the third round. Detroit had run away with the Presidents' Trophy that year, and they had some fierce battles during that season in '96. In the last game of the playoffs, Claude Lemieux hit Kris Draper into the boards, and he suffered a horrific injury. He broke his jaw and nose. Draper needed a lot of surgery. Lemieux got kicked out of the game, of course, and then the Avalanche went on and won the game. There basically was a bounty on the head of Claude Lemieux, and the next year, he had surgery and didn't play until March.
>
> The Avalanche had a game in Detroit in March. I remember vividly landing in Detroit. We had played the night before in another city. The Avalanche had a police escort from the airport to the hotel. I was at the hotel, and it was completely encircled with police. In the paper the next day—the day of the game—they put up Lemieux's picture. Believe me, he was a wanted man. During the game, you could tell that there was blood in the air even before anything happened. The Avalanche came out to a big lead in the game. Lemieux was out on the ice and a fight started not involving him, and Darren McCarty jumped Lemieux from behind and bloodied him. Then the goalies, Patrick Roy and Mike Vernon, fought at center ice. It was an absolutely unbelievable moment. Not necessarily the proudest moment in hockey history. I'm not sure brawls should be a defining moment, but as far as that rivalry—and I really do think that Colorado–Detroit rivalry was one of the best ever when you go back in history with the cups those teams won and the players they had—that night in Detroit

at Joe Louis Arena was as memorable a night as I've ever had. There's no question both teams would have won more cups if the other wasn't in the league. That's how good they were.

Later that year (1997), Detroit was on the victor's side of the mid-ice handshake with Colorado before sweeping the Philadelphia Flyers for their first Stanley Cup in 42 years. These two initial playoff series created, like Kelly notes, what was soon seen as hockey's greatest rivalry. Haynes explains,

> There was a period of time when the Avalanche and Red Wings had the best rivalry in sports. They were the two best teams in hockey. They hated each other, and it was legitimate hate. Legitimate fights. For nine years, every game was great. In April of '98, the Avalanche went to Detroit, and Patrick Roy and Chris Osgood fought. It's hard to explain unless you were really there watching. Roy beat up their goalie and there was a full on-ice brawl. It was my most memorable game.

The Avalanche lost the game, 2–0. The contest featured 228 minutes of penalties, including 48 between goaltenders Roy and Osgood, who received a game misconduct each. The two would not face one another in the playoffs later that year, but they would do so in three of the next four postseasons, adding to hockey's biggest rivalry. Today, with the competitive embers cooling after the departure of the Red Wings for the Eastern Conference, the fans inside the Pepsi Center occasionally add a little kindling for old time's sake. Haynes comments, "It seems like almost every game, if the crowd's getting a little restless, some 'Red Wings suck' chants happen."

A "RAY" OF SUNSHINE

Amid this increasingly heated rivalry between the Avalanche and Red Wings was the final stop of an inspiring journey by one of New England's most beloved sports figures, Ray Borque. Having won the James Norris Memorial Trophy for the league's top defenseman five times—not to mention the Calder Memorial Trophy his rookie season and the King Clancy Memorial Trophy for his leadership and humanitarian efforts—the longtime Boston Bruin, during the 21st season of his career, realized that his quest for a Stanley Cup championship was more likely to be fulfilled in a location outside of Bean Town.

Four-fifths of the way into the 1999–2000 season, Borque went from (dirty water) to spring water and joined the Avalanche just in time for a deep playoff run. Unfortunately for Borque, his arrival at the NHL's summit would have to wait another year, as Colorado fell to the defending Stanley Cup champion Dallas Stars in seven games. Not to be deterred, the defenseman would return for a 22nd season and, this time, reach the top, outlasting the defending Stanley Cup champion New Jersey Devils in seven games and sharing a special moment mid-ice with his elusive, alloy-rich friend. Among the witnesses to Borque's long-awaited smooch of Lord Stanley's Cup was New York Rangers TV broadcaster Sam Rosen, who shares,

> There are so many things that happen during the course of a lengthy career. There are things that happen, whether on the ice or off the ice. I remember Ray Borque being traded from Boston to Colorado because he wanted so badly to win the cup. He won it with the Avalanche in 2001. They handed him the cup and I remember him kissing it and how emotional a moment it was because, after all these years he had played in Boston—and on some really good teams—and had never been able to win the Cup, and there he was in Colorado. Just the tears in his eyes when they handed him the cup as he kissed it on the ice.

Needless to say, a satisfied Borque hung up his skates and began the wait for his inevitable enshrinement into the Hockey Hall of Fame.

THE AVS TODAY

With the Borques, Simons, Lemieuxs, Sakics, Forsbergs, and Roys long since retired, the snow hasn't exactly been, as former Colorado Rockies baseball broadcaster Wayne Hagin would say, "Falling off Pike's peak with the decibel level" inside the Pepsi Center, as the "Avs" haven't been past the first round of the playoffs since being ousted by (who else but) the Red Wings in the 2008 Western Conference Semifinals. In 2013–2014, however, a familiar face stepped behind the Avalanche bench rather than taking his usual spot in the crease, as Patrick Roy, in his first year as head coach of the Avalanche, led the team to the division title and 112 regular-season points before being upset in the first round by the Minnesota Wild.

Although it's unlikely Roy, in his business suit, will be calling opposing coaches out to center ice for a scrap, as team vice president of operations, he has been building up the Avalanche roster with such acquisitions as center Carl Söderberg and defenseman François Beauchemin to help team captain Gabriel Landeskog and veteran Jerome Iginla try to return the Stanley Cup to a mile-high altitude. With the Red Wings dancing in the other conference bracket, who knows? Perhaps these two will become playoff opponents once again, only this time on hockey's grandest stage, where a rivalry once so heated belongs.

• 9 •

Columbus Blue Jackets

$\mathcal{D}$ating back to 1890, which was so close to the Civil War it's debatable whether the Union Army boys suited up for a game or two, the Ohio State Buckeyes have dominated the sports landscape in Columbus, Ohio. Aside from LeBron James' improbable NBA Finals run in 2016 and the "Big Red Machine" and "Nasty Boys" Cincinnati Reds championships of 1975, 1976, and 1990, Ohio sports glory since the Browns' last NFL title in 1954 and the Indians' last World Series championship in 1948 has taken place in the state's capital, thanks to five Buckeye national championships under coach Woody Hayes and two more with Jim Tressel (2002) and Urban Meyer (2014). With Cleveland's Barons surviving only three seasons in the NHL before merging with another struggling Upper Midwest team, the Minnesota North Stars, hockey, on its grandest stage, eluded the "Buckeye State" for a quarter-century.

In 1997, with the city "wooing" NHL commissioner Gary Bettman and other members of the league's top brass, major U.S. corporation Nationwide Insurance announced the building of an arena in downtown Columbus. Less than a month later, the city was awarded an NHL franchise. Rich in history from its involvement in the Civil War for the Union Army, the Columbus team would be named the "Blue Jackets." In the fall of 2000, the country's Upper Midwest was once again booming with professional hockey, as the Blue Jackets and the Minnesota Wild emerged as the league's 29th and 30th teams. On October 7, 2000, with most of the city scrambling to Madison, Wisconsin, to watch the Buckeyes take on the Badgers, the remaining 18,136 Columbusites stayed home to watch their Blue Jackets fall, 5–3, to the Chicago Blackhawks. The Buckeyes, however, defeated the Wisconsin Badgers, 23–7. The Blue Jackets would have to wait half a season to step out of Ohio State's shadow.

50

GROWING PAINS

Despite losing their home opener to the Blackhawks, the Blue Jackets, in their inaugural season, would best their fellow expansion team, the Minnesota Wild, by three team points and take *that* consolation prize home for the summer. Led by Geoff Sanderson, Espen Knutsen, and veteran goaltender Ron Tugnutt, Columbus, although the newborns of the league, played with a relatively older squad and were near or just below the league average in practically every offensive and defensive category. Unlike most expansion teams before them, the Blue Jackets did not get better with age.

In the three seasons that followed the 2000–2001 slate, Columbus failed to reach the team point mark set during the inaugural campaign, finishing, at best, fourth in the division the first four years. With seasoned veterans Ray Whitney, Andrew Cassels, Adam Foote, and disbanded "Russian Five" standout Sergei Fedorov treating Ohio's capital like a halfway house, the team was never really able to sew that "C" patch onto a uniform long enough for it to stay there, and an 82-game season became the standard for the Jackets their first seven years in the league.

Finally, during the 2007–2008 season, Columbus would have a captain who was not a flight risk in the form of Rick Nash, who had been donning the team colors since his rookie season, at the age of 18. Under Nash's leadership, the Blue Jackets finally qualified to play in the postseason in 2009, reserving a seat in the Western Conference Quarterfinals against the defending champion and eventual Stanley Cup runner-up Detroit Red Wings. Although the Jackets would fail to win a game in their first postseason appearance, their 92-point regular-season showing satisfied the appetites of playoff-starved fans, shortening that spring–fall gap, albeit by only a week.

DO YOU HAVE A PERMIT FOR THAT CANNON?

At about the same time that the changing of the guard brought the captain's patch to Rick Nash, another military tradition was being introduced at Nationwide Arena for the 2007–2008 season. Throughout the Civil War, cannons sounded on the battlefields, alerting those within ear's reach of each army's presence. More than 150 years later, Columbus was once again host to such pyrotechnics, only this time the only thing in danger was the average fan's hearing. Columbus Blue Jackets TV play-by-play broadcaster Jeff Rimer describes the team's distinguishing tradition:

Certainly the tradition in the last several years has been the cannon. The cannon goes off after a goal. It's terrific. I think the players were getting a little tired of it during the All-Star Game because it went off so many times. Whether it's a broadcaster or the players, they tend to forget after a Jackets goal that the cannon will go off, and, nine times out of ten, you're going to hear the cannon scare the you know what out of them. I can't tell you how many broadcasters told me they jumped out of their seat when the cannon [went] off after a Blue Jackets goal. It's really caught on, and, of course, with the history of Columbus and the Civil War, the fans wanted a cannon for the longest time, and after Doug MacLean was replaced by Mike Priest as president of the hockey club, the cannon was approved. It's become a staple in Nationwide Arena, as well as an attraction within the building when fans come from other cities, even longtime Blue Jacket fans who want to get a picture taken with it. They've really gravitated to that. It's right there on the main concourse at one end of the ice. It's become quite a talking point in the building and certainly around the NHL. The cannon's really something special and is a staple of Blue Jackets hockey.

HOW ABOUT ANOTHER GO AT THE POSTSEASON?

With the team finishing fifth in the division in the three seasons following their first playoff appearance, Nationwide Arena's cannon feeder wasn't exactly putting the fuse distributor on speed dial. A strike-shortened 2012–2013 season put the Jackets up a slot in the Western Conference's Central Division but still not enough to qualify for the postseason. In 2013–2014, the league's realignment had Columbus joining the Eastern Conference ranks, slightly lowering their playoff odds by more than 3 percent. The new weighted schedule in the east seemed to work more for the Blue Jackets than playing the likes of the Kings and Blackhawks on a continual basis, as the team finished with 94 regular-season points, their most since 2008–2009.

Arriving in the postseason for just the second time in the franchise's 13-year history, the Blue Jackets, without a team captain on the ice for the second straight season, were led up the steps of Pittsburgh's Console Energy Center for the 2014 Eastern Conference Quarterfinals by Ryan Johansen, James Wisniewski, and Brandon Dubinsky's scoring, Jack Johnson's defense, and Sergei Bobrovsky's goaltending. After a 4–3 loss to the Penguins in the opening game, the Blue Jackets were still in search of the franchise's first-ever playoff win. In the second overtime of game two, the score was again 4–3, but this time Columbus had the deciding goal, by left winger Matt Calvert; his second of the night.

With the monkey off their back, the Blue Jackets returned to Columbus for game three in hopes of securing their first playoff win at home. Once again, the score was 4–3, but again Columbus was on the lighter side. Amazingly, game four ended in another 4–3 tally, the fourth time in the series' four games. With the fourth being the "forth" in Columbus and Pittsburgh's back and forth, the Blue Jackets not only banked their first home playoff win in franchise history, but also tied the series at two games apiece. Rimer, who did pregame and postgame for the Montreal Canadiens in the 1970s during one of their four-peat campaigns, looks back on game four of the 2014 Eastern Conference Quarterfinals against the Penguins as one of his most memorable:

> They'd never won a playoff game. They won two games in that series. One thing about that playoff series with Pittsburgh was it was back and forth. No two-goal lead for either team was safe in the series until the Penguins kind of took it over in game five. The one game here at Nationwide, between Brandon Dubinsky and Nick Foligno, the Jackets' come-from-behind win to tie the series was something memorable; perhaps as memorable as any game that I did for any team. It was the 24th of April. . . . The Blue Jackets came from a two-goal deficit and won the game, and all of a sudden they had Pittsburgh on the ropes. I've got the game on tape, and, from time to time, when I'm looking for something to do just to get a smile on my face, I'll put the game on and get a look at it and just relive the memory of that night. It was game four, and, of course, the Jackets came back and tied the series at that point and certainly made things quite interesting. I'm probably going to keep that game for the rest of my life.

The Penguins ended the string of 4–3 decisions in game five but resumed the trend in game six at Nationwide Arena. After yet another 4–3 loss, the Jackets began their summer vacation, and the Penguins went on to lose in game seven of the following round to the eventual Eastern Conference champion New York Rangers. The Blue Jackets, although not advancing past the first round, were still able to again shift the focus in Columbus away from the gridiron for a brief, springtime moment—this time for two games longer than in 2009.

THE COLUMBUS SPORTS SCENE TODAY

With the Ohio State Buckeyes being named National Champions in 2014, it's a bit difficult to step into the sports spotlight in Columbus if you're not wearing scarlet and gray, but the Blue Jackets aim to one day redirect attention away from those "college boys." Rimer adds,

> One of the biggest, if not *the* biggest, fans of Blue Jackets hockey is Kirk Herbstreit, who, of course, is renowned for his college football work. Kirk and I did a talk show for a couple of years here in Columbus before he moved to Nashville, and Kirk would always say to me, "If the Blue Jackets were ever to put it all together and go deep in the Stanley Cup Playoffs, it would be every bit as big as college football and the Buckeyes." Kirk's told me on many occasions his kids just eat it up, and, now living in Nashville, they're still Blue Jacket fans. His young guy would just as soon go to a Blue Jackets hockey game or go down and meet the Blue Jacket players as opposed to going to a national championship.

While it's not likely that the majority of Ohio's capital has the same devotion as Herbstreit's youngster, it's possible many might tilt the scales of their fandom should the Blue Jackets some day parade the Stanley Cup past the Ohio State University campus. With left winger Nick Foligno filling a captain's seat that remained empty for three seasons, the Jackets, with the help of veterans Brandon Dubinsky and Scott Hartnell and recent import Brandon Saad, are looking to get over yet another playoff hump and win their first-ever playoff series so that the boom of Nationwide Arena's cannon can resonate throughout the summer before fading into the sounds of marching bands, cheerleaders, and 105,000 screaming fans inside Ohio Stadium.

Dallas Stars

In a move questioned by the entire sports universe, the Minnesota North Stars, members of the NHL's "second six" expansion teams of the 1967–1968 season, moved from the Upper Midwest to Dallas, Texas, where the only use of ice at a major sports level up to that point was on Texas Ranger Nolan Ryan's pitching shoulder. Local Minnesota fans, regardless of how poorly their North Stars had played that season, weren't exactly displaying their finest form of "Minnesota nice" toward team owner Norman Green. Former Stars TV/radio play-by-play broadcaster Mike Fornes, who was on the ground floor when NHL hockey arrived in the "Lone Star State," describes the unanimous mood in the "Gopher State," saying,

> In the spring of 1993, the North Stars left the Twin Cities under very bad conditions. They had an owner named Norman Green, who didn't feel the way he wanted to run the team in Minnesota was going to work, so there was animosity between him and the fans. He decided to move the team, and here they were; moving right down Interstate 35, all the way to Texas.

Given that the only thing Dallas, Texas is north of is Mexico, a change in the team name would have to take place. After the debate about the name deferred to the team simply being labeled the "Dallas Stars" and not the "Dallas South Stars," the next graphic to be considered would be "demo." Considering a southern city with a deep-rooted tradition in another sport, the spring and summer prep time for fall hockey proved to be quite the challenge. Fornes continues,

> The first thing a lot of us found out was there were two sports in Texas: football and *spring* football. The Stars bought an ice rink that was located

right next to the Dallas Cowboys training complex, which was like the Taj Majal. The rink the Stars bought for their practices was like an oversized garage. They knew right away they were going to have to put a lot of money into making that not only a twin ice sheet, but also an office complex. It has since evolved even more to this day.

Living in the shadow of the world's second most valuable sporting franchise wasn't the only obstacle the Dallas Stars would face after their exodus from the Upper Midwest. Fornes notes:

One thing that was a big factor for everybody—especially the players coming from a northern climate—was the heat. I can remember walking off the plane. Just going through the jet way, I thought I was in an oven. That was something I wasn't used to, and, over time, I acclimated to it. They worked really hard at keeping the ice good, and that was a challenge, not only at the practice facility, but at Reunion Arena as well. Once you got through the winter months and into spring, that temperature started to warm right up, and they had to really be on their game to keep that ice playable. It was never like the ice in Winnipeg, but I think they did a good job with what they had. The learning curve took over there. They got a lot of advice on how to take care of the ice, and I think that helped.

Hockey's learning curve applied to not only ice resurfacers like Bruce Tharaldson, but also the nearly 17,000 fans who would be in attendance. Fornes explains,

Early on, they would have this public address announcement that explained the rules and what was going on. They would tell the fans if it was icing and when the play was offside. You wouldn't hear that in any other city, but it was necessary for a short while in Dallas. The people had to be educated. They didn't know what the Zamboni did. It was an experience just to watch some of the fans at the games. I used to enjoy some of the comments I would hear in the crowd.

At that time, the league was trying to institute new face-off procedures, and they were instructing the linesmen to make sure the wingers lined up appropriately on the hash marks and the circle, and that the centers came in at the same time. When that didn't work, the linesman would stand and throw one or both of the centers out of the face-off and bring in somebody else. I remember one night it got real quiet after the second time the linesman had a problem getting the puck down to these centers. Some fan yelled out, "Just open yuh hand. It'll fawl out." We were from a foreign environment coming in there. The Texas hockey fans learned to adapt when people from up north would say "eh" or "aboot" and "ootside," and, at the same time, we got used to learning about "y'all," "fixin to," and the southern nomenclature. It was an adventure culturally. Even going to restaurants provided a totally different lifestyle than what many of us had seen in the northern states or Canada.

Regardless of the nomenclature, climate shift, or Dallas-Cowboy-attention-envying quest for fan popularity, the basic question of "Will it work?" ultimately depended on the product that was being put on the ice.

FROM "MOTOWN" TO "HOEDOWN"

Along with the Stars' migration south on Interstate 35, the league itself was going through some changes to start the following season. No longer separated into the Clarence Campbell and Prince of Wales conferences, the NHL would simply be Eastern and Western. Joining the Stars in the Western Conference's Central Division was a familiar face from their old Norris Division days in the Campbell Conference, the Detroit Red Wings. The two teams, which finished 11 games apart in the standings in the previous season, were set to match up on October 5, 1993, for the Dallas Stars' grand debut at Reunion Arena. Calling the team's first-ever game, Fornes describes opening night as follows:

> There was such a sense of anticipation for that game because you had Norman Green, who was the owner, practically booed out of the building when he left Minnesota. He was heralded as the man who brought hockey to Texas. Those people really cheered for him that night. Opening night, the team beat the Detroit Red Wings, and that was a big deal. That proved our hockey team was going to be a good team. This was not an expansion team. This was a team that was already competitive, and to beat Detroit on opening night, it couldn't have gone better as far as a way to start a franchise history. Here we were playing the Detroit Red Wings, a very established franchise. Of course, this team was established, too, but fans didn't know or care about that. Hockey was brand new to most of those people, and they saw this whole entertainment package in front of them and then this great game was played.
>
> Neal Broten scored the first goal in the history of the Dallas Stars, and Mike Modano scored the second one. It was known that it was going to be a defensive-minded team. The coach, Bob Gainey, who had won five Stanley Cups with the Montreal Canadiens, was defensive minded. For them to be a couple of minutes into the game and be up 2–0, that was pretty cool. It was a great start. Hockey had landed in Texas. It really had an impact on hooking a lot of fans for the first time. A lot of people were saying, "I'll be back to see this again." If you're going to have a great debut, nothing could have gone better.

It goes without saying that the phrase "Y'all come back now, ya hear?" couldn't have been more sincere than it was to those exiting Reunion Arena after the Stars' 6–4 victory.

NOW THEM'S FIGHTIN' WORDS

Going 19–13–7 in just under a half-season of play, the Stars were doing all right for themselves; however, it would take almost that half of a season for the Dallas crowd to realize that the tough sports guys in the area weren't just the ones on the gridiron but those on the ice as well. Fornes comments,

> New Year's Eve the first season, the team went to Chicago and played in the old Chicago Stadium. They played against the Blackhawks in a game that was refereed by Paul Stewart, who was a former player in the WHA and had a career in which he was known for his pugilistic prowess. He would let the guys go a little longer with some things. He had a command of the game, yet gave the players a little more room. We were seven seconds into that game, and the gloves dropped right from the opening face-off. There must have been three fights in the first 21 seconds. It was a New Year's I'll never forget because I think the team really came together after that game.
>
> There was something in the air that night. Chicago Stadium on New Year's Eve. A lot of people were partying already. It was electric, and that kind of set the stage for some future games we had with the Blackhawks that were very memorable. I will always remember that game because I didn't know how the team would do in that respect. We were already up to New Year's, but we'd never seen a blowout where everybody dropped the gloves. They did real well that night, and they kind of took off from there. They were more unified as a team. Calling those fights was the introduction for a lot of people to hockey. I used to get people who would come up to me and say that was the first game they ever saw on TV, and that was halfway through the season. That might not have been the first game fans saw, but it was the first one they remembered.

Surely among the dropped gloves on the ice on that New Year's Eve in Chicago were those of former Stars right winger Shane Churla. Fornes continues,

> There were lots of guys who could take care of themselves with the Dallas Stars over the years, but there's only one name you want to mention when it comes to the early days with the Stars and that was Shane Churla. Here's a guy who had over 2,000 penalty minutes in his career. He had more than 300 of those his first season in Dallas. The fans really appreciated him. You

had a football mentality there. He was a combination of a football player, rodeo rider, pro wrestler, and stock car driver all in one package as a hockey player, and the Texas fans just bought it. They thought it was great.

He had a penchant not only for taking care of business on the ice, but, when he would go to the penalty box, he would end up taking all his equipment off from the waist up. He insisted on spending the five-minute penalty time completely redressing himself from the waist up. Women in Texas loved that. They would get shots of him up on the video screen. Here's this guy who's very muscular and had just taken part in this fight, and he would be taking everything off and putting everything back on. I don't know why he did it, but it became an added attraction. He took on all the big guys. Anybody who came through, he was there to take care of business. His record was good. He didn't lose. Even in other team's buildings. I was amazed Don King didn't get ahold of him at some point. He was that type of attraction. When he was on the ice, you just knew something was going to happen. If he started a game, that was a pretty good sign of what was coming. He was known for that and bought into it. He was willing to be part of the promotional efforts that sold the game to that element of fans in Texas.

Adding to Churla's theatrics was superstar Mike Modano and a supporting cast of Russ Courtnall, Neal Broten, and team captain Mark Tinordi, who would lead Dallas to the second round of the playoffs their first year in town.

THAT CUP AIN'T FOR YER DIP, PARDNER

In 1998, with Churla, Broten, Courtnall, Tinordi, and even Mike Fornes now gone from the organization, the Stars were about to embark on a season that would have spurred envy from the Dallas Cowboys themselves. With Mike Modano still leading the team's scoring, the Stars were about to get some more help in the form of future Hall of Famers Ed Belfour, Joe Nieuwendyk, and the "Golden Brett" himself, Brett Hull. With defenseman Derian Hatcher now promoted to team captain, the Stars would dominate the league with 51 wins, the most in team history up to that point.

Sweeping through Edmonton in the first round, the Stars faced the St. Louis Blues in the Conference Semifinals, where Brett Hull scored two goals and logged four assists against his longtime former mates, en route to a Conference Finals showdown against Patrick Roy, Joe Sakic, Peter Forsberg, and the mighty Colorado Avalanche. Overcoming a 2–3 deficit, the Stars won the final two games by identical 4–1 scores to advance to the Stanley Cup Final for the first time since 1991 as their former identity, the North Stars.

Facing a Buffalo Sabres team that was seeking its first Stanley Cup title as well, Dallas and Buffalo split the first four games before Dallas took command in game five at Reunion Arena. In game six, which featured three overtimes, Hull scored one of the most controversial goals in playoff history on Buffalo goaltender Dominik Hašek, handing both himself and the Stars their first-ever Stanley Cup. While the debate concerning the validity of Hull's goal continues to this day in many hockey chat rooms and senseless sports discussion panels, Hull and Hašek later reconciled as teammates in Detroit in 2002, where Hašek's own dream of a championship was fulfilled.

With many of the team's stars returning, the Stars gave it another go during the 1999–2000 season. Dallas once again beat the Avalanche at home in game seven of the Conference Finals. Going from Patrick Roy to Martin Brodeur—the defensive equivalent of going from Wayne Gretzky to Mario Lemieux (or vice versa)—the Stars came up short to Brodeur and the New Jersey Devils in the Stanley Cup Final, losing on a Jason Arnott double-overtime goal that would not be open for debate for years to come.

After the second-place finish in 2000, the two-time Western Conference championship machine would slowly disband, starting with the departure of Hull for Detroit. Nieuwendyk would follow suit, joining the same New Jersey Devils team that had beaten him in 2000 and winning a Stanley Cup with them in 2003. With Belfour and Hatcher walking the same line as their departed teammates, the only one left standing was Modano.

Aside from one season cut short due to injury, Modano played 20 of his 21 NHL seasons for the Minnesota North Stars/Dallas Stars, setting franchise records for goals, assists, points, and total games played that will likely never be eclipsed. In fact, Modano, with his 561 goals and 1,374 career points, is the highest-scoring American-born player in NHL history. A "no-brainer" for nomination to the Hockey Hall of Fame, Modano's number "9" hangs high above the ice inside the team's current home at the American Airlines Center.

Since before Modano's departure from the team in 2010, the Stars have only made the playoffs twice in nine seasons. While the next Modano may spring up elsewhere, the Stars continue to build, with such young skaters as brothers Jamie and Jordie Benn, Tyler Seguin, and John Klingberg, as well as veteran imports Jason Spezza, Antti Niemi, and Aleš Hemsky, looking to again bring the Stanley Cup down Interstate 35 before the Cowboys' next Super Bowl win, suggesting perhaps that the green star—not the blue one—should reign supreme in the Lone Star State.

• *11* •

Detroit Red Wings

$\mathcal{D}$ecades before songwriter-turned-music-producer Berry Gordy Jr. coined the phrase for his music label, "Motown" was releasing a different set of "hits" at the Olympia. Referred to as the "Old Red Barn," the Olympia in Detroit opened in 1926 and hosted the NHL's Detroit Cougars, who, after a two-year marketing test as the Falcons, changed their name to Red Wings for the 1932–1933 season. One of the NHL's "original six," the Detroit Red Wings, thanks to such players as Marty Berry, Syd Howe, Normie Smith, Ebbie Goodfellow, and Sid Abel, were able to hoist three Stanley Cups in their first 11 years with a team name that would forever stick with the franchise.

"MR. HOCKEY'S" PRODUCTION LINE

While the first batch of Detroit legends was nearing the end of its career, a new class, which some may consider part of the greatest hockey dynasty ever, was coming to the front of the team line. Beginning in the mid-1940s, newcomers Leonard "Red" Kelly, Ted Lindsay, and "Mr. Hockey" himself, Gordie Howe, joined veteran Sid Abel, and, with Kelly on the defensive side of things, Howe, Lindsay, and Abel formed what was nicknamed the "production line." The group would win two Stanley Cups together before Abel finished his career with the team's rival Chicago Blackhawks. With a name like "Mr. Hockey," it can only be expected that Howe would make his mark on the sport by the time he retired at the age of 51. Having accumulated 1,850 points in his 26 years in the NHL, he retired as the game's all-time leading scorer, only to be surpassed by Wayne Gretzky, Mark Messier, and Jaromír Jágr years later.

Although playing nearly two decades during what would be considered by most to be their "twilight years," Howe maintained his presence on the ice. Having grown up in Detroit, Red Wings radio broadcaster Ken Kal saw Gordie Howe live for the first time in 1969, more than 23 years into Mr. Hockey's career. Kal notes, "He actually scored a goal in that game. He was such an amazing player, even at that age. I could only imagine what he was like in his prime." With a "prime" including four championships, Howe continued to compete with ferocity long after the champagne had dried into his inscriptions on Lord Stanley's Cup. Kal continues,

> If he needed room out there, he was going to get it one way or another. If he had to hit you over the head with a stick or hit you with an elbow, he was going to do it or go right through you. People didn't like that. They feared him, and that's what gave him his room, and that's what made him such a great player. He had the skills obviously, but, even late in his career, nobody messed with him because he was Gordie Howe. I remember Scotty Bowman talking one time about Gordie when he was coaching the Canadiens. When asked what was the game plan when he played against someone like Detroit, he said, "Don't wake Gordie up. Let him go out there and do his thing, but you don't want to get him riled up because that's when he's at his best."

During one of the times Howe was at his best, one of major sports' greatest traditions was born in the "Motor City."

ICED OCTOPUS, A DETROIT SPRINGTIME DELICACY

Right about the time the "production line" was losing one of its key "belts" to the Blackhawks, Detroit brothers and fish aficionados Pete and Jerry Cusimano were finding ways to "haul" championship symbolism in from the Atlantic. Kal comments,

> Back in 1952, the tradition started where they threw the octopus out on the ice. There was a guy who owned a fish market whose last name was Cusimano. At that time, you had to win eight games to win the Stanley Cup, so what a perfect idea to throw an octopus on the ice so that it'd have eight tentacles and each tentacle represented a win. If you won all eight games, you won the Stanley Cup. Since that time, for years, it's been the longstanding tradition of somebody throwing the octopus, wishing the team good luck. Now, I guess you'd have to throw two of them on the ice. I encourage fans, "Don't throw one. Throw two, because you need 16 tentacles to win the Stanley Cup."

A key figure in this interactive experience is Al Sobotka, who, although not dressed as a mascot, is the next best thing for Detroit fans. Kal elaborates, "Al has been around since the Olympia days. He's the guy who swings the octopus over his head when someone throws it on the ice. He'll grab it and twirl it over his head. He's been doing that for a long time, too, and that gets the crowd going. That's been a tradition come playoff time." Even though Sobotka wasn't twirling any (let alone two) octopi above his head in 1955, it's unlikely the Atlantic Ocean was suffering any shortage of cephalopods during that time, as the Red Wings were about to begin the longest cupless drought in team history.

FORTY-TWO YEARS OF DRY ICE

Despite having stars like Gordie Howe, Ted Lindsay, and Alex Delvecchio, the Wings fell five times in the Cup Final between 1956 and 1966. In fact, during the following 17 seasons, Detroit only qualified for the postseason twice, failing to reach the second round on both occasions. In 1979, amid this playoffless fury, the team found a new home just off the banks of the Detroit River, moving out of the Olympia and into Joe Louis Arena. Much like the heavyweight champion after which it was named, Joe Louis Arena saw its fair share of fights, especially during the late 1980s, with the arrival of Joey Kocur and Bob Probert, otherwise known as the "Bruise Brothers." Accepting the enforcer rule as a young rookie in 1985, Kocur racked up a team record 377 penalty minutes, only to be bested by teammate Probert's 398 two years later. While not reaching the Stanley Cup Final during their reputable years as a tandem, Kocur and Probert made their message clear on many occasions. Kal explains,

> Before I was announcing Red Wing games, I watched Kocur and Probert. Those were the two ultimate heavyweights for a long time. Detroit was lucky to have them both when every team seemed to have an enforcer. I remember talking to St. Louis Blues enforcer Kelly Chase one time. He said, "If I ever did anything to Steve Yzerman or Sergei Fedorov, the penalty wasn't the two minutes. My penalty would be I'd have to fight either Kocur or Probert." If you wanted to go after a star player, you had to go and face the music, which was Bob Probert or Joey Kocur's fists. I remember one game Rick Tocchet stuck his knee out to Steve Yzerman coming over a line. Yzerman goes down and Tocchet gets the penalty, and as soon as he came out of the box Kocur went after him and fought him. I can't imagine what Tocchet was thinking in the penalty box, knowing sooner or later he was going to have to fight Kocur or Probert.

The Bruise Brothers disbanded during the 1990–1991 season, which, as Red Wings fans know, started a string of postseason success never before seen outside of Boston, St. Louis, or Chicago.

STEVIE-Y, THE BUILDER, AND THE RUSSIAN FIVE

While second fiddle to the Bruins' 29 and the Blackhawks' 28 consecutive playoff-qualifying seasons, the Red Wings' showing of 25 straight from 1990–1991 to 2015–2016 was good enough for third best all time. Before this annual qualifying past game number 82 commenced, the Wings received a huge boost from eventual team captain and Hall of Famer Steve Yzerman, whose 1,755 career points in 22 seasons—all with Detroit—are second only to Mr. Hockey himself in team history. In just his fourth season, Yzerman took on the moniker of team captain, with the team finishing lower than second in the division only twice for the remainder of his career. Halfway into Stevie Y's tenure, the Wings got a giant boost from behind the bench, as head coach William "Scotty" Bowman, already having "built" six Stanley Cup–winning teams in Montreal and Pittsburgh, took the reins for the 1993–1994 season. Two seasons later, Detroit would be known as "Hockeytown." Kal notes,

> I remember when it first started and came through our marketing department. They wanted to create an idea that Hockeytown was not a fictitious place but a place where you get away from your 9-to-5 job. Where fans can leave their work behind and come to a place where they can get away from it all for three hours just to be caught up in the whole scene of the Red Wings in a place where it's been around for a long, long time. From there, it just grew. We grew into a place where you say, "Yeah. This is Hockeytown." When you think about it, all the great players and coaches—broadcasters around here who deliver the message to the fans—this is the place to be. It's kind of like your escape from reality, so to speak. To come into a place or arena that's great for the fans to cheer, forget about the world, and just concentrate on the Red Wings and their hometown team. Next thing you know, everybody around the league looks at Detroit and says, "Well, it's Hockeytown." It's been like that for 18, 19 years.

Behind Scotty Bowman, Steve Yzerman, and the latest edition of the "Russian Five," the city would immediately find itself quite worthy of carrying such a title.

During the 1995–1996 campaign, the Red Wings, with Yzerman and future Hall of Famers Brendan Shanahan, Paul Coffey, and Nicklas Lidström, as well as the famed "Russian Five," which included Viacheslav Fetisov, Vladimir Konstantinov, Vyacheslav "Slava" Kozlov, Sergei Fedorov, and mid-season import Igor Larionov, would win an NHL record 62 regular-season games and finish with 131 points, second most all time (first, 1976–1977 Montreal Canadiens).

Leading the scoring for the Wings on this record-setting squad was Fedorov, who, by the end of his Hall of Fame career, would hold the record for most NHL goals scored by a Russian-born player, at least until Washington Capitals star Alex Ovechkin passed him seven years later. A witness to both Russian superstars was Washington Capitals TV play-by-play broadcaster Joe Beninati, who, despite calling games for Fedorov while in a Capitals uniform, recalls perhaps his most memorable game as a broadcaster being one with Fedorov on the other side of the face-off circle. Beninati reflects,

> In my first full season as an NHL television announcer, Sergei Fedorov scores five goals in the same game in a 5–4 overtime win against Washington at Joe Louis Arena. It's not a happy moment for the Caps, obviously, but how many times am I going to call a game with a guy scoring five times? All five in a 5–4 overtime. Not only was it five goals, the Detroit Red Wings, at that time in '96, were stunning. They were incredible. All five goals were tic-tac-toe beauties.

Despite burning through the NHL and Western Conference for seven and a half months, this "stunning" and record-breaking Wings team met their match against the relocated and rebooted Colorado Avalanche, who, thanks to Patrick Roy, Peter Forsberg, Joe Sakic, and Claude Lemieux, would see the cupless drought pass through Detroit for a 41st consecutive season. Colorado, having worn out its welcome, left a parting gift in the Motor City during their game-six clincher, when Lemieux checked Red Wings defenseman Kris Draper into the boards, breaking his jaw and leaving the team and the fans stewing going into the offseason. The famed "Blood Feud" between Detroit and Colorado, which would see five Stanley Cups between the two teams over a seven year period, was born. Red Wings TV play-by-play voice Ken Daniels, who came into the organization a year and a half after the incident between Lemieux and Draper, describes what many believe to be major sports' greatest rivalry of the late twentieth century, saying, "Unlike other sports, beyond the fans hating one another, it was the true hatred of the players. Dino Ciccarelli couldn't believe he shook Claude Lemieux's hand in '96, but he hadn't seen how badly Kris Draper was beaten up and what his face had looked like when he was in the handshake line because Draper had left to go to the room. I've spoken with Dino since, and I think what pissed him off even more was he didn't know the extent of how badly Draper looked at that time." With a 62-win season scrapped, it would be another 10 months before Lemieux returned to the ice at Joe Louis Arena; only this time, his hands wouldn't be used for a mid-ice shake.

MARCH 26, 1997: ROUND 2 . . . *FIGHT*

Ten months, 40 stitches, and one wired jaw later, Kris Draper and the Red Wings, not nearly with the record and statistics of the year before, brought the spirit of Joe Louis back into his arena. With their hated rival back in town, the Red Wings tended to some unfinished business late in the regular season. In what is clearly his most memorable game in more than 20 seasons broadcasting for the Red Wings, Ken Kal describes the fire that ignited beneath the team's skates:

> I think the game that most people remember around here—certainly I remember it—is when we had the big battle with the Avalanche. It was a really good rivalry when the Red Wings and the Avalanche played each other. From '96 all the way through 2002, it was big. They had so many great players on both sides. Future Hall of Famers. Guys like Yzerman, Larionov, Shanahan, and then you had Forsberg, Sakic, Adam Foote, just to name a few. It was great hockey, and, not only that, it was pretty intense. That one game March 26th of '97, when they had the big brawl at Joe Louis Arena, was the game that turned everything around for Detroit. Prior to that time, the Red Wings had always made it to the dance but could never get over the hump. They went to the finals against the Devils and lost in '95. They won 62 games my first year here in '96, and then they played the Avalanche and lost in the Western Conference Finals. The Avalanche went on to win the Stanley Cup that year against Florida.
>
> That particular season, in the three meetings they had prior to that game, the Red Wings lost all three. They just could not get over the hump. About a year before in that Western Conference Finals game, Claude Lemieux hit Kris Draper along the boards and kind of rearranged his face. The Red Wings never forgot that, so when this game happened on March 26th, all hell broke loose at the Joe. As far as changing the outcome of the game, how can you not think of Darren McCarty, who had that brawl with Lemieux? Ironically, it all started with Igor Lirianov and Peter Forsberg in a wrestling match, and then the next thing you know, this brawl happens. You've got Patrick Roy and Mike Vernon charging at each other and Brendan Shanahan intercepting Roy and Adam Foote, so that they wouldn't get at McCarty and Lemieux. McCarty was pummeling Lemieux at center ice and

then dragged him over to the boards. He was working him over pretty good there. Then the next thing you know, the goaltenders go at it.

Throughout the entire game, I think there were six or seven fights. I was really surprised there were no ejections in the game. In today's game, there would be ejections all over the place. McCarty always played well against the Avalanche. He always scored big goals against them. He was the guy who was out for blood in that game against the Avalanche, and he ends up scoring the game-winning goal in overtime. From that point on, that changed everything for Detroit. That game right there really propelled the Red Wings to get to the top, and what a way to do it.

During the next 10 weeks, 42 years of heartache, playoff futility, and "coulda, shoulda, wouldas" were swept from the ice by the proverbial Zamboni, and on June 7, 1997, the Red Wings finished a four-game sweep of the Philadelphia Flyers in the Stanley Cup Final. With the drought having begun before he was even born, Kal details the Red Wings' return to glory:

> The first cup in 42 years against the Flyers was pretty exciting because, as a kid, for me personally growing up in Detroit, I always wondered, "When are we going to win a Stanley Cup? We haven't won one since 1955." Little did I know growing up that I was going to be the next guy to call it. It's something you dream of but you never think is going to happen, and then when it does, you think back and go, "Wow! That's exciting!"

Sadly, the 1997 cup clincher would be one member of the Russian Five's final game, as Vladimir Konstantinov was permanently disabled in a limousine crash that also sent teammate Viacheslav Fetisov to the hospital. Despite playing without Konstantinov and '97 Conn Smythe recipient Mike Vernon, the Wings went on to defend the Stanley Cup the following year against the Washington Capitals in yet another finals sweep, but not before "handling a little business" with their Rocky Mountain rivals in Colorado and Detroit's first regular season matchup since "The Brawl." With the 1997–1998 season being his first in the TV booth for the Wings, Ken Daniels describes the broadcast "manna" he received coming into "The Blood Feud," saying, "A lot of that rivalry was built before I got there. I was there for '97–'98. I remember the buildup before the start of the game. It was a UPN50 game at the time. You knew it was happening. Darren McCarty and Claude Lemieux. Claude Lemieux knew he had to answer—after the turtle incident in '97—in the opening faceoff. I remember seeing the opening lineups and seeing Lemieux and McCarty. That's when you're in contact with the production truck on my talk back button. We're about to opening faceoff, and, following the anthem and seeing McCarty line up against Lemieux, you just knew as soon as this puck is dropped, they're going to drop them, so you waited for that." Not to disappoint those in attendance at Joe Louis Arena and tuning in all over the country, McCarty and Lemieux's gloves hit the ice perhaps even before the puck itself, and the two commenced a "turtle free" scrap that would carry over into the next millennium for both teams.

Even with Lemieux going back to New Jersey to win a fourth career Stanley Cup against the same Avalanche team with which he started the season in 1999–2000, Detroit and Colorado's rivalry would spill into the postseason during both 2000 and 2002. The 2001–2002 Red Wings, with imports Dominik Hašek, Brett Hull, Luc Robitaille, and Chris Chelios, were labeled "a hall of fame team," but, with future hall of famers spread across the Avalanche lineup as well, the 2002 Western Conference Final proved to be the biggest hump for Detroit. Colorado had Detroit "on the ropes" with their overtime win in game five, taking a commanding 3–2 series lead. Dominik Hašek, perhaps the most discussed offseason acquisition for the Red Wings, would prove to be the team's most important with two straight shutouts in game six and seven. For the second time in six seasons, Detroit punched Colorado's plane ticket home. Five games later, including Dominik Hašek's record sixth shutout of the 2002 playoffs, the Red Wings bested the Eastern Conference champion Carolina Hurricanes for their third Stanley Cup in six seasons. Just moments after the final horn, Scotty Bowman, having won his NHL-record ninth Stanley Cup, announced to opposing team captain Ron Francis his retirement from the game but not before lacing up his skates one final time for a victory lap with the cup.

In 2008, with a relatively fresh Mike Babcock standing behind the bench, Chris Osgood once again stewarding the crease, imported Devils defenseman Brian Rafalski handling both sides of the puck, Pavel Datsyuk and Henrik Zetterberg serving as an upstart combo, and Lidström, Draper, McCarty, Chelios, and Dominik Hašek still figuring on the roster, the Red Wings won their fourth Stanley Cup in 12 years, cementing a fair share of their core roster's eventual enshrinement into the Hockey Hall of Fame.

The 2008 postseason would also mark the sixth and final time Detroit and Colorado would meet as Western Conference foes past game #82, as Detroit, following the 2012–2013 season, would join four of the other "original six" in the Eastern Conference. With a regular season schedule reduced from four to two games and a playoff matchup going from probable to highly unlikely, the "blood" in this feud has become quite watered down compared to its ice-staining days of the late 1990s. Ken Daniels notes, "I think it's going to be some time before that rivalry is renewed. It will never be what it once was because it was so violent—and by violent, I'll say wonderful—at the time; except for if you're Kris Draper. You can certainly understand that not being the case. The unfortunate thing about Colorado/Detroit is it's not there anymore because we moved to the East. Red Wings going East, in part, ended that rivalry. You're not seeing Colorado and Detroit in the playoffs again unless they're in the Stanley Cup Final, and that's going to take a number of years. They play twice a year now. In terms of rivalry and those who have hated us, it's built on playoffs."

HOCKEYTOWN TODAY

While the Stanley Cup hasn't made its way down Woodward Avenue since 2008, a handful of players from that championship roster still don the red and white, including Niklas Kronwall, Darren Helm, and Henrik Zetterberg. As if parting with the Yzerman's, Federov's, Datsyuk's, Larionov's, McCarty's, Lidström's, and Bowman's wasn't enough, the Red Wings departure from the Western Conference before the 2013–2014 season left behind not only the Avalanche but other long-time and budding rivals like Chicago, San Jose, St. Louis, and Nashville. However, as they say, one's departure is another's arrival, and, in the case of the Toronto Maple Leafs, Detroit's arrival in the Eastern Conference may just rekindle the rivalry the two shared in the Western Conference decades before. Ken Daniels adds, "The way Toronto is coming—and hopefully Detroit will get back to where they can be in the next 3–5 years—you can maybe build a rivalry with them and say they're rivals because they really always were. They're both original six, and, you'll remember, Toronto was in the west for a while. I think that rivalry will be renewed much more quickly and maybe get a hate on, but it's a new NHL. I don't know how much of a 'hate on' you can get in this league anymore. The game's changed." With the rookie record-breaking Auston Matthews handling business north of the border and the young talent and speed of Tomáš Tatar, Andreas Athanasiou, and Dylan Larkin practically setting the ice aflame inside the team's new home of Little Caesars Arena, who knows? The Wings and Leafs may once again find themselves "skipping each other's lake" to the tune of a late spring seven-game series.

• 12 •

Edmonton Oilers

$\mathcal{I}$n the fall of 1979, the NHL opened its doors to the World Hockey Association (WHA)—at least what was left of it. A year before the merger left the association as one of the "odd men out," the WHA's Indianapolis Racers had boasted two 18-year-old Canadian players who would eventually turn the NHL on its head, en route to a combined 10 Stanley Cup championships in a 12-season span. Mark Messier—a native Albertan who would play the following year for the soon-to-be-defunct Cincinnati Stingers—and hockey's eventual all-time leading scorer, the "Great One," Wayne Gretzky, would rejoin one another in Edmonton once the merger was complete, leaving the Racers, Stingers, and Birmingham Bulls to host a human yard sale for prospective talent.

During the 1979–1980 season, Gretzky won the first of his eight consecutive Hart Memorial Trophies for league MVP, scoring 137 points and leading the Oilers to a playoff appearance their first year in the league. A quick three-game sweep by the eventual league runner-up Philadelphia Flyers had Edmonton thinking, "Next year." With that in mind, the 1980–1981 season brought forth Paul Coffey and Glenn Anderson, as well as defenseman Jari Kurri, who, although teamed up with Gretzky and Messier, helped the team barely qualify for the postseason; however, the Oilers advanced one round further than in the previous year before losing in six games to the eventual Stanley Cup champion New York Islanders.

During the next several years, before the two teams were finished building their respective dynasties, the road between Edmonton and Long Island became a well-worn path for Oiler and Islander fans. While the Oilers' 1980–1981 season heralded five different goaltenders, most of them ceded the passage to 19-year-old Albertan Grant Fuhr the following year.

Fuhr joined the team during the 1981–1982 season, by far the team's best showing. Edmonton accumulated 111 team points and a first-place finish in the Clarence Campbell Conference's Smythe Division. The 1981–1982 season would also be the first one behind the bench for team-builder Glen Sather. Despite 212 points from Wayne Gretzky in his third straight Hart Trophy showing, the Oilers were bested in the opening playoff round by the Los Angeles Kings, thanks to their improbable "Miracle on Manchester" comeback win in game three. Instead of moving forward into the postseason, the team appeared to be doing quite the opposite.

During the 1982–1983 slate, Edmonton advanced further than they ever had in the team's brief but playoff-filled history, making it all the way to the Stanley Cup Final against a New York Islanders dynasty that, after a four-game sweep of the Oilers, would go on to win their fourth straight championship. This would not be the final postseason meeting between the two teams.

After five seasons in the league, the Oilers' 1983–1984 campaign proved to be the "next year" the team had been hoping for. Scoring an NHL-record 446 goals, the 1983–1984 Oilers had their best regular-season showing ever, with 119 team points. With Gretzky winning his fifth consecutive Hart Trophy, the team stormed into the playoffs. Aside from a seven-game battle with the Calgary Flames in the Division Finals, the Oilers had virtually "no car trouble" on the road to the team's first-ever Stanley Cup, including ousting the four-time defending league champion New York Islanders in five games in the 1984 Stanley Cup Final. Edmonton Oilers TV play-by-play broadcaster Kevin Quinn discusses how the team's success of more than 30 years ago still holds a lit torch for the city of Edmonton:

> It was a team that wasn't the original six. It wasn't part of the NHL. It came from the outside. There's that idea that this is an outside team that wasn't around the league, and when they became part of the NHL they dominated it. There's a lot of pride that runs deep through the city when it comes to the Oilers. The legacy of Gretzky, Messier, Kurri, and Coffey, and winning a championship early in terms of the team coming into the league from the WHA, having success not long after, and then having a great run of cups. It's the biggest game in town.
>
> Everybody, whether the team is doing well or poorly, follows this team. When you're out and about, everybody is wearing Oilers gear. They've got the flags on their cars, and the radio talk shows here every day are dominated by Oilers talk, whether it's the offseason, the preseason, or the regular season. It is a big part of the community. The city, like any other place, feels good about itself when the team wins, and there's a pride that comes with it. I think this city takes a lot of pride in the success this team had with the dynasty. Even the fact that the players grew up here. The

Gretzkys and Messiers started here and moved on to other places, but some of their best years were spent here.

Following the team's fourth Stanley Cup title in five years, Oilers owner Peter Pocklington traded the "Great One" and his eight straight Hart Trophies to the Los Angeles Kings, leaving Edmonton fans in a haze of bewilderment. Fittingly, Gretzky, although failing to win a ninth straight Hart Trophy, beat his former teammates in seven games during the Division Finals, ending Edmonton's bid for a third straight Stanley Cup. Without Gretzky but still with Kurri, Fuhr, Anderson, and Messier, the Oilers rebounded during the 1989–1990 season to win the team's fifth Stanley Cup of the decade, solidifying their position as an NHL dynasty.

THE NONMARQUEE NAMES OF THE OILERS DYNASTY

With 5 Stanley Cups, 5 Hart Memorial Trophies, 2,648 goals, and 332 wins in a seven-year period, Edmonton, although some may not believe it, consisted of more than just Gretzky, Messier, Kurri, Fuhr, Coffey, Anderson, and Sather. To have a fully functioning hockey dynasty, every aspect of the game must be covered. Former Oiler and current TV analyst Louie DeBrusk, who missed the team's last Stanley Cup parade by just two seasons, discusses some of the role players of Edmonton's dynasty:

> The enforcer role in the Oilers dynasty was instrumental in their success. Wayne Gretzky has often talked about what guys like Dave Semenko, Pat Price, Dave Hunter, Don Jackson, Kevin McClelland, Marty McSorley, Jeff Beukeboom, Kelly Buchberger, and Dave Brown meant to the Oilers in their cup wins. It was a very sticky and chippy game in the '80s and '90s. Teams genuinely disliked each other. Even with guys like Messier, Lee Fogolin, Kevin Lowe, Charlie Huddy, and Randy Gregg—guys who could easily take care of themselves—there were always at least a couple of designated enforcers to take care of business and send the message.
> As skilled as the team was, the Oilers were easily one of the toughest— if not *the* toughest—teams of that era as well. Glen Sather was incredible at surrounding his talent with guys that would protect them, and, as a result, he empowered them to be a big part of the team on and off the ice, often playing with a star for periods of time just to let everyone know who was off limits. They did not get pushed around, and the stars were very protected so they could go and do what they do best, which was win. There was always retaliation when an Oiler was wronged—certainly

different levels of it—but, if a star was hit high or stuck, it was typically immediate, and not only from that game. It would usually carry over for years. They didn't forget, and it would be from many players. Not just one. I think that's why the game was so different. Sure, there were situations where the Oilers were the instigators. Dave Semenko and Kevin McClelland were great protectors, but they also understood it was their job to put the opposition on edge, and they were terrific at it. Agitate at any lengths, and, when all this was going on, guess who was just playing. The stars.

With Jari Kurri eventually rejoining Gretzky in Los Angeles, Paul Coffey skating on to Pittsburgh to win a Stanley Cup alongside another offensive superstar in the form of Mario Lemieux, and Mark Messier and Kevin Lowe teaming up again to bring the New York Rangers their first Stanley Cup in 54 years, the Oilers dynasty officially disbanded after the 1991–1992 season. The team wouldn't return to the postseason for another four years.

AN IMPROBABLE RUN

After their furlough from playing past game 82, the Oilers, under the direction of a committee of team-builders, including former players Kevin Lowe and Craig MacTavish, qualified for the playoffs in five straight years, making it to the second round only twice. In fact, going into the 2005–2006 season, it had been six years since Edmonton hadn't seen, at best, a first-round exit in the postseason. Following the NHL lockout of 2004–2005, the 2005–2006 Oilers posted their best regular-season showing since their fourth Stanley Cup–winning season of 1987–1988, winning 41 games and finishing third in the Northwest Division.

As the Western Conference's eighth seed, Edmonton upset the Detroit Red Wings, winner of 58 games, in six contests. Going into the Conference Semifinals against the Sharks, the Oilers lost the opening two games on the road in San Jose. Returning home, thanks to a Shawn Horcoff goal in triple overtime, they made sure they didn't leave the building with an 0–3 deficit. Horcoff's goal proved to be the turning point of the series, as Edmonton went on to win four straight and play in the Conference Finals for the first time since 1992. Nearly sweeping the Mighty Ducks of Anaheim, the Oilers took the series in five games and returned to the Cup Final. Playing in the same venue with five Stanley Cup championship banners from the 1980s hanging from the rafters, the Oilers once again packed Rexall Place in the spring of 2006. Kevin Quinn notes,

The times I've experienced a playoff game, the noise level at the arena was so much stronger than even when the team was doing well during the regular season. It's a fan base that is very knowledgeable, but come playoff time they just go crazy. I was so surprised when I first was in the building in '06 with just how loud it was before, during, and after the game as opposed to what happens in the regular season. During the regular season, the crowd, in my experience, is not as loud as some other buildings, like San Jose or Winnipeg, but come playoff time the town is all Oilers all the time, and the sound inside the arena is deafening. It really gets cranked up in that building.

Although the Oilers' magical run came to an end during the seventh and decisive game of the Cup Final against the Carolina Hurricanes, the team breathed life back into its fan base and the community, bringing late spring hockey back to Alberta.

TAKING "CHAMPION" OUT OF "CITY OF CHAMPIONS"

Since their Cup Final run of 2006, the Oilers failed to make the postseason in 10 straight seasons from 2006 to 2015. In fact, having burned through seven builders in that span, the team engineering department finally decided to just put a paint can and brush by the coach's parking space. In 2015, with things going so badly on the ice in Edmonton, the city council voted to have the slogan "City of Champions" removed from the outdoor welcome signs; however, amid this playoff vacancy and personnel shakeup lies broadcaster Kevin Quinn's three most memorable games, which took place in the spring of 2010. Quinn recalls,

> Back in March of 2010, it was a game in Columbus followed by a game in Chicago followed by a game at home against St. Louis. In those three games, Andrew Cogliano scored the game-winning goal in overtime. That's never happened before where one player scored a game-winning overtime goal in three straight games. He did it the third time at home. It was unbelievable. The first time, they won the game in overtime in Columbus. That's fantastic, and then holy cow! He did it again against Chicago. Then to come home and have him do it against the St. Louis Blues, the place went crazy. We went crazy. I was working with Ray Ferraro at the time, and Ray exclaimed, "I can't believe it!" It was a pretty special moment. Andrew's gloves and stick went to the Hall of Fame because it had never been done before. Winning in overtime is always exciting, but to do it three straight games, and, for me, to be able to broadcast those three straight games was something I will always remember.

With Cogliano having taken the path most traveled by Oiler super-stars—which is out of Edmonton—today's Oilers, with the young offensive talent of team captain Connor McDavid, Jordan Eberle, and Leon Draisaitl, as well as team-builder Todd McLellan, who is hoping to disrupt the trend of coaches not sticking around long enough to get a Christmas card, have not only brought the team back to the postseason but have made them a legitimate Western Conference threat. Riding the heels of McDavid's speedy skates, the Oilers are looking to bring Lord Stanley's Cup back into town and past a welcoming sign once again worthy of the slogan "City of Champions."

• *13* •

Florida Panthers

*W*hile retirees, meteorologists, and virtually everyone south of Atlanta, Georgia, were still shaking their heads at how professional hockey found its way to the "Sunshine State" before baseball in the form of the Tampa Bay Lightning, South Florida was gearing up for its own shot at some on-ice action in the fall of 1993. Even though the record low temperatures of most of its surrounding cites still wouldn't be enough to freeze water, the city of Miami welcomed the NHL expansion Florida Panthers to its downtown sporting facility, Miami Arena. After five seasons, including a trip to the Stanley Cup Final in 1996, the Panthers packed their things and traveled north on the Sawgrass Expressway to (then-named) National Car Rental Center. Sparing pregame commentators and a boat load of printer ink in the season ticket office, the Panthers' home would go with the trendier acronymic option and be renamed the BB&T Center. Today, with the nearest freezable pond three states away, the Panthers are celebrating 20-plus years of professional hockey near the Everglades.

THE "RAT TRICK"

Throwing wildlife onto the ice is part of professional hockey. In Detroit, during playoff time, they throw an octopus. In Nashville, they throw catfish. In Florida, the proverbial Pied Piper appeared to have "missed a spot" during the 1995–1996 season, as another member of the animal kingdom was about to join center ice. Early in the season, right winger Scott Mellanby killed a rat in the team locker room before the game and went on to score two goals against Calgary. Mellanby's goaltender, John Vanbiesbrouck, coined the term "rat trick" that night and would quickly regret his cleverness once back in his pads and between the pipes, as a swarm of plastic rats made their way onto the ice, delaying the game and surfacing a league rule that had since been collecting dust. So as not to penalize the team and risk altering the course of the game, the plastic rats would be holstered until the final period came to a close. Panthers radio play-by-play broadcaster Randy Moller notes, "We've had a history of fans throwing rats on the ice after a big win. I don't think that's ever going to go away. Of course, it started back in '96, with the 'rat trick' and the team going to the Stanley Cup Final. They've kept that up."

Although the team hasn't made it past the first round since their only trip to the Stanley Cup Final in 1996—and the arena store stopped selling them for fear of league backlash—fans continue to litter the ice with the toy rodents. They may not admit it, but the ice resurfacers at the BB&T Center, if they listen closely enough, can hear the sound of Vanbiesbrouck laughing every time the broom nudges the rat a little too hard.

ARE THOSE CHEERS FOR ME OR FOR THEM?

Much like its Sonoran Desert counterpart out West, the warm climate of South Florida draws the postretirement crowd. Doing their best impersonation of birds and monarch butterflies, those in the Great Lakes region and on the northeastern seaboard eventually make their way down the Florida panhandle for a permanent residence once terms like "401K" and "social security" start becoming everyday conversational material. As would be expected from fans whose team roots predate those of the Panthers by—at the very least—three generations, local team fandom isn't part of the moving package. Moller discusses the pitfalls of a new market clashing with old loyalties:

> There's a very small percentage of the population that was born and raised out here who's over the age of 40. Everybody's from somewhere else. We have a large population that turns in a fan base from the northeast everywhere from Boston through New York to Philadelphia, Washington, and Baltimore, so a lot of our fans are transplants. They were huge sports fans—huge hockey fans—when they lived up north, wherever they were. The challenge we have—and we've done a pretty good job of it—is if the team starts to improve and becomes a pretty consistent playoff team, will we change those fans from the Canadiens, Maple Leafs, Bruins, Flyers, Rangers, Islanders, and Devils to becoming full, 100 percent Panther fans? We have a lot of Panther fans who, out of 40 or 39 games of the year,

they're wearing Panther jerseys. The other two are when the Rangers come to town and they're wearing Rangers jerseys. There's a lot of teams who are like that, whether it's Nashville or Phoenix or Tampa. With the nontraditional markets, you're still going to have that. Go to a Calgary Flames game when the Montreal Canadiens come to town or the Toronto Maple Leafs and over half of the stands will be wearing visiting jerseys. Fans are fans, and that's what you're going to get.

Luckily for the Panthers, the arena seats match the home jerseys, creating an optical illusion of support, as the team has finished in the bottom two in average attendance two of the past four seasons (2013–2017).

FLORIDA BEARS MORE FRUIT THAN JUST ORANGES

The seats weren't always half empty at BB&T, as the Panthers finished second in the division the first two seasons inside their new home, making the playoffs for the first time in three years during the 1999–2000 season. While they would only play the bare minimum four games in a sweep by the eventual Stanley Cup champion New Jersey Devils, the team brought another attraction to the ice in the form of Paul Laus and Peter Worrell, the Panthers' most notorious enforcers to date. Former Panthers TV play-by-play broadcaster Jeff Rimer, who called the team from their inception until the lockout of 2004–2005, discusses Laus's presence:

> Paul Laus was a very physical defenseman and very tough; probably the toughest player in that role I've ever been around. He never lost a fight. Oftentimes, it was just one punch and it was over. With all the fighting he did over the years, he certainly made the Panthers a better hockey team. In the inaugural year, they just about made the playoffs and would have been the first team to join the National Hockey League as an expansion team and make the playoffs. He was an incredible part of that team, as he was in '96, when the Panthers went to the Stanley Cup Final. Laus kept the opposition honest. He was one of the leaders on that hockey team.

Randy Moller adds to Rimer's sentiment saying,

> Paul Laus was the original enforcer for the Panthers. He played 5, 6 years here in Florida and became a very big fan favorite. The two toughest guys were probably Paul Laus and Peter Worrell, the largest black man to ever play the game. My goodness he was big. Peter was 6-foot-6, 250 pounds. When he played, you couldn't miss him. He played an important role for the Panthers for only a few years, but his time here, he played the role to a T.

With his physique more than big enough to play for the NFL's Dolphins just down the road, Worrell tangled with the NHL's not-nearly-as-heavy-as-his-weight enforcers during his time with the Panthers, including Bob Probert, Tie Domi, Rob Ray, and, on one occasion, virtually the entire 2000–2001 New York Rangers club. Former Panthers TV play-by-play voice and Hall of Famer Ken "Jiggs" McDonald explains,

> Pete Worrell, you just knew, once he came over the boards, something was going to happen, provided something had led to him coming over the boards. He was going to make sure a price was paid for taking any liberties. He was probably pound for pound one of the toughest guys I've seen in this game.

With a broadcasting career spanning more than six decades, McDonald's claim puts Worrell in an elite class.

THIS TIME, A LITTLE TOO MUCH BLOOD ON THE ICE

While Panther fans relish any edition of "Peter Worrell versus the World" or anything that crimsons the ice, on February 10, 2008, against Buffalo, they would get a sobering dose of "be careful what you wish for," courtesy of team left winger Richard Zedník. Moller recalls,

> It was my first or second year doing play-by-play when Richard Zedník got his neck cut with a skate in Buffalo. He just about died on the ice. To see him skating off the ice with blood shooting yards in the air. It cut an artery in his vice jugular vein in his neck. I'm glad that he survived that (knock on wood). That was a surreal experience as far as broadcasting goes.

Cheating death, Zedník would return the following season and play 70 games, racking up another 17 goals before hanging up his skates for good.

LET'S PLAY A GAME OF MUSICAL ~~CHAIRS~~ LOCKERS

Much like the team's former and interim broadcaster, Jiggs McDonald, the Panthers' playing roster had its fair share of journeymen throughout the years. Seasoned veterans like Pavel Bure, Sandis Ozolinsh, Joe Nieuwendyk, Rob Niedermayer, Igor Larionov, and Jaromír Jágr; goalies Ed Belfour, Kirk McLean, and Mike Vernon; and even fellow broadcaster Randy Moller bore the Panthers crest at one point or another in their careers. Unfortunately, the majority of these men suited up during what would be considered their "twilight years," having already used up their proverbial "make-a-wish" bid for the Stanley Cup on another team.

The seat behind the bench was apparently just as hot, as the team burned through seven coaches during a 10-season playoff drought. Finally, during the 2011–2012 season, the Panthers, under the direction of new team-builder, Kevin Dineen, and with the play of Tomáš Fleischmann, Stephen Weiss, Kris Versteeg, Brian Campbell, and goaltenders José Théodore and Scott Clemmensen, tallied 94 points, good enough for first in the Southeast Division and the third seed in the Eastern Conference playoffs, where the team's opening-round opponent would be the New Jersey Devils.

While there were still three rounds of playoff hockey to go once their series was over, the Conference Quarterfinals between the Panthers and Devils played out more like the headliner than the opening act. With each team stealing a win on the road in the series' first four games, the Panthers shut the Devils out, 3–0, in game five before traveling up the coast to Jersey with a chance for the team's first playoff series win since 1996. The sixth-seeded Devils rebounded in game six and won in overtime, necessitating a flight to the Glades for a decisive game seven. Down 0–2 in the third period, the Panthers scored twice to force overtime. Facing the winningest goalie in NHL history in the Devils' Martin Brodeur, the Panthers were fruitless in their last 27 minutes of playing time, as Devils center Adam Henrique's double-overtime goal past Théodore sealed the game and the series for a Devils team that would go on to reach the Stanley Cup Final against the Los Angeles Kings. While on the losing side of the contest, Moller, in an interview from 2015, recalls his most memorable game as a broadcaster:

> Three years ago, when the Panthers last qualified for the playoffs, game seven against the New Jersey Devils was really something. The place, the electricity in the air, and the fans. Games one and two were very exciting in that series, but game seven, for me as a broadcaster, was probably one of the most exhilarating games to be involved in. It was back and forth, and the Panthers lost in overtime. It was a crushing blow, and the Devils went on to the Stanley Cup Final that year. For me, personally, to be able to call that game—a game seven—was absolutely fantastic.

THE FLORIDA PANTHERS TODAY

With two additional teams coming to the Eastern Conference party in 2013, in the form of the Columbus Blue Jackets and playoff staple Detroit Red Wings, a ticket to the postseason has become harder to come by for Florida.

However, in 2015–2016, thanks to an offense spearheaded by veterans Jaromír Jágr and Jussi Jokinen, as well as the youthful Aleksander Barkov, Jr. and Jonathan Huberdeau (whose ages combined were *still* not greater than that of Jágr), the Panthers' 103 regular season points were enough for first place in the Eastern Conference's Atlantic Division. Jágr's 66 regular season points led the team, which, unfortunately was ousted in the first round by a New York Islanders team long overdue for a postseason advancement. Panthers TV play by play voice Steve Goldstein describes the anomaly inducing dynamic with the (now) 45-year-old Jágr, saying, "It's amazing to watch him with his young teammates. These guys are half his age. He's like a renaissance man. He gets along with everybody at an age where a lot of people in society start to get that 'back in *my* time' when they talk to young people. Jágr is completely the opposite. He's not like that at all. For anybody to be as passionate about anything as he is about the game of hockey, it's really fascinating to watch." During the 2016–2017 season, Jágr passed Mark Messier for second on the NHL's all-time scoring list. Witness to the milestone, Steve Goldstein notes, "I grew up in Brooklyn, New York, and I was a Rangers season ticket holder when Jágr broke into the league. I remember a playoff series with Mario Lemieux and Jágr against the Rangers. The Penguins were just deadly eliminating them when they won their cups. He's only a little bit younger than I am, so every time he's on the ice and I'm calling games, it's amazing to me and it's also an honor. He's been passing guys over the last three years with the Panthers. I kind of pinch myself sometimes and say, 'What the heck am I doing here calling these legendary milestones for Jaromír Jágr?" With the right wingers' 1,914 career points still 943 shy of "The Great One" Wayne Gretzky's all-time mark, Jágr may need a Gordie Howe length career to reach that summit, but, as the saying that's as timeless as the Czech superstar goes, "stranger things have happened." One thing's for sure; you won't likely find Jaromír kicking around any nearby Florida retirement communities once he hangs up his skates for good.

Los Angeles Kings

$\mathscr{F}$or 35 years, the NHL's "original six" seemed more like an exclusive club, with a sign that read, "You must be on this side of the Mississippi River to enter" outside the door. Prior to 1967, even the "gateway to the West" was too far for the league's liking, as the St. Louis Eagles so painfully found out after one season of futility before folding. In 1967, however, the league not only gave it another go in St. Louis, but also all the way to the West Coast, introducing the Los Angeles Kings and California Seals as part of the NHL's first-ever expansion, doubling the league to 12 teams.

Having only one other team in their time zone, let alone state, for the initial years of their existence, the Kings had their own struggles "joining the club," especially after their Bay Area cohorts from the north moved east to Cleveland in 1976. Kings radio play-by-play broadcaster and Hall of Famer Nick Nickson describes the added hardships for Los Angeles in its infancy:

> When I started back in '81, the only team west of the Mississippi River was the Kings. When Vancouver came in the early '70s, they were our clos- est rival to the north, and that's a two-and-a-half-hour plane ride, so the Kings were kind of isolated there for a number of years. I truly believe it prevented the Kings from reaching their potential because of the weighty travel schedule. We just didn't have a rival we could get on the plane the night before, play, and come back—a one-night jaunt like we have with San Jose. Anaheim is a bus trip. Phoenix is a one-hour trip. Colorado is only a couple of hours by plane. The fact the Kings were isolated as far as where they were located in respect to other teams in the league hurt them immeasurably over the years because of the grueling travel schedule.
>
> You've got to remember up until 20 years ago, all of the teams were traveling commercial. Now all the teams have charters. That's pretty much

the norm of professional sports in North America. The travel's a lot easier in that regard. It would have been easier back then if the Kings chartered everywhere. I look back on it because the broadcasters traveled with the team wherever they went. So many flights were 6:00 a.m. to get back to L.A. When you got to L.A., the players had to go practice, and they had played the night before, so you know they didn't have the rest they needed or should have gotten. That happened on a number of occasions. Then you lost practice days when you left to start a trip because you were at the beckon call of the travel schedule of the airlines and not when you wanted to go.

Now, if we play a game on a Saturday at home and have a game on Monday in St. Louis, Sunday, we could practice at the normal time— 10:00, 10:30 at home—get on the plane at 1:00, and be in St. Louis by 5:00. In past years, you were going commercial, and maybe the only flight leaving for St. Louis was 8:30 in the morning to get you in at a decent hour. Then you missed the practice that day. A lot of that came into play. I think anybody would be foolish to say it didn't affect the Kings' performance on the ice at certain times during the year.

Battling through cabins filled with screaming babies and autograph-seeking hockey enthusiasts on commercial flights, one would assume these Kings would have a hero's welcome upon their return home to the Los Angeles Forum; however, this was not the case for the budding franchise. Kings TV play-by-play broadcaster and Hall of Famer Bob Miller describes the half-empty Forum nights, saying, "The Forum, in the year I started, a good attendance would be 8,500 to 10,000. Jack Kent Cooke, when he owned the team, said, '250,000 Canadians live in Southern California. It must be they moved here because they hate hockey.' He didn't see them coming out to the Forum."

THE NEW KIDS ON THE MANCHESTER BLOCK

In the 10 years that preceded the Kings' arrival in Los Angeles, two of the sporting world's most storied franchises, the Brooklyn Dodgers and the Minneapolis Lakers, were making some of the country's biggest headlines by moving out West from their respective East Coast and Upper Midwest homes. The Dodgers would win three World Series titles and four league pennants in their new home by the time the Kings came into the NHL, and just as they were settling in, so, too, were the Los Angeles Lakers, who would sign superstar center Wilt Chamberlain to start the 1968–1969 season. With players like Koufax and Drysdale on the mound and Chamberlain on the hardwood, it was difficult for the Kings to grab the attention of an average Los Angeles sports fan. Nickson comments,

> When you look at where the Kings were when they started as one of the original six expansion teams in 1967, they developed a fan base. The sport was new. A lot of people who had never seen a hockey game before got exposed to the sport. As the franchise became established, it started to have a little measurable amount of success in the early '70s, when they had players like Butch Goring, Dan Maloney, and Terry Harper. Then, in the mid-'70s, Marcel Dionne—really the very first superstar player in franchise history—came on board. With the expansion in 1967 creating an interest because it was new, and then with the fact that they started to have some success in the early to mid-1970s, it kind of grew. Fans became more aware of what the sport was all about.

While the team qualified for the playoffs 10 of their first 14 seasons, their only series win would be against their intrastate rival Oakland Seals in 1969. While the Gorings, Dionnes, Maloneys, and Harpers were teaching newbie Los Angeles hockey fans the playing side of the game, players like Randy Holt and Dave "Tiger" Williams were familiarizing them with another facet of the sport. Randy Holt, a defenseman and journeyman who would only spend one and a half seasons of his 10-season career in a Kings uniform, was still there long enough to make the record books; just not necessarily in a good way. Pete Weber, lead radio play-by-play voice of the Nashville Predators, began his career in Los Angeles. During his time calling games for the Kings with Bob Miller, Weber was present for Holt's record-setting night on March 11, 1979, against the Philadelphia Flyers. Weber recalls,

> Randy Holt, the Kings' tough guy, set the all-time record for penalty minutes in a game. Jim Dorey of the Toronto Maple Leafs previously had the record, with 46 minutes in one game. Randy had 67 minutes in penalties handed out to him in that game, ending up with a triple game misconduct. There was sort of a strategic reason for that, too. The league had just put in that if you get three game misconducts, you automatically have another suspension coming up. They wanted to make sure Randy had one right there. He finished with 67 minutes, and I don't think anybody's even come close to that ever since.
>
> When Bob and I were working the games, especially those in Philadelphia, we didn't have overtime in the NHL then. Because of the line brawls, etc., we could pretty much count on being on the air for at least three hours and 45 minutes to four hours because it took so long to clean the garbage—if you will—off the ice and get things straightened out. The Kings, at one point, went 30 some games without beating the Flyers, so

there was a definite feeling of malevolence on both sides when you came down to it. That night with Randy Holt is one I will never forget.

The following season, Holt would move to the relocated Calgary Flames, where he would have another one-and-a-half-year stint with a team.

A few years after Holt's departure came the arrival of another NHL journeyman to the Kings in the form of Dave "Tiger" Williams. During his 14-season career, Williams, much like Holt, set marks designated for the *back* of the record books. Williams's career total 3,966 PIM's are the most in NHL history by more than 400 (second, Dale Hunter, 3,565). In six of his 14 seasons, Williams accumulated more than 300 penalty minutes, coming within six on three more occasions (1975–1976, 1978–1979, 1983–1984). Known by many for his fighting, Williams, in his three-and-a-half-year stay with the Kings, is remembered by Bob Miller for his other antics both on and off the ice. Miller notes,

> In those early years, Tiger was one of the players who brought attention not only to the NHL, but [also] to himself. A lot of the players in those years weren't outlandish in their actions on the ice. It was a team game and they weren't going to call attention to themselves, but Tiger would score a goal and ride his stick like a horse down the ice. Everybody loved that. I don't know if the other team liked it. He was a different kind of guy. We didn't interview him live very often because you never knew what he was going to say.
>
> I remember one game in Edmonton, he scored a goal late in the third to put us ahead before Edmonton tied us up, and it ended up in a tie. Nick Nickson interviewed him after the game and said, "Tiger, we thought you had the game-winning goal," and Tiger, putting him on a little bit, said, "Mr. Nickson, I thought it was the game-winning goal, but every time this team gets a chance to win a game, we just" (grabbing his throat with both hands and making a choking gesture) and started choking himself. It was pretty funny. You just never knew what he was going to do.
>
> I knew probably more of his off-ice things that went on. I wouldn't hear what he had said on the ice, but people would tell me he'd really rip the goaltender, stand in front of him and just berate him. I never heard any of that. He was certainly someone who got everyone's attention in the arena. One time, he was so mad over a penalty, he slammed the penalty box door and the whole pane of glass fell out onto the ice. Another time, he was with Toronto and we had Dave Hutchison, who was a big tough guy for us. They got into a scrap, and Tiger went into the penalty box and started throwing folding chairs out onto the ice. He was something to watch. His actions were always entertaining.

Williams would ship over to Hartford during his final season in the league in 1988, which, as anyone in Southern California—or anyone on the planet for that matter—knows was the season before the "Great One," Wayne Gretzky, was unexpectedly traded from the Edmonton Oilers to the Los Angeles Kings.

THE GREAT TRADE

Before LeBron James "took his talents to South Beach," David Beckham jumped the pond to join the L.A. Galaxy, and Alex "A-Rod" Rodriguez traded the sushi rolls of Seattle for the barbecue beef of Texas, arguably the biggest player shift in sports history took place on August 9, 1988, when Oilers owner Peter Pocklington traded away his eight-time Hart Memorial Trophy recipient and four-time Stanley Cup championship–winning captain to the Los Angeles Kings. If ever the term "it takes a team" could apply, as far as trades are concerned, the Oilers–Kings exchange prior to the 1988–1989 season would definitely suffice, as the rate for the "Great One" came to 55 goal-scoring Jimmy Carson, first-round pick Martin Gélinas, three future first-round picks, and $15 million. While Mark Messier, Jari Kurri, Randy Gregg, and Glenn Anderson stayed in Edmonton to win a fifth Stanley Cup, Gretzky was giving the sports landscape in Los Angeles a cooler look. Miller explains,

> The biggest difference now from the time I started in 1973 with the Kings is the awareness of the Kings franchise and the passion of the Kings fans. It actually goes back to the day Wayne Gretzky was traded here. All of a sudden, everybody got excited about seeing the greatest player in the world. Ticket sales increased, and so did souvenirs, jackets, hats, and jerseys. That's been a huge difference in this community here. The Kings before were a team that was here, but they weren't real successful. They did have some good years back in the '70s where they actually outdrew the Lakers a couple of seasons, but it was never sustained.

While a spike in the sale of tickets and sports paraphernalia is great, the real question was, How would the "Great One" fare on the ice in Southern California?

Prior to Gretzky's arrival, the Kings, in their 21-year history, had only advanced past the opening round of the playoffs twice, one of which occurred against Gretzky himself in the wake of the "Miracle on Manchester" game during the 1982 Division Semifinals. In his first three seasons with the Kings, Gretzky, winning his record ninth Hart Memorial Trophy in 1989, led the team into the Division Finals each year, including the team's first (and, to this day, only) division title during the 1990–1991 regular season. Nickson comments on the Gretzky factor in Los Angeles, saying, "The Gretzky trade in 1988 catapulted the whole franchise into another level. They did have a lot of exciting times in the Gretzky era, especially in the first four or five seasons. I think we all felt from '88 to '93, those were teams that could compete every year, so the interest there picked up."

Interest peaked during the 1992–1993 season, as the team advanced past the second round for the first time in team history, setting up a Conference Final matchup with Wendel Clark and the Toronto Maple Leafs. With the teams splitting the first four games, Gretzky's former teammate Glenn Anderson put the Kings on the brink of elimination with an overtime goal in game five. In game six, Gretzky, staying in despite a—depending on which side of the U.S.–Canadian border you are on—suspension-worthy high stick to the face of Doug Gilmour, scored the game-winner in overtime to force a winner-take-all game seven in Toronto. The morning of game seven, the only person in Toronto *not* familiar with Wayne Gretzky was apparently a security guard in the hotel where the superstar was staying. Miller recalls,

> Gretzky is going down to a morning skate, and he's in the elevator. There's a security guy in there, and Wayne says, "How's it going?" He says, "It's going great now, but, tonight at 10:30, it's going to be tough." Wayne says, "Why is that?" He says, "This city is going to be going crazy at 10:30 tonight." So they get down to the bottom and the door opens. Wayne steps out and says, "Don't worry about your job at 10:30." The security guy asks, "Why not?" and Wayne says, "Because mine starts at 7:30." Then he goes out and gets the hat trick, and the Kings win to go to the Final.

Scoring 10 points in the series to add to his eventual 40 for the playoffs that year, Gretzky led the Kings to their first-ever Stanley Cup Final appearance. Miller looks back on what is still known in L.A. as "The Series," relating,

> In '93, that series against Toronto was unbelievable. The two captains, Wendel Clark of Toronto and Gretzky of the Kings, just standing up and leading their teams. We had to win a game six to force the game seven back in Toronto. In the final minute, we're ahead by one goal, and they're buzzing around our goalie. I was shaking I was so nervous, thinking, "We're so close to getting to the Final." That was just a classic series.

Unfortunately, the Kings' next opponent would be the incomparable Patrick Roy and the Montreal Canadiens, who would thwart Gretzky and Los Angeles four games to one, winning the team's record 22nd Stanley Cup in franchise history. While the Kings wouldn't return to hockey's grandest stage for another 19 years, there was still plenty of room in Los Angeles for Gretzky and his milestones. Having already passed "Mr. Hockey" Gordie Howe on the all-time scoring list in just his second season with the Kings, Gretzky, on March 23, 1994, would pass Howe in a category nobody would have ever reasonably expected to be eclipsed. Howe, after 26 seasons in the NHL, was the only player to have scored 800 career goals, and it took a one-season return after an eight-year absence to do so. Gretzky, thanks to record-breaking seasons early in his career with the Oilers and a continual barrage of offense with the Kings, found himself tied with Howe going into the late 1993–1994 regular season matchup against the Vancouver Canucks. With fans all over the country tuned in, Gretzky would stand at hockey's scoring summit by night's end. In the ESPN booth for this historic night was Gary Thorne, who notes, "Gretzky's goal at the Forum that made him the all-time leader, you knew going in that this was a moment. This was going to be a record that would stand and people were going to talk about forever. I was getting a chance in broadcasting the game not only to be there and see it but to actually call it. I never practice calls or have anything made up as to what I'm going to say. I said whatever I felt at the moment and then I just sat back and kind of became a fan. Watching the reaction of Gretzky's teammates and the fans who were there at the Forum, I wanted to remember that. That was a moment I wanted to be sure I was on the outside looking in because this was something I would remember forever." Gretzky would play with the Kings for almost two more seasons before rejoining his former teammates Glenn Anderson and Grant Fuhr—as well as Brett Hull and a roster filled with eventual Hall of Famers—in St. Louis for a half-season active-player version of the "old-timers' game." Upsetting the Toronto Maple Leafs in the opening round of the 1996 playoffs, Gretzky and the Blues then ran into the Detroit Red Wings, winner of 131 regular-season points, and lost in seven games.

Next Gretzky rejoined another former teammate, Mark Messier, in New York. While Messier dabbled in British Columbia for a few seasons with the Canucks, Gretzky retired as a player following the 1998–1999 season. Gretzky's 894 goals, 1,963 assists, and 2,857 points are the most ever by any player in NHL history. On November 22, 1999, just a few months removed from his retirement, Gretzky was inducted into the Hockey Hall of Fame. Shortly thereafter, Gretzky's number 99 was retired by the NHL, making him the only player in league history to receive such an honor.

THE GREAT "ONES"?

Following Gretzky's departure during the 1995–1996 season, superstars of another L.A. sport stole the spotlight back from the Kings, as Kobe Bryant and, eventually, Shaquille O'Neal led the NBA's Los Angeles Lakers to three straight titles from 2000 to 2002. In the meantime, it was back to "one-and-done" or no-playoff hockey for the Kings for 16 of 17 seasons following the 1993 Stanley Cup Final run. While Kobe was lifting five NBA titles, the Kings were firing five team-builders, including two during the 2011–2012 season; however, as the Kings demonstrated at the start of the 2012 postseason, the team's record through 82 games isn't what matters. It's what the team does after those 82 games.

Under Darryl Sutter, their third team-builder of the season, the Kings entered the 2012 playoffs as the Western Conference's eighth seed, where they would play the top-seeded Vancouver Canucks. Calling the team's playoff games on the radio, Nickson reflects on the Kings' return to postseason relevance in 2012:

> I had been with the Kings for 31 years. Bob Miller, at that time, had been with the Kings for 39 years, and neither one of us had ever experienced a Stanley Cup championship team. I think whether you're a player, a broadcaster, a coach, or a fan for a team, that's what you're looking for. You're looking for your team to be crowned the champions. For me, there are a lot of exciting broadcasts I'll always remember once that playoff season started in 2012, but a couple of them really stand out.
>
> The Kings had beaten Vancouver, the number-one seed that year, in five games in the first round. The game-five winner in Vancouver on the Jarret Stoll overtime goal clinched the series. Then the Kings' second-round opponent was the second seed in the West that year, the St. Louis Blues. The Kings had won in game one. It was a close game, but in game two, they came out and they scored four goals in the first period. I think Anže Kopitar scored the fourth goal, and I remember turning to my broadcast partner Daryl Evans and we didn't say anything. We were still on the air, but the crowd was still reacting to the Kings scoring four goals in the first period. I looked at Daryl and he looked at me, and it was like we were both reading what each other was thinking. It was like, "Oh my gosh. Who's going to stop this team in the postseason?" They were playing so well night after night.
>
> That game will always stand out to me because at that point in the playoff run, I thought to myself, "I'm expecting this team to win now every single night." You get through stages—coaches and players talk about it—when you develop a team, you hope you can win, you think you can win, and you know you can win. For me, I was expecting them to win every night because they were playing that well in the playoffs. That was kind of a turning point for me in the way I regarded what the team was starting to accomplish in the 2012 playoffs. I've got to say that second game of the St. Louis series would stand out for me not so much as the final score of

the game or any calls of the goals, but because of the mindset I started to develop in following that team throughout that playoff run.

Although not the three-digit regular-season powerhouse the Blues and Canucks were in 2011–2012, the (then-named) Phoenix Coyotes were still the Western Conference's third seed and, in being so, had the home-ice advantage in the Conference Finals. Much like they had done in the previous two series, the Kings kept winning on the road, taking all three games in Arizona, including the game-five clincher on an overtime goal by Dustin Penner. The Kings, once again, were in the Stanley Cup Final. Nickson continues,

> Once they got to the Stanley Cup Final and played New Jersey, they didn't have home ice in any of those four rounds. They start games one and two in New Jersey. They win game one on the overtime goal by Kopitar, and then, when they won game two on the overtime goal by Jeff Carter, that's when I got that this is really going to happen. Up 2–0, you win the first two games on the road, and now you're coming home and you've got home-ice advantage.
>
> Game two of the final would stand out during that run only because that's when I felt—after Carter scored to give the Kings the victory—this is going to happen this year. The Kings are going to win a Stanley Cup. Then, of course, in game six, when the Kings win it on home ice, from a broadcasting standpoint, we all knew midway through the game when it was 4–1 in the second period, everybody in the building knew it was going to be a Kings victory. Nobody was going to score more than two goals that year against Jonathan Quick in the playoffs.
>
> In the third period, we all had to kind of just relax, soak in the moment, soak in the atmosphere, and then you know, once the clock got to 15, 12, 10 seconds left, you could count it down and you knew there was no doubt as to who was going to win the game. That was special. You always wonder as a broadcaster how you would handle a moment when a team was clinching a championship. That would stand out because of how the game transpired and how I was able to wrap up the whole season.

Although turning his TV play-by-play broadcasting duties over to the national networks, Miller looks back at the Kings' first-ever taste of winning Lord Stanley's Cup, saying,

> In 2012, the Kings just did get into the playoffs as the eighth-seeded team, and no eighth-seeded team had ever gone on to win the Stanley Cup. They won 10 straight games on the road. That had never been done before. They led each of the first three series three games to none, and that had never

been done before. There were so many firsts in that first Stanley Cup the Kings won, the series were just so memorable. It was tremendous for me to be a part of it because it was 39 years of being with the Kings at that time until they won the cup. I told people my biggest fear is I'm going to retire and they'll win the Stanley Cup the next season.

I don't think anything will replace winning the first Stanley Cup. It's great to repeat and it's great to win it twice in three seasons, but the first time was special. The buildings were sold out obviously for every game, and the whole city was taken with the fact the Kings were not only in the Final, but [also] had a chance to win the Final. There was such excitement here with all the fans and the programming on the radio and TV and in the newspapers. There were 350,000 people in downtown L.A. for the parade. The cup, as I recall, made 500 appearances in Los Angeles that summer, going to all the different landmarks. They brought it to Dodger Stadium and so many parties. It was just great to be part of it.

Two years later, Bob Miller's colleague, Nick Nickson, would have the chance to "wrap up" another Kings championship season. While losing the first three games of the 2014 postseason, Los Angeles would rebound by winning six straight, including four straight against the third-seeded San Jose Sharks, becoming the fourth team in NHL history to overcome an 0–3 deficit to win a seven-game series. Another three-game losing streak in the middle of the Western Conference Semifinals against Anaheim put Los Angeles in another hole; however, the Kings finished the series the way it started against its Southern California neighbors by winning two straight games and eliminating the Ducks in seven.

In the Conference Finals, it was the Kings who almost relinquished the series, as the team, having once led the defending Stanley Cup champion Chicago Blackhawks three games to one, needed an overtime goal by Alec Martinez in game seven to advance to the Stanley Cup Final, the team's second such appearance in three seasons. There would be no second four-game comeback from an 0–3 deficit in the 2014 Stanley Cup Playoffs, as the Kings, winning the first three games of the Final against the New York Rangers, clinched the series and the Stanley Cup on yet another overtime goal by Alec Martinez.

Miller and Nickson, having waited a collective 70 years for their first chance at being a part of a Stanley Cup champion, only had to wait another two apiece the second time around. Miller states, "We were thinking, 'This ain't never happening again,' and then, two seasons later, it does happen again. It's great to win it and say our team now is one of the dominant teams of the league, winning twice in three seasons." Nickson signs off on the team's most recent success on hockey's grandest stage, saying,

As we have seen over the last couple of years, it's crescendoed to the point where it's now one of the hottest sports tickets in the market. I think when you talk about the Kings franchise, there are only six teams in the league that are older. The original six, of course. It's been a process of building a fan base and a stamp in the market for the Kings brand. "What is Kings hockey?" "What is it all about?" I think if you charted a graph, it would have started down near the bottom in '67. Right now, it would be near the top with what they've accomplished the last two or three years. I don't know if you could say that for a lot of the other teams. It's been partly because of the durability of the franchise here and partly because of how management has attacked building a fan base, which has gotten the Kings to where they are today, and that is one of the more visible and successful franchises in the league.

Having sold out every regular-season and playoff game since December 3, 2011, the Los Angeles Kings, still with 14 players from their 2014 championship roster, including team captain Anze Kopitar and goaltender Jonathan Quick, are looking to join their occasional Western Conference playoff tango partner, the Chicago Blackhawks, and go from what was once reserved as a vacation slot in the visiting team's travel schedule to NHL dynasty. Who knows? With one more June parade through downtown, the Kings may just take the title of "L.A.'s team" from their purple-and-gold-clad Staples Center roommates and the "Boys in Dodger Blue."

Minnesota Wild

Having a background in professional hockey going back as far as 1883, the "North Star State," Minnesota, finally got its invitation to participate at the game's grandest level in 1967, when the league doubled in size. Among the "second six" of the NHL were the North Stars, who would play 26 seasons in the Upper Midwest before taking an uncharacteristic trip south to Dallas, dropping the word "North" from the team name and leaving a state full of angry fans wearing bright green and yellow sweaters with faces begging the question, "Why?" Considering it is the U.S. state that has birthed the most current professional hockey players, a lack of an actual professional team, at least at the NHL level, was sure to be short-lived. Seven years after team captain Mike Modano and company trekked southward, trading their "hot dish" diet for barbecues and buffets, NHL hockey returned to the Land of 10,000 Lakes in the form of the expansion Minnesota Wild.

SHEDDING THEIR SKIN

After much deliberation, fan polls, and several sessions of corporate brainstorming, the "Minnesota *not* the North Stars" became too much of a mouthful to be considered a team name, but the sentiment remained the same. Minnesota Wild radio play-by-play broadcaster Bob Kurtz, who called games for the North Stars as well, describes the Wild's quest to step out of the shadow of their predecessor:

> I was there for the North Stars, but then I was in Boston working for the Red Sox when the North Stars moved to Dallas. Then I came back

with the Wild. They're two different organizations. In the beginning, the Wild wanted to separate themselves from the North Star identity in terms of maybe the North Stars failed to draw enough people and finally wound up packing and moving to Texas. The Wild wanted their own identity and a fresh start. We have a lot of North Star people. The guy I broadcast with, Tom Reid, also did the North Stars. A number of people in our front office worked with the North Stars, but then there's a lot of people who haven't.

The North Stars were out in suburban Bloomington, which is where the Mall of America is now. They went from a suburban setting basically to the other side of the river into downtown St. Paul. The Wild are well marketed and draw a lot from the East Metro, although they still get a lot of fans from the West Metro. It seemed the North Stars grew primarily from the West Metro out. There's quite a contrast. A lot of fans that went to North Star games purchased season tickets for the Wild, but there were a number of them who the North Stars were the end of it and ripped it off and didn't necessarily attach their loyalty to the Wild. There's a huge number of them who picked right up where they left off, but some have never forgiven Norm Green for moving the team. There's a lot of people who think the Wild should be named the North Stars. You run the gambit. In a lot of ways, it's an entirely new crowd.

The Wild weren't the only ones trying to separate themselves from tradition, as the city of St. Paul itself felt it had something to prove. For a place nicknamed the Twin Cities, the Minneapolis/St. Paul area of Minnesota had, for decades, displayed more fraternal than identical traits, especially in the world of professional sports. Separated from its urban sibling by the mighty Mississippi River, Minneapolis, in the business world, would have been served for antitrust activity by its eastern kin had the NHL and its expansion market not stepped in during the summer of 1998 and broken ground on the Xcel Energy Center. Being *literally* left out in the snow all those years prior to 2000, St. Paul finally got its chance at the "big leagues." Kurtz notes,

The area at West Seventh and Kellogg was not particularly the greatest place in the world. The old Civic Center was famous for its clear glass boards. They tore down the Civic Center and built the Xcel Energy Center, their current building, right on the same site to welcome back the Wild. They had this magnificent new building that really breathed some life into downtown St. Paul. They did a terrific job. My broadcast partner, Tom Reid, owns a pub a couple of blocks down from the Xcel Energy Center that he bought just before they opened the new building. You can go to his place for a pregame drink and then walk up towards the rink. There's a number of establishments on West Seventh. There's just excitement in the air, especially when you get that little winter nip and a little snow falling—hockey weather—it dominates, and it has really helped to revitalize downtown St. Paul.

HOCKEY~~TOWN~~ STATE

Although their "brothers of a different lake" in Detroit, Michigan, claim citizenship in what is known as "Hockeytown," Minnesota could probably make the case for "Hockeystate," as the game's competition—on all levels and with both sexes—is as present as the ice on which it is played. Kurtz describes the hockey community found throughout the "Gopher State," saying,

> Obviously, with the name Minnesota rather than St. Paul, they incorporate pretty much the whole state. In Minnesota, the Wild are obviously at the top of the pyramid, but then you have the University of Minnesota, the University of Minnesota Duluth, St. Cloud State University, Minnesota State, Mankato, I could go on and on. Plus all of the high school tournaments makes it unique. They sell out a high school tournament and put 19,000 people in the building. At Xcel Energy Center, they have the jerseys/sweaters of each Minnesota high school hockey team, and they have them on display up on the suite level. They pay tribute to basically every high school that has a hockey team in Minnesota. They do a terrific job of tying in with the pee wees, the bantams, the high school, and the university, and no better job is done.
>
> They have this thing called "Hockey Day Minnesota," which was put together by the TV people of Fox Sports North. They do a telecast starting in February, where they pick a site outside. This year, it was on the Tarmac of Holdman Field, which is the St. Paul airport. They'll have a girl's high school game, a boy's high school game. The Minnesota Gophers would play, and then the Wild would push their start time back to 8:00 to play, and this is all televised. It's wall to wall hockey all day. There's people putting together outdoor rinks and all kinds of interesting stories.

Perhaps the most interesting of all stories predated Hockey Day Minnesota, when the Stars changed states from "lone" back to "north" during the Wild's inaugural year.

UN-WELCOME BACK, STARS

While it took only six seasons for the Dallas Stars to do what they couldn't in 26 in Minnesota—win a Stanley Cup—there weren't any parades awaiting them upon their return to Minnesota on December 17, 2000. Considered by many Wild fans to be the team's most memorable game to date, the Stars return north was significant for Kurtz as well, at least from a nonplayoff standpoint. Kurtz recalls,

> One of the most memorable games I've done with the Wild was the first time the Dallas Stars came back to town. They packed the building, and it was really jumping. The emotions were high. You talk about wide-eyed excitement, all the kids had their eyes wide, and all the old North Stars people came back. Neal Broten went up on stage to do the "let's play hockey" tradition they had. He was wearing a Dallas sweater. He took it off and had a North Stars sweater underneath. Everybody went nuts. The crowd roared. Minnesota beat Dallas that day, 6–0. The real homecoming back for the Stars. The bloom was off the rose, and Dallas was basically just another team. That's the game I remember the most.

While it wasn't necessarily the father's welcome to his prodigal son, North-Star-turned-Wild fans, having received some form of closure with a 6–0 drubbing of their Bloomington brothers from another time, still reserve a place in their hearts for the star-topped, golden "N." Kurtz continues, "As they've moved along, they're reaching back a little more into the North Stars and now they seem to be embracing the North Stars even more."

THE TRAINING WHEELS COME OFF

Sadly, most of the games not involving the Dallas Stars didn't have the same result on the scoreboard for the Wild, as the team finished fifth in the Western Conference's Northwest Division their first two seasons, missing out on the playoffs both years. In 2002–2003, however, the Wild, thanks to Marián Gáborík, Pascal Dupuis, Cliff Ronning, team tough guy Matt Johnson, and the goaltending tandem of Dwayne Roloson and Manny Fernandez, improved 22 points on the team's total of the previous season and finished third in the division, good for the conference's sixth seed. Two seven-game series later, the Wild found themselves in the Conference Finals, going up against another "underdog" opponent in the Mighty Ducks of Anaheim. Although the Wild lost four straight to Anaheim, their first playoff appearance made more noise throughout the league than any of the team's appearances since 2002–2003. Having broadcast the team during their first playoff run, Kurtz describes the Wild's unexpected success, saying,

> No matter which game you pick, as far as the most memorable goes, it's always going to be a playoff game. We've had a couple of real decent

playoffs. In 2003, we played both the Colorado Avalanche and the Vancouver Canucks, and, in both of those series, we were the underdog, and, in both series, we fell behind three games to one. In the first series against Colorado, Andrew Brunette scored an overtime goal in game seven. That night I'll certainly never forget. Then in the second series that followed against Vancouver, we won two big games. Game six at our place and game seven at their place. Any of those game sevens or any of those overtimes you always remember, including the bad ones.

While it's likely one of those "bad ones" included the double-overtime opening-game loss to the Ducks, the Wild had finally given a showing worthy of a North Star nod.

THE MINNESOTA WILD TODAY

While the team has not made it back to the Conference Finals since 2003, the Wild, having waded through a brief four-year playoff drought, once again find themselves contenders in the NHL's Western Conference. Be it the departure of the Columbus Blue Jackets and Detroit Red Wings to the Eastern Conference—increasing their playoff probability from 53 to 57 percent—or the emergence of offensive-minded players like Zach Parise and Jason Pominville, the Wild have qualified to play past game 82 the last five seasons (2013–2017), making it to the second round in two of the last three. With the ponds and lakes throughout the state serving more as frozen springs of talent, chances are a healthy batch of high school or university players featured during Hockey Day Minnesota will go from the tarmac to the "show," representing their home state to the tune of a Stanley Cup title, raising a banner into the rafters of the Xcel Energy Center, and giving St. Paul a "one up" over its twin brother to the west.

· *16* ·

Montreal Canadiens

$\mathscr{W}$hile "original six" is certainly a jacket to wear with great pride and honor in the NHL, the "original" is a patch that can only be sewn on one. The sport of hockey has many origins. The game's founder, James Creighton, hailed from Nova Scotia, while his first organized contest took place on March 3, 1875, in Montreal, at the Victoria Skating Rink. Some of the contestants of the exhibition, particularly the students of McGill University, where Creighton attended school, formed the first hockey team at the collegiate level in 1877. Another 25 years down the road and across the U.S.–Canadian border, Portage Lake became the first hockey team to legitimize itself as professional and make the boys to the north pose the question, "We've been doing this for *free* this entire time?"

Realizing they could quit their day jobs, players formed the Eastern Canada Hockey Association (ECHA) and the National Hockey Association (NHA), the latter consisting of two teams from Montreal, the Wanderers, and, for French-speaking spectators, Les Canadiens. After the ECHA dissolved, Montreal's second team dropped the article "Les" and went on to compete in the NHA, earning their first trip to the playoffs in 1914. Two years later, the Canadiens, the representing champions of the NHA, went on—as was customary—to play the West Coast Hockey League champion Portland Rosebuds for the Stanley Cup. With the series coming down to the deciding fifth game, the Canadiens outlasted the Rosebuds, 2–1, and captured the first of what would eventually become an NHL-record 22 Stanley Cup championships, second in the four major sports to Major League Baseball's New York Yankees and their 27 World Series titles.

A year after raising their first cup, the Canadiens, as well as the Wanderers, the (original) Ottawa Senators, and the Quebec Bulldogs, detached themselves—

specifically from Eddie Livingstone, owner of the Toronto Torontos—and formed what is now known as the NHL. With enough dynasties to rival a world history book, the Montreal Canadiens have served as the NHL standard for nearly a century, turning the seed planted by Mr. Creighton into a blooming maple.

AS COULD BE EXPECTED

With the game originating in the "Great White North," one can only assume hockey dominates the Canadian sports landscape from Vancouver to Newfoundland, but with the city of Montreal, it's a little different for Canadiens radio play-by-play broadcaster John Bartlett, who says,

> It's more than just being an original six team. The franchise itself has such a strong history and is really a cultural tie to the city of Montreal and the province of Quebec. The Montreal Canadiens are a part of the fabric. There's a strong cultural impact with the Canadiens across Canada and even around the world. They are the known brand in the sport, sort of like the New York Yankees or Manchester United. Anywhere you go, people know who the Montreal Canadiens are, and a lot of people, even if they're not necessarily as familiar with the sport of hockey, can still name the Canadiens, probably tell you a little about the Montreal Forum, and maybe even name a couple of the superstars over time, whether it's Jean Béliveau or "Rocket" Richard. That's where it's extra special when it comes to the Canadiens and the connection the people have with the team.

For some, the connection goes beyond the ice. Bartlett continues,

> It's really like a religion. I know the sport of hockey is considered a religion in Canada, but the Canadiens are tied in a different and special way, even to the point where the University of Montreal offered a program for students which looked at hockey as a religion with the impact it has on the people and their lives in this province.

Considering the seemingly endless list of Canadien Hall of Famers, there would be little difficulty finding a pastor to lead that particular denomination.

WAS THERE EVER A TIME WHEN
THERE WASN'T A DYNASTY?

Before Derek Jeter, Mariano Rivera, Andy Pettitte, and Jorge Posada—otherwise known as the "core four"—won five World Series championships in a 14-year span, MLB's "known brand," the New York Yankees, shared the sports spot-light with the Montreal Canadiens, with each franchise having won 22 league championships. Even spread out during a period spanning nearly a century, a club doesn't win that many titles without creating a dynasty or three along the way.

Montreal's first dynasty began in 1955, when the team, led by Jean Bé-liveau, Doug Harvey, brothers Henri and Maurice "Rocket" Richard, Bernie Geoffrion, goaltender Jacques Plante, team-builder Toe Blake, and about a dozen other names gracing the Hockey Hall of Fame in Toronto, won the first of its NHL-record five straight Stanley Cups. After the Toronto Maple Leafs had their little dip into the dynasty pool, winning three straight titles in 1962, 1963, and 1964, it was back to business as usual in Montreal. During the five seasons between 1964–1965 and 1968–1969, the Canadiens, thanks once again to Bé-liveau, Henri Richard, Ralph Backstrom, Yvan Cournoyer, and another couple of future Hall of Famers, won four more Stanley Cup titles. With the team's only nonchampionship year (1967) belonging to the Maple Leafs, Montreal completed the sandwich with another back-to-back Stanley Cup campaign.

During the 1969–1970 season, the collective wishes of the rest of the original six were answered all at once, as Montreal, for the first time in 22 seasons, finished fifth in their division and failed to reach the postseason. The team rebounded the following season, during the swan song of Béliveau, the Yogi Berra of professional hockey, who would finish his career in 1971 hav-ing hoisted 10 Stanley Cups. After Mr. Béliveau's storied departure came the arrival of Scotty Bowman, who, after four years of futility in St. Louis, came to Montreal for eight seasons that would both define and set the precedent for winning as a team-builder in the NHL.

Under the charge of Bowman, the Canadiens won five Stanley Cups, in-cluding the franchise's second run of at least four straight between 1975–1976 and 1978–1979. The second of the four (1976–1977) came in what still stands as the greatest single-season record in NHL history, as the Canadiens finished with 132 team points. The only other team that has come close was the 1995–1996 Detroit Red Wings, who, although playing in two more games, still came up one point short. Current Columbus Blue Jackets play-by-play broadcaster Jeff Rimer, who was a pregame and postgame commentator for the Canadiens during this, the third of the franchise's dynasties, looks back on the early part of his career, saying, "One season in Montreal, the Canadiens lost eight games all year, including the playoffs. That's certainly a memory in its own right." After coaching the team to their fourth straight title, Bowman shot down the Saint Lawrence River, skipped over Lake Ontario, and landed in Buffalo for seven seasons. With one memorable Canadiens' departure came another's arrival, but this particular player was better known for his play away from the puck rather than with it.

WITH A NAME LIKE "KNUCKLES" . . .

Chris "Knuckles" Nilan, referred to by former player/current play-by-play broadcaster Randy Moller as "pound for pound, the scariest, toughest guy he ever played with or against," began and ended his career with the Montreal Canadiens. Being one of only nine players to eclipse the 3,000 career penalty infraction minutes (PIM) mark, "Knuckles" Nilan had more than 200 PIM's during 11 of the 13 seasons of his career, all of which took place during a period in which game misconducts were not issued for starting or instigating a fight. A witness to Nilan's presence and prowess, Rimer describes the right winger, saying,

> My real recollection of the enforcer started in Montreal. I was there from '77 to '84. Their enforcer was a guy who, when he first came up, wasn't necessarily much of a player but made himself a player, Chris Nilan. He certainly was a tough guy. As tough as they came. His nickname was "Knuckles," and he certainly held his own. He protected the likes of Guy LaFleur, Yvon Lambert, and the rest of the Canadiens. He certainly was a tough guy.

Nilan's knuckles, presumably caked with blood during the spring of 1986, were washed clean by the champagne dripping from Montreal's 21st Stanley Cup.

A REAL SHOWSTOPPER

While Chris Nilan was protecting such players as Guy LaFleur, Yvon Lambert, and Mats Naslund, a young Patrick Roy was protecting the net. In his second year in the league, Roy started and won all 15 of the team's postseason games, raising the 1986 Stanley Cup at the age of 20. Roy would man the pipes for seven more years before taking on Wayne Gretzky's upstart Los Angeles Kings. Even the "Great One" wasn't great enough to get past the star goaltender, as a veteran Roy won an astonishing 10 overtime games during the team's 1993 Stanley Cup campaign, including three straight against Buffalo. Making an overwhelming 601 saves in 20 games, Roy boasted his second Stanley Cup, as well as his second Conn Smythe Trophy. After a spat with Canadiens coach Mario Tremblay two seasons after leading the team to glory, he was traded by team GM Réjean Houle to the Colorado Avalanche, formerly the Quebec Nordiques, Montreal's biggest rival.

Roy, in the team's first year in Denver, stymied the aforementioned 1995–1996 Detroit Red Wings team before sweeping the Florida Panthers in the Stanley Cup Final. His fourth and final Stanley Cup came in 2001, with newly acquired teammate Ray Borque, formerly a longtime member of the Boston Bruins, who, thanks to Roy's third career Conn Smythe–worthy performance, finally had the opportunity to kiss Lord Stanley's Cup and put a bow on his soon-to-be Hall of Fame career. Roy played for two more seasons, adding to his already NHL-record playoff wins as a goaltender to finish with 151, besting Martin Brodeur by almost 40. Today, Roy plays the role of the man he stared down skating to the bench in Montreal all those years, serving as Colorado's team-builder. It's quite likely he gets the itch to suit up from time to time.

LIFE AFTER THE FORUM

Having served as home to the Montreal Canadiens for 70 years, the famed Montreal Forum eventually gave way to the team's current home, the Bell Centre. After nearly 20 years in their new venue, the Canadiens have yet to raise a banner to the rafters. Nonetheless, the team support is still there, as always, in "La métropole." Bartlett notes,

> It has always been a special experience to go to a Montreal Canadiens game. Back in the early days of the Forum, it was almost like going to church. People would dress up for it, and it was an event. I think some of that, to an extent, still carries across today. The fans at the Bell Centre have a deeply rooted passion towards the game and the team. As great and electric a building as it can be when things are going well and the team is winning, if it's not going well, you're going to hear about it, too. It can become a very tough building for all the things that make it so exciting for the home team to play in. It can also become tough for the home team when they're struggling a little. Being in all 30 buildings, there is no better in-bowl experience than at the Bell Centre. When that building gets rocking, you can just feel it. The rafters are shaking, and the crowd is like a roaring jet engine. You really do feel the passion of the fans there, and the players feed off of that.
>
> Both Canadien players and the visiting teams that come in love playing in the Bell Centre because they love feeding off that energy. When it first opened, it was a big change for the fans. The Forum was smaller and more intimate, and had such a history to it, but it was time to move on to a new building. I think the most important part when they originally built the (then-named) Molson Centre was to try and keep that sense of intimacy and feeling that the Forum had with a new building, and I think, to a certain extent, they were able to do that. Every time you come in and look up

and see all those Stanley Cup banners and retired numbers, you understand the history and the legacy the Montreal Canadiens are and what they mean to everyone. Whether it's the photos, the statues, the banners, or the team pictures everywhere, that is where the experience carries over. It's always something special to play in Montreal. I believe there's no better experience than when you're in the building in the actual seats.

WHEN ARE WE GONNA GET NUMBER 23?

While 24 years is hardly the 50 currently being suffered by the Maple Leaf neighbors just down the Saint Lawrence River, it certainly seems like a hockey lifetime in a city that has won 22 Stanley Cups. In a 2015 interview, Bartlett describes the "patient" Canadien fans as follows:

> There was sort of a time period in the late '90s and early 2000s where the team struggled and the expectation was lowered a little, but, for the most part, the goal is to win the Stanley Cup because that's what the team has done over the years. This is the longest drought they've ever gone through. Now the team is built around a young core group. Players like Carey Price, P. K. Subban, Max Pacioretty, Alex Galchenyuk, and Brendan Gallagher. All of these youthful pillars to building a team towards the future. Being a much better, more competitive club, I think people now start to have that expectation level come around again where they want the Canadiens to be able to compete for the Stanley Cup and do it each and every year. I think that's where Marc Bergevin has done a great job of building that foundation to not just take a short-term run at it but be consistently good and a long-term club that can compete and at least challenge for the Stanley Cup every year. That's the direction they're going in now and I think that's what has fans the most excited.
>
> The game's changed and times have changed back from when the Canadiens were in their dynasty years, and fans understand that now. It's a different game and a different world. It's very hard to win the Stanley Cup, especially with the amount of teams and the parity in the league; however, I think what you do want to have is a chance to win every year, and that's where I believe the fan base sees things are going once again.

Of all the "youthful pillars," none stands stronger than team goaltender and 2014–2015 Hart Trophy winner Carey Price. Having won a team-record 44 games during his league MVP–worthy season, Price rose above an elite class of past Montreal Canadien goaltenders, including Ken Dryden, Patrick Roy, and Jacques Plante. With the "you must have at least four Stanley Cups to enter" sign posted outside the doors separating Price from his predecessors, it may only be a matter of time before the 2014–2015 MVP is wearing his own "members-only" jacket. Speaking about Price, Bartlett comments,

> Night after night, Carey Price continues to amaze you. It almost becomes a routine where you expect him to make the big save. He's such a treat to watch, not only in games, but in practice, too. He works just as hard in practice as he does in games and doesn't like the pucks to get by him. His strongest skill set is he makes so many saves look easy because he's in the right position. When he does make one of those acrobatic saves, it's spectacular because he's not often caught out of position where he's forced to make those kind of moves and go that extra distance to make sure he can go there and get the puck.
>
> There's some nights where you almost feel he's going to be unbeatable. Some of the shutouts he's had, it's been probably the end of the first period or early in the second where you just know it's going to be a shutout night because they're just not going to get a puck by him. If you feel that as a broadcaster, or even as a fan, imagine how the players feel on the ice and the confidence it gives them. That's what he does night in and night out. There goes the history of the Canadiens. Another incredible goaltender. There's Carey Price adding his name to a list of legends. Patrick Roy did that in '93 with all those overtime victories in the cup. He had a way of just convincing the team and the opposition you weren't going to score on him. They started to get that into their heads and squeezed their sticks a little too tight. It becomes a really interesting mind game when that happens.

With Price between the pipes, it's hard to believe there are another 19 mates on the team, but the Canadiens, with youthful pillars stacked on the ice, are out to bring the Stanley Cup back to the birthplace of organized hockey and finally raise—rather than import—a championship banner into the rafters of the Bell Centre and add "born again" to the University of Montreal's "hockey as a religion" curriculum.

Nashville Predators

*M*emphis, Tennessee, may be the birthplace of the "King of Rock and Roll," Elvis Presley, but its intrastate rival, Nashville, is known as the "Music City." Home to the Country Music Hall of Fame and the Grand Ole Opry, the stage upon which many of the Country Music Hall of Fame's inductees once played, Nashville "one-upped" its "Volunteer State" counterpart once again in 1997, when it was granted the National Football League's Houston Oilers, keeping both the logo and the name for two seasons before becoming the Tennessee Titans. While Nashville's being awarded the franchise left many southwest-residing Tennesseans—including Tom Hanks in *Cast Away*—scratching their heads, another sports franchise would bypass Memphis along Interstate 40, as expansion hockey introduced the Nashville Predators as the NHL's 27th franchise in 1998.

Considering it was a state best known for such figures as Davy Crockett, Dolly Parton, and "Machine Gun" Kelly, many of those along the Cumberland River may have been skeptical as to how a sport from the north would fare this close to the Heart of Dixie. Having broadcast for the team since day one, Nashville Predators voice Pete Weber describes the city's preparation for the "fastest game on earth":

> Country music played a large role in the team's first season-ticket drive before they ever played a game. In '97–'98—that preparatory year, if you will—when the team had coaches and managers and scouts out looking for the expansion draft, there were these billboards up around town, they had Lorrie Morgan, Garth Brooks, and other country music stars with their teeth blacked out, saying, "NHL hockey's coming to town. Got tickets?" That was a tremendously helpful drive the country music people were all fully behind.

With some of country's biggest stars holding season tickets at (then-named) Nashville Arena, the "puck dropped" in October 1998, and hockey was born in the Music City. Weber recalls the night, saying, "The fans from the very onset—from that first face-off on October 10, 1998—I've never seen it before. From that first game, there was a standing ovation for the first face-off in NHL history in Nashville." Before a standing-room only crowd, the "Preds" fell, 1–0, to Ray Whitney and the Florida Panthers; still, a Grand Ole Opry–worthy stage had been set for hockey.

A CÔTÉ FROM ~~MUSKOGEE~~ MONTREAL

As can be expected from a venue playing music featuring a fiddle and a steel guitar between periods, fights have been welcome inside (now-named) Bridgestone Arena since 1998, and no scrapper was found in these melees more than former Predators left winger Patrick Côté. Before his troubles with law enforcement for his participation in two Montreal bank robberies in 2014, Côté left an impression as the Predators' enforcer in their inaugural year, collecting 242 penalty infraction minutes (PIM), the fourth highest in the league. Weber notes,

> I think what helped sell hockey here in the early years—certainly in the first season—was Patrick Côté. He had 30 majors that first season for Nashville. No one's come close to that since. I'll assure you that. That first season, he fought Bob Probert twice. He was a colorful guy who went on to that Quebec senior league and was one of the highest-paid players. In a much shorter season, he had 15 fights in that league, where they're essentially playing just on the weekends.

While equipment necessary to play ice hockey (e.g., blades, sticks, wrapping tape, etc.) would preclude its inception into any penal leagues, it can only be assumed Patrick Côté continues to master his craft on the "yard" and not the ice.

A *RED WING* IN A BLUE-COLLAR PIPELINE

Hockey tailors itself to its fan base and vice versa. There is no other sport where tossing a 25-pound dead octopus onto the playing surface would be classified as normal. One thing to consider in a hockey town is that for 18,000-plus fans, there's another world outside the arena doors once the final horn sounds. As they wait for that next puck to drop, a considerable number of these fans carry a blue-collar workload so that they can feed their families and afford tickets to the next game. Once in a while, expansion hockey drops a team in the middle of this hustle and bustle, turning a hockey fan's world on its side.

Detroit, the Motor City, known for its auto industry, blue-collar work-force, and octopus-draped ice from April to June, extends its manufacturing seed to auto plants in Nashville and beyond. In 1998, with their labor dedicated to the mother corporation in Detroit but their fandom to the newborn Predators, hockey fans in Nashville began to create their own traditions. Weber elaborates,

> The Predators always had a rivalry with Detroit. They started out the first 14 years in the same division. There are so many Michigan people—auto workers—who, over the years, had been moved down to middle Tennessee, first for a Saturn plant, then a Nissan plant. The tradition started in Detroit—years ago at the Olympia—of throwing the octopus out for good luck for the Red Wings. Nashville wanted to answer that back, and, so, somehow or another—no help from the club—what do they begin throwing out when Detroit came to town? Catfish. They began to throw catfish over the glass. Can you imagine walking into the building with a catfish taped to the inside of your coat—or right up against your body—and waiting for the appropriate time?

With an odor better reserved for a practical joke and a texture better handled by the pros at Pike Place Market, the Nashville catfish has been known to backfire on occasion. Weber continues,

> The catfish started very early. When we had the unfortunate death of a young girl struck by a puck in the stands in Columbus, they put the mesh netting at the ends of the rink. One guy—who forgot to calculate the mesh had been put up there—threw his catfish and it sprung back on some poor soul sitting in the front row.

While not living up to the "predatory" nature of the team name, it's likely the stench of a rebounded catfish will scatter even those season ticket-holders paying premium prices.

STANDING ROOM ONLY

While too far from the ice to throw a five-pound catfish, a special group of "nosebleed-suffering" patrons make Predators games memorable for some and forgettable for others. Weber relates,

We have a rather raucous group that sits upstairs in Section 303. They have organized cheers they do throughout the course of the game. It seemed so similar to what I experienced doing baseball games for years. In a way, Section 303 is in the outfield. It's in the upper deck. They have their cheers and put the opposing teams—particularly goaltenders—through the ringer.

This raucousness includes the use of large foam fangs and, in the case of economic-minded fans, forefingers and middle fingers curled down during power plays to pantomime their predatory prowess.

While putting opposing goalies "through the ringer" is a great way to display team support, a little positive reinforcement, every once in a while, goes a long way. Such is the case for Predator fans. Throughout the team's 18-year history, Nashville has qualified for the playoffs 10 times, making it past the Conference Quarterfinals only four times. In 2006–2007, the team lost in the opening round to the San Jose Sharks. This unexpected defeat, coupled with an owner's itchy *un*-signing hand, led to an interesting offseason prior to 2007–2008. Weber comments,

> The '07 season had been the most productive one in team history. They had 110 points and lost in the first round of the playoffs to San Jose. There was Peter Forsberg, Paul Kariya, J. P. Dumont, Jason Arnott, Alex Radulov, Stevie Sullivan on that team. There were six 20-goal scorers, but then the founding owner, Craig Leopold, decided he was losing too much money in Nashville. He had the chance to buy the Minnesota Wild, so he put the team up for sale, and, in doing so, the roster was stripped. There was no offer to Paul Kariya. Scotty Hartnell and Kimmo Timonen were dealt off to Philadelphia. Tomáš Vokoun was sent to Florida because he was a $5-million-a-year goaltender at that point in time.
>
> That team had it tough to make the playoffs, but make the playoffs they did. In the spring of '08, it was getting very close. The team had a tight game going at home with St. Louis, and, just spontaneously—no prodding from the scoreboard or public address—going in to what turned out to be the last television timeout of the game, the fans just stood as one and gave the club a deafening standing ovation. That spurred them on. They won. They've pretty much continued that ever since. I think that probably is the one tradition that has been established—and that truly was established in '08—that has continued on to this day.

FROM PRETENDERS TO CONTENDERS

With the crowd still standing three seasons later, the Predators finally faced a California team not named the Sharks and defeated the Anaheim Ducks in six games. Having escaped Anaheim's Honda Center with an overtime win in game five, the Preds journeyed home to Bridgestone Arena with a chance to clinch the franchise's first-ever playoff series win. Thanks to two goals by team center Nick Spaling and 25 saves by goaltender Pekka Rinne, Nashville sent the "not-so-mighty" Ducks home and packed their own bags for Vancouver. Reliving the franchise's first mid-ice handshake as the victor, Weber states,

> After all of the frustration over the years in the playoffs—to finally win a playoff series—and they finally did so against the Anaheim Ducks in 2011, then went on to play Vancouver. Two series with long, long road trips involved, but winning that game against the Anaheim Ducks to wrap it all up. The Preds have always been underdog types. When the game was over, I just had to call upon Rocky Balboa, and, as the time ran down, I said, "Yo, Adrian. They did it. The Predators have won this series over the Anaheim Ducks."

While Nashville fell on the losing side against the Vancouver Canucks, the team returned to the playoffs the following year and defeated the Red Wings, four games to one, before being bested by the (then-named) Phoenix Coyotes in the Conference Semifinals.

With the team returning to the playoffs only once in the three seasons (2012–2015) since their back-to-back Conference Semifinals run, the catfish on the ice at Bridgestone Arena were likely so few that team mascot "Gnash" was able to clear the rink in one sitting; however, with the recent play of Viktor Arvidsson, Ryan Johansen, Filip Forsberg, and Mike Ribeiro, who have been leading the team's scoring, and "old reliable" Pekka Rinne manning the area between the pipes, the Predators have been finding themselves looking down—not up—in the Western Conference standings. With two straight seasons playing past the postseason's opening round—including the team's first ever trip to both the Conference Finals and the Stanley Cup—the city of Nashville has quickly become "Smashville" when it comes to hockey, suggesting that the tune playing on Music Row might soon be "Gold on the Ceiling" rather than "Heartache Tonight."

· 18 ·

New Jersey Devils

If there were to ever be a motivational poster for the phrase "third time's the charm," the New Jersey Devils franchise would make the sporting world's best case for the cover image. In 1974, to give the somewhat-isolated St. Louis Blues some company, the NHL brought another team along Missouri's Interstate 70. Aside from team logos that would likely support Native American protest groups in their suit against the NFL's Washington Redskins, there was little buzz surrounding the Kansas City Scouts their first season in the league, as the team would go 15–54–11. The following season, a 12–56–12 record, including a 44-game span with only one win, resulted in a practically empty Kemper Arena. With owners hemorrhaging money and a lack of promise that the fans would restore it, the Scouts relocated to Denver and became the Colorado Rockies.

Going through more coaches than seasons played in the Mile High City, the Rockies didn't do much better than they had done as the Scouts. Despite a 19–40–21 record during the 1977–1978 season, the team made its only playoff appearance before losing out to the Philadelphia Flyers. This would be the beginning of the end of NHL hockey in Colorado—at least until 1995—as two different owners shifted their focus to the New Jersey Meadowlands. After an 18–49–13 record during the 1981–1982 season, the team was sold to John McMullen, shipped as far east as they could go without falling into the ocean, and renamed the New Jersey Devils to start the 1982–1983 season.

A "NEW JERSEY" STATE OF MIND

Being just on the other side of the Hudson River from the "City That Never Sleeps," New Jersey often tries to differentiate itself from its metropolitan neighbor. New Jersey Devils TV play-by-play broadcaster Steve Cangialosi describes the sense of pride the team exudes in its "Garden State" fan base:

> The Devils are New Jersey's team. They are the only major professional sports franchise that can say that in terms of the team's name and location. The fan base is not entirely New Jersey–based, but there is a great sense of pride from hockey fans in the Garden State in terms of "our team." In the NFL, the Jets and Giants play in New Jersey, but the team name is New York. The New Jersey Nets could once lay claim to being "Jersey's team" but of course at the end were plotting the move to Brooklyn. The Devils also play in New Jersey's largest city. Newark was never a hockey town before the Devils arrived, but I see a great sense of pride in the community as well. A lot of Newark residents work in the arena, and many of those have adopted the Devils as their team.

Reaching into a bottomless bag of clichéd phrases, once the team set up in the Meadowlands and "talked the talk," the question—especially with their "original six" neighbor hogging the marquee at Madison Square Garden—became, "Could they walk the walk?" Steve continues,

> There is tremendous pride in hockey operations, having built a perennial contender that peaked with three Stanley Cup championships in a nine-season span between 1995 and 2003. Those accomplishments dwarfed what their biggest rivals across the Hudson River were able to produce in that era. Those titles remain a badge of honor. Devils fans know they're outnumbered. Many of them are sons and daughters of those who root for the Rangers because there was a time New York had the only team in town. New Jersey might not be able to match the history of the original six franchises. But the fans understand that the team can win the battle moving forward.

THE DEVILS' FIRST VOICE CALLS THE DEVILS' FIRST CUP

Anyone south of the U.S.–Canadian border watching hockey on the national broadcast, especially during the Stanley Cup Final, will recognize the voice of U.S.-born Mike "Doc" Emrick, who has been calling deep-round playoff games and All-Star Games for more than 20 years. Emrick's first job in the NHL was with the Devils when they moved to New Jersey in 1982. After a brief stint in Philadelphia during the late 1980s, he was back in New Jersey in 1993. Much like he did in Philadelphia, Emrick broadcast games for the Devils but also covered national broadcasts.

During the strike-shortened 1994–1995 season, "Doc," unlike many of his broadcasting colleagues who would defer to the networks once the teams got past the second round of the playoffs, instead called the Devils all the way to their first-ever Stanley Cup championship at the hands of the Western Conference champion Detroit Red Wings. Easily his most memorable broadcast for the team, the Hall of Famer gives his account of the Garden State's first-ever major sports championship:

> The cup-clincher in '95 stands out because there were other championships after that and there were many other national broadcasts after that, but this was the one involving the team I had followed all year for two seasons. Here was this team that had been able to scrap their way into the Stanley Cup Final, and it was a year in which the East did not play the West at all. The Devils were a team that scored goals. The thing that stuck out the most was how well they played their system and took advantage of mistakes and how little they needed to do that to get a lead in a game. Here they were going up against the imposing offensive juggernaut that the Detroit Red Wings were. Going into that series with Detroit, most everybody had conceded that Detroit would win and that it might be a sweep.
>
> The Devils won the first game. Stéphane Richer got the first goal of the series, and it was one of those games where Detroit hadn't played the Devils all year and they didn't know what to expect other than what videotape would tell them. Now, they'd actually played them a game and they lost.
>
> It's game two at Joe Louis Arena. I'm standing next to Peter McNab during the third period, and we're just watching the game near the end. I always valued what he had to say because he looked at the game with a different perspective than I had. I was just watching the puck and who had it and who was playing well, and he was watching the flow and how things were either being figured out or not. At one point in the third period, the Devils and Red Wings were tied. He turned to me and said, "The Devils are going to win the Stanley Cup, and it might be a sweep." Peter's tall. He's 6-foot-4, and I'm only five seven, and I thought maybe I didn't hear him. I said, "I beg your pardon?" He said, "I'm telling you the Devils are going to win this thing, and it might be a sweep." It was just about that time Scott Niedermayer scored the goal that wound up being the winner.
>
> The Devils had taken two out of two in Detroit and were coming back home. Bill Clement was doing the ESPN Stanley Cup Final. He and I had worked together quite a bit so we talked about the series before he went to work the third game in New Jersey. He said, "It's almost like after the first game, the Red Wings said, 'Okay. We've seen them now,' and after the second game, 'Boys, we're in trouble here.'" You could see that they

hadn't figured it out, and now they were going into New Jersey, where the Devils had their fan base.

The fourth game was the one that will always stand out in my mind. I remember during the third period, there was a stoppage of play. We took a commercial break and one of the cameramen alerted the truck that Mike Peluso was sitting at the bench, waiting for his next shift, and he was crying. We showed a close-up, and it turned out he had missed a shift with his line mates because it was such an emotional experience for him. I think that showed an awful lot, not only about Mike, but it also showed a lot about how incredible an experience this was going to be for the team that had been branded at one time "Mickey Mouse." All of these other things that had taken place in their young history in New Jersey.

They arrived in '82, and Dave Lewis, one of their defensemen, said it was the best bunch of guys he ever played hockey with that couldn't win a game. They were rising out of this now. Mike Peluso sort of reflected what the fan base did. "Can you believe our names are actually going to be on the Stanley Cup?" It was at another commercial break after Shawn Chambers had scored to make it 5–2 that my partner, John Davidson, turned to me and said, "Doc, these last few minutes are going to go by fast, so make sure you enjoy them." He knew we were on a national telecast, and he also knew I prided myself on being fair, but this was a sweep and it was a decisive win in the fourth game. I told him, "I know in the final minute, you're going to want to pay tribute to the whole playoff run and how exciting it was. Just leave eight or nine seconds at the end." He said, "No problem." Of course, if you know John, I looked up at the clock and there were 10 seconds to go and he handed it off to me. That enabled me to deliver a prepared line, which I had rarely been able to do, but, in decisive wins, it's not up for grabs and the goalie is not pulled in the final minute. In a decisive game, you can do it, so I said, "The championship to New Jersey. The Devils win the Stanley Cup." That's the most memorable game to me.

It was the final emergence out of such modest beginnings when they came from Colorado. It was finally the emergence into a championship. They had gotten to the seventh game of the third round the previous year and lost in double overtime, but that was still not there. You still don't reward losses. That's not the Lou Lamoriello way. This was something that was the total payoff of all things, sweeping the Red Wings in the Stanley Cup Final. It was the first one, and for that reason, it's the most lasting one in my memory.

Emrick would continue his "double duty," broadcasting to the tune of two more New Jersey Devils Stanley Cup titles in 2000 and 2003, before leaving the team in 2011, to work exclusively on national broadcasts for NBC.

RED, WHITE, BLACK, AND BLUE

Considering the team won three Stanley Cup championships in a span of nine seasons, while its red, white, and blue counterpart in Manhattan has only won one of its four in a more than 77-year span, the New Jersey Devils have developed a "history" of their own against the New York Rangers. Round one of this "Hudson River Rivalry" went to the Rangers during the 1994 Eastern Conference Final. In the booth to witness this incredible rivalry birth was another Devils play-by-play broadcaster turned national spotlight voice, Gary Thorne, who notes, "That is probably still the most heated conference final I have ever seen. It brought everything about the Devils and the Rangers into real focus because the Devils were a very good team. The Rangers had made the Messier tied deals to get the people they thought would finally get them the cup, which, in fact, it did. That series was just hell bent for leather. In game six, where Messier made the promise that the Rangers would win, he ended up with a hat trick in the third period. Then they won game seven in double overtime on Stefan Matteau's goal. It was as good a series as you'd ever want to see. It had all of the passion that had been built over time between the Rangers and the Devils. It was magnificent hockey, but it was really tough. There was no room. There was no give. As the series went along, you ended up with the Devils actually having a chance to win it in games six and seven. The pressure got even greater for both teams. Game six is a game that marks the rivalry and brings out everything these two teams always had to some degree when they played one another, even during the regular season." While a trip to the Stanley Cup Final was the ultimate goal for these two teams, their geographic proximity to one another brought out another important aspect. Thorne continues, "It was about the teams and who they were. It was about the franchises. It was about the Ranger history and always dominating with publicity in the New York area. It was about the Devils trying to gain their piece of that and trying to show that they were the equivalent NHL team. It wasn't about individuals. Mark Messier made that an individual game, but the entire series was marked by ferocious hockey played by everybody. It wasn't bad blood between individuals. It was bad blood between franchises, and that's the way it stayed. As tough as that series was, it didn't vary from that." Although the two squads wouldn't face off the following year in the postseason, 1995, as history would show, became New Jersey's turn to hoist Lord Stanley's Cup.

While losing the next playoff matchup in the Hudson River Rivalry in 1997, four games to one, the Devils would be the first of the two teams to return to the Cup Final. New Jersey, thanks once again to the winningest regular-season goaltender in NHL history, Martin Brodeur, as well as defenseman Scott Niedermayer, team captain Scott Stevens, and returning enforcer

Claude Lemieux, won their second Stanley Cup in six seasons by defeating the defending champion Dallas Stars on a double-overtime goal by Jason Arnott. The Devils returned to the Stanley Cup Final the following season but were upended by the only goaltender with more playoff wins than Martin Brodeur—Patrick Roy—and his Colorado Avalanche, who, much like the New Jersey squad they were facing, sported a roster with at least a half-dozen future Hall of Famers.

Two seasons later, the Devils claimed their third title at the hands of the (then-named) Mighty Ducks of Anaheim. Brodeur, although outshined by Jean-Sébastien Giguère, winner of the Conn Smythe Trophy, was still the winning goaltender during the final mid-ice handshake of the 2002–2003 NHL season. Aside from Brodeur, Niedermayer, and Stevens, Ken Daneyko and Sergei Brylin were part of all three Stanley Cup championship teams for the Devils.

While the last Stanley Cup to be lifted between either the Devils or the Rangers took place more than 14 years ago, the Hudson River Rivalry still kindles the ire of even the team-builders. Steve Cangialosi recalls a matchup between the Rangers and Devils that summoned the ghosts of the league line brawls of yesterday:

> Pete Deboer and John Tortorella are excellent coaches, and when they were counterparts with the Devils and Rangers, one of their games began with three fights at the drop of the puck. One coach took a look at the other's starting lineup and decided that "anything he can do I can do better." One second ticked off the clock, and there were six fighting majors. Both teams were good at the time too. Deboer and Tortorella weren't fans of each other. Apparently, Tortorella talked about their verbal exchange on the benches the next day. I'll never forget Pete saying, "I'm done discussing it. It's over. I'm not the one who needed 24 hours to sort out my feelings!"—or something to that effect. It was an obvious jab at John.

It's rare that a rivalry reaches as far as the league rulebook, but during the 2008 Eastern Conference Quarterfinals the Devils and Rangers did just that. Cangialosi explains,

> In the 2008 Stanley Cup Playoffs, Sean Avery screened Martin Brodeur on a Rangers power play, not with his back to Brodeur, but facing him and waiving his stick in front of him in the crease. There was no rule in place to prevent Avery from doing this, but the NHL quickly put one in place. The Devils actually won the game in overtime on a John Madden goal, but the Rangers won the series in five. The whole episode brought the rivalry to an even more intense place. Brodeur refused to acknowledge Avery on the handshake line at the series' conclusion.

As if rule-change inspiring tactics and coach-staged line brawls weren't enough, the Hudson River Rivalry's most recent installment featured yet another Conference Finals matchup, but this time New Jersey took the winning side to advance to the Cup Final, where they lost in six games to the Los Angeles Kings in 2012. Two seasons later, the Rangers followed in their neighbor's skates, losing to virtually the same Los Angeles team, four games to one, in the 2014 Stanley Cup Final, briefly making the Devils the Kings' biggest fans.

SUNSET/SUNRISE (AND NOT VICE VERSA)

Throughout the years, the Devils have picked up a couple of rivalries outside of New York, including the Philadelphia Flyers, but it was against two nonrival opponents that Steve Cangialosi gathered his two most memorable games with the Devils. Cangialosi relates,

> There are two games that are completely in contrast in terms of agony and ecstasy. I was in the host role for game seven of the 2009 Stanley Cup Playoffs between the Devils and the Carolina Hurricanes and the collapse in the third period of that game. The Devils had the lead with two minutes to play. Traditionally, that's a situation this team lives for. New Jersey allows a goal with just over a minute and a half remaining. Tim Gleason makes a tremendous dive for the Carolina Hurricanes to keep the puck in the Devils' zone. They set up Jussi Jokinen for a sharp angle goal, and the Hurricanes tie the game.
> The Devils pride themselves on having an ability to protect the lead unlike any other team in the NHL. As a franchise, it's defense first, and, of course, Marty Brodeur was always the last line of defense. At that point, I'm standing in the Zamboni area, waiting to interview the star of the game at center ice as Jokinen scores that goal. Suddenly, the game is tied. At that point, you think, "We're going to overtime." Instead, Eric Staal scores with just over 30 seconds remaining in the game on a goal that Marty Brodeur should have had, and the arena is in disbelief. You've gone from advancing to the second round of the playoffs to being eliminated, and it all happened in a span of roughly one minute of hockey time. The crowd was stunned. It was a complete reversal of what you thought the epilogue of the night would be. We made the transition of setting up a second-round playoff series to suddenly, it's your final show of the year. Disappointed fans were stunned in disbelief. I always thought of the beat writers who covered the team in that situation, too. They have to make that quick transition where the story is basically written, "The Devils survive a seven-game se-

ries." Then the whole tone changes. It's suddenly the last game story you write for the season.

   The Devils' best line in 2009 couldn't get off the ice. It was Travis Zajac, Zach Parise, and Jamie Langenbrunner who were trapped on the ice for a minute and 29 seconds. They just couldn't get off. They were exhausted. They just could never get to the bench, and then Carolina tied it before Staal had the game-winning goal. That was surreal. That moment was one of the few times I'm witnessing a sporting event and I'm just standing there saying, "Did I just see that?" This is the team that played better with the lead than almost any other in the National Hockey League for the longest time. You just did a double take on the whole night.

Having gotten the "agony" out of the way, now for the "ecstasy." Three seasons later, New Jersey, still with the 2009 opening-round collapse monkey on its back, was looking to finally get the fans their redemption in the 2012 Eastern Conference Quarterfinals against the Florida Panthers. Cangialosi remembers,

The last Stanley Cup Playoff game I've ever called was in the spring of 2012. That's the season in which the Devils went to the Stanley Cup Final and lost to the L.A. Kings. There was great belief the Devils would never move past the disappointment of that series against Carolina in 2009 until they won another playoff series. In 2012, they're facing the Florida Panthers in the opening round of the playoffs. While the Panthers were the higher seed, the consensus was the Devils were a better team; yet, New Jersey trailed in the series, 3–2. The Devils survived game six when Travis Zajac scored in overtime, and that set up game seven. There was so much on the line for this team because if New Jersey doesn't win game seven, you were starting to think the ghost of what happened in Carolina would never leave them.

   New Jersey had a two-goal lead in game seven against Florida. The Panthers came back to tie, and the arena in Sunrise, Florida, was rocking. The Devils let a multiple-goal lead slip away, and you're thinking to yourself, "Uh oh. It's all happening again. This team is not going to be able to get out of the abyss. They're going to come up short again." You're trying to forget about the disappointment of '09. The overtime was riveting hockey, and then in double overtime, Adam Henrique wins it by darting out in front with a simple wrist shot that wins the game for New Jersey. From there, the weight of the world was lifted off the team's shoulders. You could just sense it. They dispatched the Flyers in five games in the next round, beat the Rangers in six in the Conference Finals, before falling to a superior L.A. Kings team in the Final. The memory of Henrique—who was a rookie forward at the time—saving the day for this team and taking the weight of the world off that franchise's shoulders and me calling it? That is probably an experience I will never forget.

After falling to the Kings in the Cup Final, the Devils took a sabbatical from the postseason that continues to this day.

GOODBYE, OLD FRIEND

From 1993 to 2014, number 30, Martin Brodeur, manned the crease for the New Jersey Devils. In that span of 20-plus years, Brodeur, aside from his three Stanley Cup titles, won the Calder Memorial Trophy for rookie of the year in 1994, took home five William M. Jennings Trophies for fewest goals scored against, and won four Vezina Trophies for the league's top goalie. Brodeur's 691 regular-season wins and 125 career shutouts are the most in NHL history. In fact, his two career goals scored are the most ever by a goaltender as well. Brodeur's number "30" will always be remembered as sewn on with the horned and spike tailed "J" of New Jersey. Cangialosi notes,

> The faces of the franchise have had remarkable staying power and that's really played into the identity of the team. Lou Lamoriello just completed his 28th season as general manager of this franchise. Up until this last season (2013-14), Martin Brodeur was the face of this franchise on the ice. It was a two decade relationship, and that's something you just don't see in sports anymore. The staying power of icons like that for the longest time. The biggest reason for that is the team, for the most part, has had tremendous on-ice success. The fans have enjoyed that and enjoyed the continuity of the organization as well through the years.

With the Brodeurs, Niedermayers, Stevens, and Lamoriellos gone from the game, today's on-ice edition of the "Jersey Boys" are "Working Their Way Back" to another Stanley Cup title. Thanks to Adam Henrique, veteran Mike Cammalleri, captain Andy Greene, and an imported Cory Schneider looking to "fill the pads" of perhaps the greatest goaltender in NHL history, the Devils are seeking to drop their "Rag Doll" status and once again "~~Walk~~ Skate Like a Man" until they tie their Hudson River rival's cup total.

• *19* •

New York Islanders

$\mathcal{A}$s the "Big Apple's" sole NHL representative for more than 40 years, one would think the New York Rangers should have been the one carrying an island-referencing name going into the 1972–1973 season. With New York's original hockey team, the "Americans," 30 years removed from their decade-long, fruitless battle to be counted among the league ranks, the NHL decided to take the non-Broadway/subway/Central Park/traffic jam approach to major sports in the nation's largest city and opt for the suburban alternative instead. Thanks to the influence of William Shea—a man for whom baseball fans in the New York area were quite grateful 10 years earlier—and eventual team owner Roy Boe, the New York Islanders became the NHL's 15th franchise. Much to the behest of the New York Raiders, the hopeful representative from the World Hockey Association (WHA), the Islanders' NHL status granted them use of Nassau Veterans Memorial Coliseum and sent the Raiders west to San Diego, which, in 1972, *was* an island as far as hockey was concerned.

Although now an NHL team, the Islanders would quickly find out there would be no new-arrival-doting, older-sibling-snubbing treatment in the New York market. As part of the arrangement that put the franchise in motion to begin with, the Islanders were required to pay a territorial fee to the Rangers, which, considering the film *The Godfather* would release that same year, seemed more like a "protection tax." The territorial fee would not be the only bad rap the franchise would be forced to endure. Much like William Shea's firstborn expansion concept, the New York Mets, the Islanders had to enter the league in the widely cast shadow of a deep-rooted and long-established club. Playing on the opposite bench during the 1970s and early 1980s New York Rangers defenseman turned radio play-by-play voice Dave Maloney describes the early dynamic between the two clubs, saying, "The Islanders/ Rangers rivalry basically jumpstarted when the Islanders beat the Rangers in the Spring of '75 when Jake Parise scored in overtime. That was fairly unprecedented between the two clubs. The Islanders had just been in the league a couple of years, and I think there was always a sense that the Rangers were an original six and the Islanders were an upstart from the suburbs and felt they were always under appreciated."

Adding to Maloney's sentiment is former New York Islanders and current New York Mets play-by-play radio voice Howie Rose, who explains the struggle of a "new" franchise in an old market:

> The Rangers–Islanders rivalry started in '72. When it started, the Rangers were a very good team who had just played in the Stanley Cup Final, and the Islanders everybody knew would be bad at the outset. It didn't take long before the Islanders became more competitive. Their third year in the league, they were one game away from playing in the finals. I think what defined the rivalry between the fans more than anything was the bitterness Rangers fans felt over the fact the Islanders were becoming a really good team. The Rangers, Emile Francis's team, which had been contenders for a number of years, was now on the downslide because they had gotten old together and were basically finished as contenders.
>
> Shortly thereafter, the Islanders started winning Stanley Cups. Because the Islanders won a Stanley Cup before the Rangers had broken their long drought that created a lot of bitterness among Ranger fans. I think Islander fans were especially bitter because they felt their team never got the recognition it deserved being in a New York market, but, then again, they were A) a suburban team and B) a team moving into a market that was so traditionally dominated by the Rangers. They were never going to get the kind of coverage the Rangers did, even in '79, when the Rangers and Islanders played in a great semifinal series. When the Rangers won game six to win the series, the papers all treated it as though the Rangers had beaten any other team from out of town. Things like that really pissed the Islander fans off.

The following season, the papers, regardless of team loyalty, would have no choice about what to put in print.

1980–1983: "FANTASY" ISLAND

Outside of the Montreal Canadiens, who did it on two separate occasions, the New York Islanders are the only NHL team to win four straight Stanley Cup titles. Beginning in the 1979–1980 season, the Islanders, led by team-builder

Al Arbour, general manager Bill Torrey, and future Hall of Famers Mike Bossy, Clark Gillies, Denis Potvin, Billy Smith, and Bryan Trottier, would make New York's championship tally Islanders 4, Rangers 3. Not to exclude the supporting cast of Bob Bourne, Butch Goring, Anders Kallur, Gord Lane, Duane Sutter, and John Tonelli, the Islander teams of the early 1980s compiled an astounding 183–88–49 regular-season record and a 60–18 postseason record during their four-peat, not to mention featuring four recipients of the Conn Smythe Trophy for MVP during that span. Winning an NHL-record 19 consecutive playoff series, the Islanders finally relinquished their playoff run in 1983–1984, to the Edmonton Oilers and the soon-to-be "Great One," Wayne Gretzky, who, in turn, would carry their own dynasty torch, winning five of the following seven Stanley Cup championships.

Although they would wind up winning another 10 playoff series in a row, the Islanders, and their run for the Stanley Cup, found themselves in great jeopardy against the Pittsburgh Penguins during the '82 playoffs. Hall of Fame broadcaster Ken "Jiggs" McDonald, who, to this very day, finds himself calling Islander games to start each season, was the voice of three of these four championship teams. McDonald describes the best-of-five series that almost cut down the dynasty in its prime,

> The most memorable would be the run for the third Stanley Cup. The opening round, they handled Pittsburgh easily the first two games on Long Island and then went to Pittsburgh to supposedly wrap up the series on a Saturday night. They lose in overtime to the Penguins and now have to stay over. We thought we were going home after winning three straight. It was a best-of-five series back then. They lose, have to recheck back into the hotel, stay over, and play Easter Sunday night and lose by a wide margin. They come home for game five and they're down by two in the third period and managed to tie it up. Mike McEwen, John Tonelli, Bob Nystrom, the whole combination. We should have lost in overtime. Mike Bullard was in on a breakaway, and Smitty (Billy Smith) just got a piece of it. Then they went into overtime to win the series; a series that the first two games there was really no contest. Then to go to Pittsburgh and have to come back home for game five. It was as close as it was to being all over in '82. That was one of the more memorable games. A couple of times I thought, "This run is ending at two," to be down the way they were in the third period.

Summing up the playoff juggernaut, McDonald concludes,

> The Islander teams that won four finals, the fifth year was probably the epitome of a balanced hockey team; a team that could beat you no matter what style of game you wanted to play. On some nights, I felt they'd let

you dictate the game. "You tell us how you want to play it. Do you want to get into a track meet? Do you want to just grind it out or do you want to be a physical team tonight? No matter how you establish the style of play, we'll match it and beat you by it." They had speed, they had great goaltending—whether it be "Smitty" or "Chico" (Glenn Resch)—the goaltending was phenomenal. Smitty, I don't think at that time there was a better money goaltender. If you had a game on the line or a series on the line and you had to win, the guy you would want in the goal would be Billy Smith. In fact, Gretzky told Butch (Goring) and me on the air of a game at Edmonton, Billy Smith was the best goaltender he ever faced.

Luckily for Gretzky, Smitty and the Islanders would not return to the Cup Final.

NOT TO MENTION THE "OTHER GUYS"

While goaltenders like Billy Smith were getting praise from hockey's eventual all-time leading scorer, several of the Islanders' role players were taking care of things on the other end of the ice in more ways than one. Reflecting on a time when fights were not only present but practically mandatory, McDonald states,

> We can say what we like about trying to create hockey rivalries, but fights are really what create rivalries. What puts people in the seats. That first Stanley Cup run in the playoffs against Boston, Bob Nystrom and Clark Gillies were rooming together, and on a sportscast of Boston, they see Terry O'Reilly talking about how they're going to take care of the Islanders. They just looked at one another and said, "Oh no they're not. You take so and so and I'll take so and so and we'll take care of the Bruins," and that's exactly what happened.
>
> When I got there you had Garry Howatt, Bob Nystrom, Clark Gillies, Denis Potvin. All of them could take care of anybody on the other team. You didn't want to wake up Gillies. "Don't go around Gillies. Don't upset Gillies. Don't make him mad. Just let that big sleeping guy play his game." If he was on the left side with Bryan Trottier and Mike Bossy, or Nystrom and John Tonelli, just give him a wide birth. The other thing that team had was Gordy Lane, not an enforcer, but Gordy would spear, hack, and whack. You just didn't want to come down to his side of the ice, so that forced everything over to the other side, to Denis Potvin's side. He wasn't an enforcer—not a fighter by any means—but he hit and hurt. I don't think he knew how solid he was. He got a guy on the boards and forget it. Howatt wasn't the biggest guy by any means, but he would take on the biggest guy. He would go after whoever. It didn't matter. We called him

the toy tiger. He was sensational. If something was to develop, look out for Nystrom, Howatt, and especially the big guy, number 9. He would just . . . yikes!

ONE MORE TIME IN THE SPOTLIGHT

After five straight runs to the Stanley Cup Final, it was almost another 10 years before the Islanders even made it past the second round of the playoffs. During the 1992–1993 season, the team, thanks once again to team-builder Al Arbour, delved deep into the postseason. With the high-scoring presence of Pierre Turgeon, as well as the enforcement of Mick Vukota and Darius Kasparaitis, and the goaltending of Glenn Healy and Mark Fitzpatrick, the Islanders mowed down the Washington Capitals and outlasted the two-time defending Stanley Cup champion Pittsburgh Penguins in a seven-game, overtime-winning series before falling to Patrick Roy and the eventual league champion Canadiens in five games to close out the Prince of Wales Conference Final.

Turgeon moved on to become a journeyman to close out his career, and Healy left the island for the "Garden," backing up Mike Richter on the 1993–1994 Stanley Cup–winning New York Rangers the following season. Arbour, who would be inducted into the Hockey Hall of Fame in 1996, sat on a teetering stat for 14 years, with 1,499 career games coaching the Islanders. Tipping the scale to a more even number, he was called in for one more game behind the bench at Nassau Coliseum during the 2007–2008 season.

FROM SUBURBS TO SUBWAYS

Since the team's improbable run to the Conference Finals in 1992–1993, the Islanders have only won one playoff series in eight appearances. Opposite that of Glenn Healy, Howie Rose's New York switch took him from Madison Square Garden to the suburbs, where he called Islander games for more than 20 seasons. Unfortunately for Rose, his first taste of the postseason inside Nassau Coliseum wouldn't come as quickly for him as it did in the New York Rangers booth, when he, alongside childhood hero Marv Albert, called the team's first Stanley Cup title in 54 years. Speaking on his Islander experience leading into the 2015–2016 season, Rose notes,

> In terms of memorable games, there aren't many. Without question, the most memorable game for me would be the Shawn Bates penalty shot

game in 2002, the first round against the Toronto Maple Leafs, which came in game four, as the Islanders were en route to evening that series. They would eventually lose it in seven. They were tied late in the third period. Bates was awarded a penalty shot after being pulled down carrying in on a shot to Curtis Joseph. He scored on the penalty shot, and I thought the roof was going to cave in. Sadly, in the 20 years I've been there, there haven't been a lot of seminal moments.

Perhaps one of the most seminal moments for the Islanders since their four straight championships was the farewell to Nassau Coliseum in yet another opening-round game-seven loss, this time to the Washington Capitals (2015).

Today, NHL hockey is back in the town the Americans left behind some 70 years ago, as Islander fans now call the Barclays Center in Brooklyn their home. Although the trip to and from the game isn't much farther than it was on Long Island, the commute and arrival is an entirely different experience. Rose comments,

> You go from the suburbs to downtown Brooklyn, and you might as well be going from Venus to Mars. The farther east on Long Island the fans reside, the less likely it is that they'll go to Brooklyn. It's not an easy trip by the Long Island Railroad because most of the time you have to change in Jamaica, which is just a pain in the neck. I've had people tell me in preseason games they waited 20 minutes to a half-hour for their connection. That's not going to fly with a lot of people. They're also not moving into virgin hockey territory. People in Brooklyn chose sides a long time ago. If someone from Brooklyn wanted to be an Islander fan, it was very easy for them to get in their car, drive out to the Coliseum, park their car, and go home. Doing the reverse is virtually impossible. There's very little parking down there. It's ridiculously congested. You have to take public transportation. That's not as convenient for everybody who's an Islander fan as you might think. They're very used to their suburban parking lot lifestyle.

Whether it be a parking lot, a Jamaican changeover, or an overwhelming ambiance of red, white, and blue Rangers jerseys that slows the credit-card-swiping hands of Islander fans wielding season tickets, the five borough Stanley Cup tally still shows what local papers won't: Islanders 4, Rangers 4.

· *20* ·

New York Rangers

*A*lthough an "original six" team, the New York Rangers were preceded, not only in their city, but also in their building, by the New York Americans, who took the ice at the brand new Madison Square Garden in 1925, one year before the Rangers came into the picture. Thanks to ticket sales during the inaugural year of the Americans, the owner of Madison Square Garden, Tex Rickard, lobbied for his own team, and the Rangers took the ice on what would become their home for the following 90-plus seasons. Unfortunately for the Americans, such issues as World War II, team contracts, a weak roster, and an icing-rule-inspiring, lethargic style of play exploiting that weak roster left more to be desired from the team.

After a 17-year battle, the (then-named) Brooklyn Americans, while still playing in Manhattan, were sent up the Hudson River and out of the NHL picture. During this great back and forth with Rickard, Americans owner Red Dutton, and the NHL, the Rangers won three Stanley Cup titles, in 1928, 1933, and 1940. The champagne showers and championship parades through Manhattan, however, would subside for more than half a century—the longest drought ever by any original six team—before a Stanley Cup would again grace the "rows" of Rickard's "garden."

THE WORLD'S MOST FAMOUS ARENA

While the claim of which venue was the *real* garden carried on for 70 years between Bostonians and New Yorkers, the folks from New England would have to defer the title of fame and notoriety to their "Empire State" neighbors down the coast. Although it's the fourth site bearing the name "Madison Square Garden," this sporting world landmark on 4 Pennsylvania Plaza is the oldest arena in the NHL. Located just minutes from virtually every point of interest in Manhattan, Madison Square Garden, much like its Broadway neighbor on the Upper West Side, brings in crowds from all walks of life, namely the New York Ranger fans who have been calling it their home for almost 50 years. Longtime Rangers TV play-by-play broadcaster and Hall of Famer Sam Rosen describes Rangers hockey from the standpoint of its home, saying,

> The uniqueness of New York Rangers hockey and sporting events at Madison Square Garden is because it's right in the heart of the city. Fans come by public transportation, whether it's the New York subway system or the Long Island Railroad. People will drive in as well. They'll come to games after work and then jump on the trains to go home afterwards, but that's the other part that makes it so unique. It's a gathering place everyone gravitates to.
>
> During the playoffs last spring, things were set up around the "Garden." They took over storefront space in 2 Penn Plaza to make it a place for Ranger fans to come in night after night, day after day. There was a place for activities involving the Rangers. Former Rangers stars and alumni were brought in to be part of the playoff excitement and allow the fans a chance to get closer to the team and the organization. You have the steps leading into Madison Square Garden filled with fans. Seventh Avenue packed with Ranger fans.
>
> When you say Madison Square Garden anywhere in the world, everybody knows where it is, what it looks like, and where you're going to. It's part of the fabric and the fiber of New York City. Again, that's what makes it so special to be a part of New York Rangers hockey. The other part of Rangers hockey is that it's New York, and sports in New York is *big*. Anytime you're representing New York, you're part of something big and something special. So you put all that together, and I think that's what makes New York Rangers hockey special and different from most other teams.

Ranger fans have been known to fill the steps leading up to the other 29 NHL arenas as well.

RANGER FANS: 82-GAME SEASON TICKET-HOLDERS

The term *arguably* is a paradox when discussing the NHL's best traveling fans because the New York Ranger fans would win by a "city" mile. Florida Panthers radio play-by-play broadcaster Randy Moller notes, "We have a lot of Panther fans who, out of 40 or 39 games of the year, they're wearing Panther jerseys. The other two are when the Rangers come to town." Rosen picks up where Moller leaves off, saying,

> The passion of the Ranger fans is always there. You see it as you go around the country. I saw it in my early days doing a broadcast when we were on our road trips. WWOR, channel 9, which, at that point, was called a superstation and was carried by cable companies around the country. We would go to Chicago and Minnesota, and then out to California. People would watch our games on the superstation. You had transplanted New Yorkers everywhere. Wherever we went, there were New York fans, New York Ranger fans, T-shirts, blue jerseys, and white jerseys. You always saw them. And they were always loud enough to let the players know they had plenty of support in the building.

On December 23, 1979, at Madison Square Garden, virtually the entire Boston Bruins team "saw them" and, this time, gave Ranger fans a little bit more for the price of admission.

ATTENTION FANS IN THE FIRST
FEW ROWS: YOU WILL GET ~~WET~~ HIT

In 1979, before the glass got higher and the safety nets encompassing it became mandatory, viewing a hockey game was quite an intimate experience, especially at Madison Square Garden. With the rival Boston Bruins in town just two days before Christmas, the Rangers fell, 4–3, when Phil Esposito's break-away shot on goal was stopped by Gerry Cheevers. As the buzzer sounded, a fight broke out when Bruins left winger Al Secord sucker punched Rangers center Ulf Nilsson. A skating target, Bruins enforcer Stan Jonathan got a taste of how close a front row seat gets a Ranger fan to the action at the Garden, as Ranger fan John Kaptain reached over and struck the left winger on the face. Kaptain then took Jonathan's stick, and, in the eyes of Bruins forward Terry O'Reilly, must have appeared a threat with his new souvenir, as O'Reilly proceeded to go over the glass and into the stands, engaging Kaptain with continual punches in the arena seats. Having broadcast the game for nearly four decades, Rosen looks back on the early days of his career with the team, a time when such an occurrence, although rare, was not entirely unexpected:

> When you think back to the '70s when I started out as a radio broadcaster, there were bench-clearing brawls. Every player jumped on the ice. Gloves and sticks were all over the ice. To me, that was a big negative for hockey. Eventually, they changed the rules. They eliminated players coming off the

bench and eliminated brawls. But I remember those days when you'd have brawls on the ice. Maybe the craziest night of all was at Madison Square Garden when the Bruins and Rangers got into a fight and the Bruins took it up and into the stands. They climbed over the glass, and there were fights going on between the players and the fans in the stands who were throwing things at the Bruins. It was an unbelievable thing to watch.

Among those players-turned-Madison-Square-Garden-attendants was Mike Milbury, whose role in the skirmish is perhaps the most memorable. Former New York Islanders play-by-play radio broadcaster Howie Rose, who, at the time was working Rangers games, looks back on Milbury's attempt at "shoe-jitsu," saying,

> I covered the game when Mike Milbury and the Boston Bruins went into the stands at Madison Square Garden. That was different and unique. Mike, who I consider a friend, later went on to coach and then manage the Islanders, so I always felt like we had a little bit of a connection there. When he was playing with the Boston Bruins, a skirmish broke out at the end of the game, which the Bruins won, and as players were starting to head to their rooms—I don't remember what exactly had ignited it from the fans' perspective—but, all of a sudden, we come running out to the runway to see what all this commotion is and there's Mike Milbury and a couple of other Bruins going up into the seats with their skates on and all. Milbury was in a tussle with one particular fan. While he was wrestling with him, Milbury grabbed the shoe right off the guy's foot and started belting him with it. That was as surreal as it gets in a hockey arena to see something like that go on. That's something Mike will always be remembered for infamously.

Naturally, following the incident, the league ordered the glass above the playing surface be raised to prevent similar incidents from happening.

A FAMILIAR FACE RAISING THE CUP

Having been born in Edmonton, Alberta, Canada, Hall of Fame center Mark Messier played for his hometown Oilers alongside Glenn Anderson, Grant Fuhr, Randy Gregg, Charlie Huddy, Jari Kurri, and Kevin Lowe during the team's run of five Stanley Cups in a seven-year period. Also included in four of those cups is the "Great One" Wayne Gretzky, who was picked up by the Kings before the 1988–1989 season and missed the parade in June 1990. Two seasons later, Messier, too, would leave the "nest" and head to the Big Apple, where he would give Ranger fans the drink for which they had been thirsting for more than half a century.

With an impressive 112 regular-season points, Messier, along with the offense and defense of Sergei Zubov and a supporting cast of Adam Graves, Brian Leetch, the notorious enforcement of Joe Kocur, the leadership of team-builder Mike Keenan, and the superb goaltending of Mike Richter, blew through the first two rounds of the playoffs, setting up a Conference Finals showdown with their across-the-Hudson neighbor, the New Jersey Devils. Down 3–2 in the series, team captain Messier guaranteed Ranger fans a game six victory. If there ever was a motivational poster for the saying "As good as his word," it could certainly display Mark Messier, who not only scored a hat trick but assisted on the team's only other goal in the 4–2 win over the Devils. The Rangers forced a game seven that would require two overtimes to decide who would represent the east against the Vancouver Canucks. His *second* most memorable game as a broadcaster, Rosen describes the Rangers' last stop before the Cup Final:

> There were the Rangers playing a tremendously intense series with the Devils, who were the up-and-coming team. The Rangers were the team that had the star power and were the favorites, but they were down 3–2 in the series. They came back and won game six in dramatic fashion at New Jersey and then went back to MSG for game seven. The Rangers were up 1–0, and the Devils tied the game with 7.7 seconds remaining in regulation. The game went to overtime and then to double overtime. The agony, the stress, the tension, the nervousness was beyond belief. Here they were—this close—to winning and going to the Stanley Cup Final, and yet they were a fraction of an inch away from not getting there. But they won it on the great goal by Stefan Matteau and advanced to the Stanley Cup Final for the first time since 1979. To that point, that was the best game that I had been ever involved with.

Though not yet in the broadcast booth—nor patrolling the ice on which he had played with the team for 11 seasons as a defenseman—Rangers radio play-by-play voice Dave Maloney shares his game seven experience at The Garden, saying, "I was actually at game seven. Believe it or not, I was able to score eight tickets. I took my oldest son, three of his buddies, and their dads. I remember when Zelepukin scored to tie it late and the ecstasy of the building became the forever destined 'We're not going to win here' sort of thing, Then Matteau would score in double overtime. My impression of that rivalry would have been that experience in '94. Game seven was an electrifying, dramatic evening."

Current Rangers radio play-by-play broadcaster Kenny Albert, whose father Marv was behind the radio microphone for the seminal moment in the history of this Hudson River rivalry, describes the series clincher, saying, "Game seven of '94 between the Rangers and the Devils is probably the pinnacle of the rivalry with the Matteau goal." As exhausting as a seven-game series can be—especially with the clincher going double overtime—the Rangers would have to endure yet another before season's end.

After falling 3–2 in overtime in the series opener, the Rangers proceeded to win three straight, including two in Vancouver. Coming back for game five at the Garden, the champagne would have to be put back on ice, and Ranger fans, already having waited 54 years to hoist the cup, would be delayed yet another game. A game-six victory by the Canucks set up the winner-take-all game seven in New York. In the decisive matchup, Messier scored a goal and an assist to accompany Richter's 28 saves on 30 shots. Adding a goal, Brian Leetch, with his 34 total playoff points, would take home the Conn Smythe Trophy for MVP, along with the Stanley Cup, as the Rangers outlasted the Canucks, 3–2, to earn the team's first championship since 1940.

Having been in the Rangers radio booth for nearly 30 years, Marv Albert describes what is likely the last great moment of his hockey broadcasting career, saying,

> I was fortunate enough to broadcast games involving some very good Ranger teams with a great coach in Emile Francis, but there was always Bobby Orr and the Bruins in their path or the Philadelphia Flyers and the Broad Street Bullies were always too good. There was a lot of disappointment along the way with playoff games and even once in the Finals and not being able to move further. It was a kick for me in '94 to do it. At the time, I was doing probably too much. I was doing the Knicks on television, the local 6:00 and 11:00 on NBC in New York, NFL football, and then NBA on NBC, so something had to go. Hockey is very tough on the voice, so I found myself having to be a little careful because you could really throw yourself off. At that time, I was working my way towards having to give something up, and that was it. It was a very nice touch that basically was the conclusion for me. It was just a great feeling to be able to do it.

Nowadays, any TV broadcasting duty—especially during the Stanley Cup Final—is turned over to the national networks. In 1994, however, Sam Rosen had the good fortune to not only be in the building but also call the team's long awaited return to glory. The Hall of Fame broadcaster notes,

> You start with the passion. The passion of the long-suffering Rangers fan. The team had not won the Stanley Cup since 1940. For me, the game that supersedes all is game seven of the Stanley Cup Final. For the New York Rangers to win the Stanley Cup after 54 years and ending that drought. To win it at home, at Madison Square Garden, in front of those fanatic, passionate, loving fans, there's nothing more exciting or thrilling for me. As a broadcaster, it's something you want, that opportunity to call a championship moment, and I had that in 1994.

Unfortunately, that was the last time in the NHL that the local broadcasters went all the way with their team to the final. After that, the networks broadcasting the NHL had exclusivity in the final round. Now, exclusivity starts in the second round. I did have the good fortune of working for the NHL radio network after that for a dozen years and calling Stanley Cup Finals from 1996 through 2008. Those were thrilling, but nothing compared to 1994, when the Rangers ended 54 years of frustration with one of the greatest moments in New York sports history. For the Rangers to win in game seven, that was the ultimate because that's the crowning moment.

With six Stanley Cups on his resume, Messier would play another 10 seasons and retire at the age of 43. His 1,887 career points are third only to former teammate Gretzky and former Eastern Conference rival Jaromír Jágr on the all-time scoring list.

LIFE IN THE GARDEN TODAY

With the 1994 Stanley Cup banner hanging high from the since-remodeled Madison Square Garden rafters, the Rangers have not equaled their 1994 feat in more than 20 years. In fact, four years removed from their championship glory, the Rangers would begin a string of seven consecutive seasons without a playoff appearance; however, after the lockout of 2004–2005, the Rangers returned to the postseason 11 out of the following 12 years. During four of the past six seasons (2011–2017), the team has advanced to the Conference Finals three times, making it all the way to the 2014 Stanley Cup Final against the eventual champions, the Los Angeles Kings.

On the shoulders of team-builder Alain Vigneault, offensive-minded Mats Zuccarello, J. T. Miller, and Derek Stepan, defensive studs Marc Staal, Dan Girardi, and Ryan McDonagh, and the ever-so-consistent goaltending of Henrik Lundqvist, the Rangers are looking to grace Times Square with another Stanley Cup parade well before the 54-year drought can be duplicated. With their New York counterpart retaining their name on a different "island," the Rangers are hoping to one up their Brooklyn neighbors and make the local cup tally Rangers 5, Islanders 4.

Ottawa Senators

Considering it was among the first cities to have organized hockey, Ottawa, the capital of Canada, surprisingly, was the last city of "Hockey Central" to receive an NHL franchise in the modern era. Established in 1883, the original Ottawa Senators went by names as simple as the Hockey Club or the Silver Seven, and, for a brief time, the Generals. Finally, after about 25 years of inspiring arguments between the locals as to "What's the team name this year?" Ottawa took on the name Senators just in time to win their first-ever Stanley Cup in 1911. Nine seasons later, the Senators became the first team in hockey history to receive "dynasty" recognition, as the team, led by George Boucher, Cy Denneny, and Frank Nighbor, won four Stanley Cups in eight seasons.

As was the case with many of the teams in the early years of the league, financial burdens became more of a reality, and the team, despite efforts by owners and the league, was eventually sold to St. Louis in 1934, where it became the Eagles. Having a team so distant from the rest of the league proved detrimental to both the city of St. Louis and its Eagles, as the team fell after just one season in the Midwest. Nearly 60 years later, the city of Ottawa was once again awarded an NHL franchise, and, following tradition, the players once again carried the name Senators on their chests.

While the team was on arguably the longest hiatus in the history of professional sports, Ottawa residents pledged their fandom and loyalty to teams of such nearby cities as Montreal, Toronto, and Boston prior to the Senators' inaugural 1992–1993 season, and, for many in the nation's capital, after it as well. Senators radio play-by-play broadcaster Dean Brown, who has been with the team since its inception, describes the "adoption" phase of Senators hockey as follows:

Comparatively, it's still a very young franchise. Ottawa's only 24 years old [2015]. Before that, geographically, where we are—not having had an NHL team—most of this city was either Toronto Maple Leaf fans growing up because their parents were or Montreal Canadiens fans for the same reason, or Boston Bruins fans. Those are really the three teams that split this city's fan base, so when the Ottawa Senators showed up, there were a lot of fans who were lifetime Leaf fans who were happy to have an NHL team here but were still Leaf fans.

As the old adage "only time will tell" comes into play, the Senators franchise and, with it, the Ottawa hockey scene has taken form in "Bytown." Brown continues,

> The fan base is really evolving because you're just now getting the first generation of fans where a kid growing up when he first started going to games at four or five years old has been a Senators fan his whole life. As a franchise, they're just getting to the point where they're going to start populating the building with lifetime Senator fans. I would think in the next 10 to 15 years is when you're going to start seeing the Ottawa fan base develop their own kind of personality and their own kind of idiosyncrasies.

While getting a Maple Leaf or Canadien fan to convert to "Senatorism" may be a generation-lasting chore, the presence of an NHL team and the ambassadorship that comes with it has proven impactful for the Ottawa community itself. Brown relates,

> The willingness of the athlete to be a part of the community has to be the first step. It can't be the other. Fans in the community are always going to connect themselves with the team because it's a sense of pride for them. It's a sense of "we have a major-league franchise" in whatever sport it is. In hockey, there's only 30 cities. Think of how many cities there are in North America, but only 30 of them have an NHL team. It's exciting. It's big time. It's professional sports. The athletes are like rock stars, so you don't have to worry about, "Will the fans attach themselves to the team?"—at least in hockey in Canada—but you do have to look at, "How willing will the players be to attach themselves to the community and be immersed in it?" That really goes to the personality and the makeup of your team's leadership group.
>
> Here in Ottawa, the Senators have been extremely fortunate. They've had captains like Daniel Alfredsson, Jason Spezza, and, now, Erik Karlsson. In the past, they've had Randy Cunneyworth and Brad Shaw. You look at the captains, and they're really the ones that gather together the guys and say, "Guys, were going to go do this." and then you have the team staff that makes those things happen. In Ottawa's case, one of the reasons they are so

closely connected to the community is over the years, the team leaders have been guys who have kids and families of their own. They understand the importance of connecting with kids, families, and the community. They know how important that is because they have children. They understand that connection is really important and how important it is to generate a bond between the community and the team.

In Ottawa, you now have a situation where you have a captain in Erik Karlsson, who's only 23 years old [2015]. He doesn't have any kids, yet, but he still understands because he was tutored by Jason Spezza, and, more specifically, Daniel Alfredsson. Ottawa has one of the tightest nine bonds that I've seen in professional sports with the community because Ottawa is not that big of a city. You really have to connect on a personal level because it's not like New York or Toronto or Chicago, where you're always going to make money as an organization because there's always going to be 20,000 people who want to show up just by sheer numbers. A place like Ottawa doesn't work that way. If you're not connected to the community—if you don't feel a part of them and they don't feel a part of you—it's going to hurt the business.

Ottawa has been very fortunate. The kind of connection they have with the fans here is built on the shaking of hands. It's the one-on-one meeting that overall people meet and see these guys all over town. They go to events, these guys are at them. They go to kids things, these guys are at them. You go to the children's hospital, these guys are there, and that only happens if the players are willing and have the want to do it. In larger cities, while players are still connected to the community, their connection isn't as directly affected by the business as it is in smaller towns.

While not the metropolis characteristic of its Ontarian counterpart Toronto or river-sharing Montreal, Ottawa opened its Civic Centre doors in early October 1992, to a crowd of more than 10,500 fans, which, while paltry by NHL standards, filled the venue's capacity and then some. Brown describes the team's initial home, saying,

> When they opened that first season in the Ottawa Civic Centre, people were just excited hockey was in Ottawa. Everybody knew from the very first day the Civic Centre was not just too small, but not even close to having the facilities to be able to properly house an NHL team on every level. The positioning of the seats, the size of the suites, how few suites there were. The broadcast facilities were poor, at best. People were fine with that because everybody understood this was temporary. There's no way the NHL would have brought a franchise to Ottawa if the permanent plan would have been to play in the Civic Centre. First of all, there's no team that could survive economically only having 10,000 seats.
>
> When they moved from the Civic Centre to the Palladium, I think people were just excited to get into the new building because it was huge,

brand new, and fresh. It was what they all envisioned NHL hockey would be, not this temporary shoehorn into a junior hockey building. There was nobody who was really disappointed they were leaving the Civic Centre. There weren't any teary departures. It's not like they were leaving a good old barn that everybody loved. They just put up with it for four years because they knew a new building would be coming.

While there may have been no teary eyes on April 11, 1996, when the Civic Centre closed its doors on NHL hockey, the same cannot be said for when it opened on October 8, 1992, as 20 players sporting Roman generals on their chests took the ice against the most successful franchise in NHL history, the Montreal Canadiens.

OCTOBER 8, 1992: HISTORY VERSUS A LACK THEREOF

During their inaugural season, the Ottawa Senators won 10 of their 84 games, and only one of those 10 wins came on the road. Only the 1980–1981 Winnipeg Jets (9) and 1974–1975 Washington Capitals (8) had fewer wins in a season of at least 80 games. While the team would be looking up from the division cellar by season's end, the Senators were looking down from the top when the Civic Centre lights powered down October 8. Brown notes,

> I know there's other guys, who, when they talk about this, they talk about the first time they made the playoffs or when they went to the Stanley Cup Final in '07 against Anaheim, but, for me, the biggest game—the most exciting game ever—is still the very first game back in the Ottawa Civic Centre, not so much because of the building, but because of what it meant. They played the Montreal Canadiens, and, obviously, here in Ottawa, the Montreal Canadiens have a huge fan base, so it was a team that everybody knew. The winningest team in the history of NHL hockey was in town to play a brand new team. I think it was probably and still is the most exciting game to me because I live here. This is where I bring up my family. This is my home, and it was the realization of several years and a longshot plan to get an NHL team in the first place, but they got the team and then it was all the preparations and finding a way to get things done so you can actually play games.
>
> When the very first game actually arrived, it was an amazing feeling in that building to finally realize in a real sense that Ottawa was in the National Hockey League. Ottawa was on the world map as an NHL city. The best game in the world was now at home in Ottawa, and it wasn't an exhibition game in September where two teams somewhere else rolled into town and then rolled out of town after the game was over. This team was

playing the first game of thousands they will play over the decades. Then winning that game, 5–3, over Montreal was the icing on the cake because no one expected that.

Everybody knew this team in the first several years was going to be a very bad team because they were going to try and build through the draft. The fact that they won the game as well was an amazing thing. An amazing night. I think that probably was the most exciting game for me because of what it meant. It had a huge meaning, and we have now found out 24 years later the massive changes that have occurred in our city because it's an NHL city now. The tens of millions of dollars the hockey team generates every year in business in this community that's not hockey related. The hotels, tournaments, and restaurants that have popped up. The Ottawa Senators Foundation generates more money for charity than any other organization in Ottawa, with the exception of the United Way. We only have the Senators Foundation because the Senators are here. All those things came from the start of that one game that one night in the dingy old Civic Centre, and, for me, that was and still is the most exciting game this team has ever played.

The following season, the Senators only improved their record by four wins, but thanks to a farm system bringing up such players as Alexei Yashin and eventual team captain Daniel Alfredsson, the team qualified for their first postseason in 1997 and would continue to do so for 11 straight years, including a trip to the Conference Finals in 2003 and the Cup Final in 2007, where they would lose in five games to the new-logo-wearing Anaheim Ducks. Somewhere in that decade-plus playoff run, the Senators picked up a rival in a city known for its "brotherly love."

OKAY, REFS. GET YOUR CALCULATORS

The most penalized game in NHL history went down without anyone other than statisticians, sportswriters, and math nerd hockey enthusiasts even knowing it. With 419 penalty infraction minutes (PIM) being recorded after the game by officials who had worked way into overtime, the Ottawa Senators and Philadelphia Flyers, on March 5, 2004, broke the modern-day record of 406 PIMs shared by the Boston Bruins and Minnesota North Stars for more than 23 years. Looking back on the game, Brown admits,

To be honest with you, I don't even remember who won that game. For me, it was just another game I did. I don't remember who won the fights. Probably the biggest single thing I remember about that game was guys who virtually never fight got into fights. I remember Jason Spezza was in a fight with Patrick Sharp, and those two guys never fight. Probably the funniest thing was Zdeno Chára, who was the biggest, baddest player in the league at that time. After everybody had paired up, there was nobody left for him to pair up with except for Mattias Timander, who was skating around the ice yelling, "Help," because he knew if Chára caught him, he was going to be destroyed. He didn't know how to fight, and the biggest guy in the league had no one to tie up with. Timander was legitimately frightened for his safety. He was skating around the ice, trying to get away from Chára.

Also featured in the melee were known enforcers Rob Ray versus Donald Brashear, as well as Mark Recchi versus Bryan Smolinski, Mike Fisher versus Michal Handzuš, Shaun Van Allen versus Branko Radivojevič, and opposing goaltenders Patrick Lalime and Robert Esche.

Considering the rule changes and officiating standards that had taken place in the 23 years between the Boston Bruins–Minnesota North Stars and Ottawa Senators–Philadelphia Flyers contests, the game didn't necessarily seem worthy of holding such a place in NHL history as far as PIMs were concerned, especially according to broadcasters like Dean Brown, who had seen much worse in their careers. Brown explains,

A week later, after we realized and everybody pointed out this was the most penalized game in league history, we were talking about the fact it didn't seem that way. We've all seen videos from the '50s and '60s where there's guys in the stands, guys who are fighting for 20 minutes, and there's blood all over the ice. That really wasn't what this was. I think the biggest difference was the officials were so conscious of this now as compared to years past. Penalties were given out in that game that might not have been given out 20 years earlier. Back in the old days, if two guys just took their gloves off and grabbed each other but didn't throw any punches, they weren't given a penalty.

I think one of the reasons why that game became the most penalized game ever was not so much because it was the most vicious game or had the most fights ever. The penalties were handed out in a way that had never been done before. Guys got penalties for things that in the past had never really been penalized. There might have been three fights that were real fights where you go, "There's a couple of guys who know what they're doing." The other ones were a couple of guys who threw a couple of punches and then wrestled to the ice or would get linked up and never throw any actual punches. Even though it was the most penalized game ever, I'm not sure it would even go down in the top 10 of any real vicious games between two teams. Not even close.

THE OTTAWA SENATORS TODAY

While the officials of the North Stars–Bruins game of 1981 would still be counting the penalty minutes according to today's regulations, "first-generation lifer" Senator fans are now bringing their own offspring to the Canadian Tire Centre and attempting to create team traditions specific to the Senators. Although most efforts are met with "It's already been done" feedback, the sounds of the Sons of Scotland Pipe Band and the antics of team mascot "Spartacat" fill the facility during each home game in the hopes that Lord Stanley's Cup will parade its way past Parliament Hill and along the Ottawa River before a crowd of both "lifers" and "converted" Senator fans.

· 22 ·

Philadelphia Flyers

$\mathcal{F}$or a city so rich and so rooted in sports tradition, many Philadelphians still likely scratch their heads at the fact that the "City of Brotherly Love" had to wait until the NHL's first wave of expansion before getting a professional hockey team that would actually stick around. Having received the (NHL) Pirates franchise from their cross-state neighbors just up U.S. Highway 30, Philadelphia, much like Pittsburgh, didn't have much luck holding a team in the early years of the league. After just one season, the (then-named) Philadelphia Quakers team would be suspended and never regain enough momentum to be counted among the NHL's "original six," slowly dissolving until it ultimately disappeared from the league in 1936. With the NHL doubling its size to 12 teams in the fall of 1967, Philadelphia, now with a venue more suited for major sports than the Quakers' former home of Philadelphia Arena, went from Market Street to Broad Street and opened its Spectrum doors to the Flyers, a team that—within seven years—would bring the city as much championship glory as the Phillies, Eagles, and '76ers combined.

BROTHERLY LOVE ON A CONDITIONAL BASIS

For a city infamously characterized by some of its fan base pelting Eagles season ticket-holder and Santa Claus-outfit-sporting Frank Olivo with a barrage of snowballs during a game at Franklin Field on December 15, 1968, Philadelphia, throughout the years, seems to have really taken to their youngest major sports franchise. Current Flyers TV play-by-play broadcaster Jim Jackson explains,

If it's orange and black in Philadelphia, the fans will show up. It's an amazing phenomenon. People who haven't lived here probably don't understand there's just something about the Flyers. I think it started with their cup teams in the '70s. From then, the people followed that team and passed it on to their kids, and it's become generational. There's just a huge interest in this team. They haven't won the cup since 1975, yet they still have an unbelievable fan base here. It's really enthusiastic and passionate. A lot of times, you need that championship somewhere along the line to sustain the kind of passion you see here, but they've been contenders. They've been to the finals several times, so believe me, this has been a very good franchise, and that's part of it.

Of course, with passion can sometimes come criticism, a theme to which Philadelphia sports fans are no strangers. Jackson continues,

It's just the passion of the fans in Philadelphia for all sports. It's certainly strong for the Flyers. The team could be at the bottom of the standings, and, still, the intensity of the crowd is there. They let the home team know when they're not happy, too. There's no question about that. They basically let the team know when they're not playing well, and, when they are playing well, support them better than any other market. I couldn't imagine being in a market other than this. It's the only one I've been in at the NHL level, but it's the only one I want to be in because, basically, of the passion of the fans, whether it's positive or negative. They care, and that makes it, in my opinion, a lot more fun to broadcast the game. It could be a game in the middle of December and they still are right there with all kinds of intensity. I love that.

Of course, it also doesn't hurt when your team has two championship banners dangling from the rafters, earned during the first eight years of its existence.

1974–1975 FLYERS: CHAMPAGNE AND BLOOD ON THE ICE

With their back-to-back Stanley Cups in the mid-1970s, the Philadelphia Flyers had already won as many championships as the Philadelphia Phillies had appeared in during their 85-year existence in Major League Baseball. While championship-caliber teams won their respective Stanley Cups with finesse, speed, and defense, the 1974–1975 Flyers did it with pure intimidation. With the city less than six years removed from the Frank Olivo incident, this style was probably right up a model Philadelphian's alley.

Of course, intimidation is a two-way street, and, coming in to the league in 1967, the Flyers were standing at the wrong end of theirs. Lead

Flyers radio play-by-play broadcaster Tim Saunders explains, "When the franchise first started, because of the way the league had it set up after expansion, the St. Louis Blues were the Flyers' first nemesis. Early in their existence, the St. Louis Blues bullied the Flyers in the playoffs and Chairman Ed Snyder said, 'Never again. We're never again going to be pushed out of a game physically.' General Manager Keith Allen went about building his teams with that in mind, and the Broad Street Bullies were born." The Broad Street Bullies, probably one of the most recognized groups in NHL history, set the tone for the team's back-to-back cup run, starting with left winger Dave "The Hammer" Schultz. Jim Jackson, who was just a kid when the Flyers first hoisted the Stanley Cup in 1974, describes what many fans feel boosted the team to its success in the second-round playoff series against the New York Rangers:

> In 1974, it was the semifinals series with the Rangers. They're going seven games, and, in a game they wanted to turn around, Dave Schultz just pounded Dale Rolfe, a defenseman for the Rangers, who was behind the net. No one really came to Rolfe's aid, which, a lot of people said, basically buried the Rangers in that game and obviously gave the Flyers momentum. I wasn't at that game. I don't know if it really had that impact, but certainly, as the legend has gone, that fight was really the end of the series. In terms of a fight that might have had a major impact on a game, that would be the one I think every Flyers fan who's been around for a while would go to.

Schultz, who would set the all-time league record with 472 penalty minutes the following season, lit the torch that carried his team to a further six straight series wins after disposing of the Rangers. Counted among Shultz's cohorts were André "Moose" Dupont, Bob "Hound Dog" Kelly, Don Saleski, and Gary Dornhoefer, with team leader Bobby Clarke handling things on both ends of the ice and goaltender Bernie Parent defending the crease. While the Philadelphia crowd likely reveled in the style with which the "Broad Street Bullies" played, the same couldn't be said for fans of their opponents, or the broadcasters for that matter. Los Angeles Kings TV play-by-play broadcaster Bob Miller, who called games during the Philadelphia "bullying" era, describes one night in particular, saying,

> In Philadelphia, they were the Broad Street Bullies, and that was the way they played. We got into a scrap with them in a game. Everybody was out on the ice, kind of pairing off, with the exception of Ken Linseman. I'll never forget. Ken Linseman, then of the Flyers, skated around the outside of the scrum circle, and he was trying to trip Kings players who were fighting with the Flyers. He tried to slide their skates out from under them. I thought, "That's the dirtiest thing I've seen."

Dirty or not, the team's combined 1,740 and 1,953 penalty minutes in 1974 and 1975, respectively, don't even break the top 20 for most ever in an NHL season. Incidentally, not one of the teams on that top 20 list ever raised their *own* Stanley Cup, let alone two.

1994–2006: A STANDING INVITATION TO THE POSTSEASON

For a brief time in the mid-1990s, the most recognized name in hockey, arguably, wasn't "Gretzky" or "Lemieux," or "Yzerman" or even "Selänne," but "Lindros." Coming into the league at age 19—not to mention at the price of future Hall of Famer Peter Forsberg and several others, including future Flyers general manager Ron Hextall—Eric Lindros quickly made his mark in Philadelphia, taking home the league's Hart Memorial Trophy for MVP in just his third year. Two years after that, Lindros and the Flyers made their first Stanley Cup Final appearance in 10 years, losing to the Detroit Red Wings in a sweep. After a concussion virtually ended his career—at least with the Flyers, that is—Lindros's team captain duties were passed down to Éric Desjardins and Keith Primeau, and, under these three, Philadelphia came in second or better in the division for 11 straight seasons, making it to the Conference Finals four times in that span.

Among this string of playoff appearances came the 2000 Conference Semifinals against the Pittsburgh Penguins, which, although only going six games, lasted longer than most series going the full seven. In game four, it would take 152 minutes and one second of playing time before a victor would be decided, as the Flyers and Penguins endured the NHL's longest game since 1936. His most memorable game as team broadcaster, Jackson describes the marathon game, which featured five overtimes:

> The game started May 4, 2000, and bled into May 5. Five overtimes in the second round of the playoffs. It was an amazing event. Keith Primeau won it. There were so many memories from that night. When you're involved in history like that, it's going to jump out. For a long time, that's been my most memorable game. Since then, we've had some great playoff victories, but if you had to pin me down on one, I'd probably go back to the Pittsburgh game simply because it was NHL history.

Another voice tested by May 4–5, 2000 was Tim Saunders, who adds, "The five overtime game was probably the most memorable game from a broadcaster's standpoint just because of the marathon nature of the game and what it took out of everybody involved."

It's arguable the six game series took so much out of each team, it would take eight years before they'd have enough in their tanks to give it another go in the playoffs. Beginning in 2008, the teams would square off against each other in three out of five postseasons; thus, opening the debate floor over the legitimacy of this rivalry extending beyond being just an intrastate one. Saunders notes,

> I think it's still one of the best rivalries in the NHL. You look at playoff history, if you played that particular team in the playoffs and you had a couple of good series, I think that goes a long way in creating a rivalry. When two teams don't like each other and the two cities feed on that, that's when a rivalry *really* takes off. In 2012, they had a six game series with the Penguins that I think cemented Pittsburgh as the current top rival in Philadelphia. It was a wild series. The Flyers won the first three games before Pittsburgh came back to win the next two. In the end the Flyers took the series in six, but because of the way the fan bases reacted and the nature of those games, I think that series locked the Penguins in as the Flyers' top rival of the last decade.

While the Penguins have won five cups since the Flyers' two, it may take another June parade through Philadelphia to sweeten—albeit just a little—the bitterness the team and its fans have for their Keystone State counterpart.

MARCH 5, 2004: CANCEL YER DINNER RESERVATIONS AND GET OUT YER CALCULATORS, REFS

One would think the NHL record for penalty minutes in a game, especially one involving the Philadelphia Flyers, would have occurred during the "Broad Street Bully" days of the 1970s; however, the 419 issued minutes came at the sparring hands of the 2003–2004 Flyers with the Ottawa Senators in town. Jim Jackson notes,

> On March 5, 2004, the Flyers and Senators played at the Wells Fargo Center, where they set the modern-day record for penalty minutes. By the end of the game, there were three players on each bench. As I recall, Martin Havlát had high-sticked or done something to Mark Recchi earlier on in the season, and so he was sort of a target for the Flyers. He took a penalty in this game, ended up in the penalty box, and a brawl broke out, and I mean everybody fought. The goalies fought, the fighters fought, and the nonfighters fought. It was just one fight after another. At the time, it was certainly a throwback. Even at that point, they had

pretty much started to see fighting decline in the league, but that night was just craziness.

All this happened in the third period. They'd drop the puck, and the fights would break out again. They dropped the puck again, and two or three fights would break out again. Just one after another. Fans loved it. It was just comical going down and seeing hardly anybody there on the bench. The irony of it was because he was in the penalty box, Havlát never really got involved in anything, and he was really the catalyst of it all. As far as nonplayoff games, I'm probably reminded of that game around here by fans more than any other game. It was a night you couldn't forget. You end up looking over at the benches, and there were more coaches than there were players. It was something you knew you weren't going to see very often.

With 16 different players receiving game misconducts, the referees took 90 minutes after the game to record the penalties, inspiring the "cutting into an official's personal time" call.

THERE'S ALWAYS ROOM FOR MORE HISTORY

In the postseason following the "fight where a hockey game broke out," the Flyers went as far as the Conference Finals before losing in seven games to the eventual Stanley Cup champion Tampa Bay Lightning. They returned to the Conference Finals once more in 2008, where they fell to their intrastate rival, the Pittsburgh Penguins, in a series where no game would take five overtimes to decide. Two seasons later, the team found itself in the unlikeliest of situations, reaching the Stanley Cup Final during a playoff run in which they faced a second-round, 0–3 series deficit to the Boston Bruins. Climbing all the way back to tie their series at three games apiece—a feat that had only been done five times prior in the history of the NHL—the Flyers found themselves in another 0–3 deficit, this time on the TD Garden scoreboard. Reflecting on game seven, Jim Jackson notes,

> The Flyers fell down 3–0 in that game. A game seven after being down 3–0 in the series, they tie that series. Then they fall behind 3–0 and you think, "Well, they made a good run," but they came right back and they won that game. It hadn't been done at that point since the '70s. Now only four times total. It's only been done five times ever in baseball, basketball, and hockey. You knew you were part of history there.

The Flyers would eventually fall to the cup-thirsty, dynasty-commencing Chicago Blackhawks in six games, and, the following season, become the victim of Boston vengeance, losing in a sweep to the Bruins, who, in turn, would go on to take home the Stanley Cup and end their own championship drought.

THE FLYERS TODAY

Although the team hasn't made it past the second round since their unlikely comeback of 2010, Flyer fans continue to display their "orange crush" and support the team both conditionally and unconditionally. While the team has yet to hoist the cup in their 18 seasons inside the Wells Fargo Center, the support for the Flyers is just as intense as it was on Broad Street inside the Spectrum. Jackson describes the contrast (or lack thereof):

> With all the new buildings, they had to adjust to the fact that it was bigger, and with the size of an arena comes a little less intimacy. I've heard this with just about every arena. When they went from the Stadium to the United Center in Chicago, from the Garden to the other Garden in Boston, or from the Forum to the Bell Centre in Montreal, it was always, "You're not as close to the ice. The fans aren't on top of the ice as much. There's just not as much intensity," but I think there's always an adjustment. I think the fans have adjusted, and now it's considered still very loud. You don't hear a team that doesn't come in here and say, "It's a tough place to play," and I think that's a credit to the fans because they're so into it. They aren't afraid to express their opinions, especially to the opposing team. I think it makes it a little bit of an intimidating place.
>
> The Flyers' home record is so much better than their road record this year [2015], and I don't think that's completely a coincidence. It's a tough place to come in here and play, and be at your best. As an opponent, you tend to get a little bit off your game, maybe because you're trying to show up the crowd. Whatever the reason is, teams don't play as well here as they do when they play against the Flyers in their own buildings. That's the case, I suppose, throughout the league, but I think it's the case even more so for the Flyers. The fans deserve some of the credit for that. They are the ones who were able to make that adjustment and make this a difficult place to play, because, obviously, the Spectrum was difficult. I think it's an adjustment all fans in all cities had to make because you had to have the bigger buildings, you had to have the suites, you had to have the setup to basically make them financially successful, and, in doing so, the buildings got bigger and the fans got a little farther away from the rink. They've been able to make that adjustment. I don't think anybody complains about that anymore.

With the late Frank Olivo's Santa Claus suit permanently hanging in its closet and the 1980 and 2008 Phillies pacifying the city's thirst for championship glory, the Flyers, with players like Jakub Voráček, Claude Giroux, and Mark Streit, are looking to take that proverbial Rocky Balboa run up the steps of Philadelphia's Museum of Art and once again raise Lord Stanley's Cup.

· 23 ·

Pittsburgh Penguins

$\mathscr{W}$hile it may be hard to believe, there was a time when two professional sports teams named the Pirates were gracing the "Steel City" of Pittsburgh, Pennsylvania. Dating back to 1925, the NHL's Pittsburgh Pirates began their brief five-year team history, playing against other soon-to-be-defunct teams like the New York Americans and the Montreal Maroons. Facing the same financial hardships so many other professional teams were going through at the time, the Pirates were shipped east across Pennsylvania and landed in Philadelphia, where they became known as the Quakers. Having about as much success as could be expected from a vagabond franchise during the Great Depression, the Quakers folded almost as quickly as they arrived, and it would be another 35 years before the "Keystone State" would see professional hockey. In 1967, during the league's first expansion—one in which it would double in size—the cities of Philadelphia and Pittsburgh were awarded franchises. Philadelphia's would come to be known as the Flyers, and Pittsburgh's would become the Penguins.

A Pittsburgh Pirates *baseball* championship earlier in the decade courtesy of Bill Mazeroski's season-clinching walk-off home run in Game Seven of the 1960 World Series, coupled with a budding NFL dynasty on the horizon in the form of the Pittsburgh Steelers, made it the perfect time for another black-and-gold clad franchise to cross one of the city's 446 bridges and be welcomed by some of the most faithful fans a new team could ever hope for. Hall of fame radio play-by-play broadcaster Mike Lange, who has been with the team for more than 40 years, describes the passion that is Pittsburgh fandom:

> Every city and every guy will tell you they have a tremendous fan base. I can remember back when *Monday Night Football* was so big, the Steelers were playing and Howard Cosell made the comment, "You play the

147

Steelers, you play the city of Pittsburgh." That never left me because he was right on the money. The uniqueness of this place is the whole city is an island surrounded by a mountain and the most bridges of any city in the world. To get in and out of the city becomes a focal point. The stadiums are downtown, and that's part of it, too. It is not a giant area, but it is a very distinct area. There's a lot of credence to what Cosell says because every-thing kind of filters into this one focal point, that being the city. Because of the three water ways and the travel for goods going up and down the rivers years ago, that's what kind of made the city. There's a uniqueness in the fact that everybody gravitates to that focal point. That has a lot to do with the way people perceive it. They get extremely behind these teams—sometimes almost to a fault—but it becomes their way of life. They actually become part of the teams.

The first year I came here was in 1974, and, that year, the Steelers won their first Super Bowl. I saw, firsthand, about 300 to 500,000 people in a small confined area downtown in the city for the parade. Everywhere you went, every building had signs up and down them. You were just over-whelmed. It was like that with the Penguins, too, and it will be like that again with the Pirates. There's just something about it that makes it unique in that way.

Of course, life's situations force some to leave the "island," but that doesn't necessarily mean the island leaves them. Lange continues,

> Because of the major changes here—the devastation they've had from los-ing all the corporations, the businesses, and the steel mills—we've had a whole generation of people who have moved away. They have a loyalty to this city that's second to none, and it is evident when you see games away. Invariably, whatever sport it is, you'll see a lot of Pittsburgh fans at the other buildings.

Of course, well-traveled fandom usually accompanies superstar players worthy of such frequent-flyer-mile-accumulating loyalty.

SUPER MARIO BROTHERS

Jaromír Jágr, a player born in the Czech Republic who has been in the NHL for so long the "country of origin" section on his stat sheet had to be changed, surpassed long-time Oiler/Ranger Mark Messier for the number two spot on the league's all-time scoring list. Having entered the league at the age of 18, Jágr, playing the first 11 of his 23-season (and counting) NHL career with the Penguins, has the points (1,914 and counting) and the tenure, but, as far as

Pittsburgh is concerned, no name stands above that of Jágr's former teammate, "Super" Mario Lemieux.

Having finished with a 16–58–6 record during their 1983–1984 season—worst in the league by more than 20 team points—the Penguins were given the first pick in the 1984 NHL Draft. The team selected Mario Lemieux, a Montreal native, and started the franchise on a road much different from the playoff-futility-paved one they had taken in their 17 years of existence. Although winning the Calder Trophy for rookie of the year during the 1984–1985 season, as well as both the Hart Memorial and Art Ross trophies in 1987–1988, Lemieux and the team resumed their six-year playoff drought. The following year, Lemieux won his second straight Art Ross Trophy as part of an 85-goal, 199-point campaign, propelling the Penguins to their first playoff appearance since 1982. Helping bring success back to Pittsburgh, he also assisted in bringing back one of Mike Lange's best-known "Lange-isms." The Hall of Fame broadcaster notes,

> When Mario first started, all our games weren't on TV. Players, families, and people in Canada would listen to the games instead of watching them like they do on all these packages. We were their main source. Mario's family didn't speak English. They spoke French, but they could get KDKA in Montreal, where they lived. If you know anything about me, I'm a little different. I would use the phrase, "Ladies and gentlemen, Elvis has just left the building." Mario came to me one day and said, "My mama wants to know what this Elvis thing is. Elvis, Elvis." As it turns out, Mario's mother loved Elvis. Mario had me laughing, so he went and told his mom in French. Over the years, his mother and I have become very close, and it's an Elvis moment when she sees me. She just starts smiling and says, "Elvis, Elvis." When we had the playoffs the first year, they came down and we had an Elvis in the building who would be part of it. I made sure he would go over to where she was and shake his hips and do the whole thing.

The further Lemieux got into his career, the longer it took Elvis to "leave the building."

The Penguins began their 1990–1991 season with their seventh coach in nine seasons, as team-builder and 1986 Stanley Cup runner-up Bob Johnson took over for interim coach Craig Patrick. Playing in only three fewer games in the playoffs than he had in the regular season, Lemieux, eventual winner of the Conn Smythe Trophy, along with rookie Jaromír Jágr, Mark Recchi, John Cullen, Kevin Stevens, Paul Coffey, and goaltender Tom Barrasso, brought a city that had already seen five World Series titles and four Super Bowl championships their first glimpse of Lord Stanley's Cup.

Lange discusses the Penguins' status in Pittsburgh fandom with the team's first championship, saying,

> Prior to Lemieux getting here, there were some very strong years while the Pirates and Steelers were so successful. This was the third cog in the machine, if you will, as far as being an accepted sport in the city of Pittsburgh. What was fulfilling to everybody, including myself, in trying to sell a game since 1974 is it's a slow build. With the teams they had, when the opportunity came up to draft Mario Lemieux, there were no guarantees Mario was going to be the player he was, but there was just instant credibility. It absolutely grew from there from the ground roots basis to kids starting to play hockey, people getting involved, including the Penguins themselves. There were still another six years without them brewing or doing anything of major accomplishment until they did it in 1990–91. A year where nobody—*nobody*—expected them to win the cup. That was one of the more rewarding things. Mario was able to establish himself as the best player in the league that year and really kind of cemented everything. It built a pretty long stretch of success for the Penguins and one that has continued to this day.

Shortly after their first Stanley Cup championship, tragedy struck the Penguins and their team-builder, Bob Johnson, who passed away shortly after doctors discovered a brain tumor. Before honoring their late coach's memory with the second of back-to-back Stanley Cup championships, the team, the fans, and the city of Pittsburgh honored Johnson on a more personal level. Lange explains,

> The most telling moment as a broadcaster for the Pittsburgh Penguins was the tribute to the late Bob Johnson, who led the Penguins to their first-ever Stanley Cup in one year of coaching, and, after the season, was discovered to have a brain tumor and then passed away. That game to honor and salute him at Civic Arena was unlike any moment in broadcasting for the Penguins or any other sport. I was completely off guard. The moving moment that it was for the players, broadcasters, and every person who was in that building. In the early stages, it was a light show type of thing, and you're thinking, "Oh boy," but, when it was done, there was not a dry eye in the house. There were tears of joy to celebrate his life, and that, to me, was the most moving moment I've ever had being around the Pittsburgh Penguins. The game was sort of second fiddle. It was amazingly exhilarating. It had just so much drama. It was all just Bob and all the things he had brought to the team and what happened. I think a lot of the players and people who were a part of it would probably tell you the same thing. It was a once-in-a-lifetime moment and one I will never forget.

Health would not be an issue relegated to just the builder of this budding powerhouse, but to the players as well. After leading the team to their second straight Stanley Cup championship in 1992, Lemieux was diagnosed with Hodgkin's disease—a form of lymphoma cancer—and missed more than a month of playing time. He returned to the ice in March 1993 and went on to once again win both the Art Ross and Hart Memorial trophies in one of the greatest comeback stories in sports history. The 1993 season would not be the only comeback story of Lemieux's career, as other health issues led him to announce his retirement in 1997, at the tail end of back-to-back Art Ross Trophy–worthy seasons.

Following the 1996–1997 season, Lemieux led an investment group to become part-owner of the Penguins, shifting his seat from the bench to the box. After a three-year absence from the playing surface, and still as part-owner of the team, he announced his return as a player. Five partial seasons and 229 points later, Lemieux retired for good in January 2006. His 1,723 career points are good enough for eighth most in NHL history. Having broadcast for the Penguins during Lemieux's first "go" at retirement, current Arizona Coyotes TV play-by-play broadcaster Matt McConnell looks back on one of the most memorable off-ice moments of his career:

> When I was in Pittsburgh, the first year, we lost in five games to the Flyers in the opening round of the playoffs, and that was Mario Lemieux's swan song before he came back. Full disclosure, I was a big Pittsburgh Penguins fan from high school through my professional life until I got to Anaheim in '93. We're in Philly, and we get on the plane. It's about a 45-minute flight to Pittsburgh. So I decide I'm going to walk through the plane and thank the guys for everything they had done for me. All the interviews and things like that. So I'm going along and thanking Petr Nedvêd, Ian Moran, and all these different guys. I get to the back row, and there's Mario, Craig Muni, and some of the veterans having a conversation.
>
> I go up to Mario and I say, "Mario, I'm working my way through the plane. I wanted to say thanks to everybody, and I wanted to take this opportunity to thank you. Thanks for everything. I don't think you understand that you were one of my favorite players growing up. It's been a privilege to be able to cover you here my first year in Pittsburgh. For everything you did for our broadcasts this year, I just wanted to say thanks." He looks at me and says, "No Matt. Thank you." I'm like a deer in the headlights. I'm stunned thinking, "Why is he thanking me," and the next thing he does is he pulls a cold one out of the bag and says, "Wanna have a beer?" As gracious and prolific a skater as he was on the ice in scoring and setting people up, he was that off the ice. He's just one of the best human beings that I had come across in the sport, and that was a memory I'll never forget.

Lemieux continues today as team owner, and he has a front-row seat to watch his franchise's current display of superstardom and leadership in the form of 5-foot-11 center and team captain Sidney Crosby.

SLAP US ALL SILLY, SIDNEY

Filling the skates of arguably one of the three greatest players in NHL history takes a special kind of athlete. Sidney Crosby, who, at the age of 18, came into the league, just as his 40-year-old teammate Mario Lemieux was leaving, handled the transition and torch acceptance quite admirably, scoring 102 points in his rookie season, placing second to Washington forward and Calder Memorial Trophy winner Alex Ovechkin and his 106 points. Crosby "rebounded" the following season, taking home both the Hart Memorial and Art Ross trophies in 2006–2007. Injuries the following year forced him to the bench for the better part of 2007–2008, but not the postseason. Scoring 27 points in 20 games, Crosby led the Penguins back to the Stanley Cup Final for the first time since winning it all in 1992. Facing a roster filled with "on-their-way-out" future Hall of Famers the likes of Nicklas Lidström, Chris Chelios, and Dominik Hašek, Crosby and the Penguins fell short of lifting Lord Stanley's Cup, losing to the Detroit Red Wings, four games to two.

The following season almost proved to be playoff hockey's edition of déjà vu, except, this time, when the Red Wings and Penguins met for the Stanley Cup Final, it was Pittsburgh celebrating on Detroit's ice. Crosby, although failing to score in the decisive game seven—and coming up short to teammate Evgeni Malkin for Conn Smythe Award honors—still managed to tally 31 points during the 2008–2009 postseason in helping bring the cup back from Detroit and over one of Pittsburgh's bridges. Averaging more than 1.33 points a game in his 10+ year career, the center's rookie campaign remains his only season outing without a playoff appearance.

While the "Lemieux versus Gretzky" debate of yesterday has become "Crosby versus Ovechkin," the native Nova Scotian has a "three up" on his Russian counterpart with the team's back-to-back Stanley Cup–clinching performance of 2016–2017 (first time in NHL history under the salary cap era), especially with the road to said cup traveling through a two-straight President's Trophy—earning Washington Capitals team. Lead Penguins TV play-by-play broadcaster Paul Steigerwald chimes in on the seemingly one-sided rivalry, saying

> We always beat the Capitals. We've tortured them over the years in the playoffs. It's been about seven straight series. There have been years where

the Capitals have had 3–1 leads in series, and, on a couple of occasions, the Penguins came from behind to win those series; including on the way to the Cup in '92. The Capitals have become the whipping boys of the Penguins in a lot of ways. I would think the Capitals fans have more of a dislike for the Penguins than the other way around because the Penguins have had so much success against them. They don't view them the same way they view the Flyers, who they were beaten by for years and years. The Capitals/Penguins rivalry became more heated when you had the Ovechkin versus Crosby aspect. Every time those two have met in big games, Crosby has come out the winner.

A RIVALRY FORGED IN STEEL

While the theme between Pittsburgh and Washington has become more of a "You can take the (Presidents') Trophy. I'll keep the (Stanley) Cup," the Penguins have also found themselves in battles with their intrastate neighbors to the east, dating all the way back to the "second six" expansion that brought both the Penguins and the Flyers into the league. Having grown up in the Pittsburgh area, Paul Steigerwald reflects on the history between the two, saying

> A lot of rivalries are born of playoff series, but, in the case of the Flyers, it's different because of the history between the two franchises. Going back to when the Penguins couldn't beat the Flyers in Philadelphia for 15 years, they became sort of the unbeatable foe, and, therefore, the most hated foe for years. Of course, they were a tough team. They were "bullies," so that brought out something in Penguins fans that made them really want to slay the dragon or eventually knock out the bully. As the Penguins got better and the Flyers faded back in the early 90s, that was a big deal. When the Penguins finally broke that streak in Philly in the late 80s and ended up winning the Stanley Cups in '91 and '92, things changed. The Penguins became the kings of the hill, and it really didn't matter if the Flyers were good or bad at that point. We had our own thing to be happy about.

With the "Broad Street Bullies" and Lemieux having their proverbial "star" on the rivalry wall, it didn't take long for Sidney Crosby to receive his own in the form of a bloody mouth. Steigerwald explains

> The rivalry was rekindled early in Sidney Crosby's career when Ken Hitch-cock accused Crosby of diving in a game in Philly when Derian Hatcher actually high sticked Crosby and dragged the stick along his mouth while he was down on the ice. He lost a tooth, and his mouth was clearly cut by

the stick. The fans got all over him. It was ridiculous. If you look at the video of that incident, it's clear that Crosby got a stick in the face from the big, bad Derian Hatcher. From that point on, Crosby became this villain in Philadelphia. He was the guy everybody booed as soon as he touched the puck. The fans were extremely abusive of him with signs. It became kind of a big deal in Philly to torture Sidney Crosby, and the Flyers did nothing to discourage it, by the way. A lot of the stuff that happens is not promulgated by the Flyers, but they certainly are accessories to it. Because of that, I think it's created another level of disdain between the two teams and these fan bases.

While "disdain" is a far cry from the "brotherly love" moniker the Quaker William Penn placed on the city in the late seventeenth century, it certainly fits the bill today. Steigerwald continues, "When we go to Philly, we've always been amazed at how they really like to sell violence. It's still part of their DNA even though their team isn't really noted for that anymore. It's still a part of who they are. When you go to Philadelphia, they like to run videos of things they've done over the years. The more violent side of the game, which is very appealing to some people, but, at the same time, for the visitors, it can be somewhat intimidating and infuriating."

With 12 straight playoff appearances, three Stanley Cups (and counting), and two Conn Smythes (and counting) under his belt, it's arguable none of that famous Philly intimidation has reached Sidney Crosby's skates, as the team captain takes that mouth bloodied so early in his career by Derian Hatcher's stick and uses it to—as Mike Lange would so famously say—"smile like a butcher's dog."

• 24 •

San Jose Sharks

$\mathcal{I}$n 1967, with the NHL doubling in size, the league conducted an experiment west of the Mississippi. The subjects of this "trial" were the St. Louis Blues, the Los Angeles Kings, and the California Seals, and the theme was environmental survival. Unlike the St. Louis Eagles of 30 years prior, the Blues proved the "alpha" of this experiment, advancing to the Stanley Cup Final in each of its first three seasons. The Los Angeles Kings, not exactly the success the Blues were, still advanced to the playoffs their first two years in the league. The "beta" of the group would have to be the California Seals, who, after more name changes than playoff appearances, finally left the Bay Area of Oakland, California, for Cleveland, Ohio, where they would become known as the Barons. Two seasons later, the Cleveland Barons and the Minnesota North Stars merged somewhat and continued in the "Land of 10,000 Lakes."

A little more than a decade later, George Gund, former owner of the Cleveland Barons, was looking to bring hockey back to the Bay Area. Instead of bringing the team full circle, the league awarded Gund and the city of San Jose an expansion franchise and settled for a three-quarters loop with the original team, shipping the North Stars south to Dallas, where they would understandably drop the "North" from their name. Going back to Gund's new sports baby, San Jose's expansion team would be known as the Sharks. The team, led by veteran defenseman and team captain Doug Wilson, took the ice in San Jose's neighboring Daly City at the Cow Palace. After nearly 25 years, NHL hockey was back in Northern California.

Now that Los Angeles wasn't the only West Coast team, the question, considering the short-lived days of the Seals, became, "Yeah, but for how long?" San Jose Sharks radio play-by-play broadcaster Dan Rusanowsky,

155

who's been with the team since their first game in 1991, discusses how this time around, hockey stayed in the Bay Area:

> The San Jose patriotism was a big part of why the team was embraced in the very beginning. That was a group of people who recognized San Jose had this great status in producing so much for our economy in the country. It was bigger than San Francisco. It sort of lived in San Francisco's shadow for a number of years. It's often forgotten San Jose is the largest of the three cities in the Bay Area. It's bigger than San Francisco and has a smaller city feel to it, which I think is part of its charm. When you talk about San Jose, there's a little provincialism in terms of patriotism between the individual communities, but there's also a lot of togetherness. Many people live here, and the vast majority of the sports public lives in the South Bay, as we call it.
>
> The center of economic activity in the United States is here in Silicon Valley, so there's a tremendous amount of support for professional sports. Having a team and a league that put its arms around the city and called it the San Jose Sharks, many people bought tickets just because of that. We call those people "South Bay Patriots." What's really interesting about that group is they were the ones who really fell in love with the team, the game, and the fact it was bringing business to downtown San Jose. This is a hockey city now. It became a hockey city—in part—because of all the patriotism. You can't call San Jose a nontraditional market anymore. It's a hockey market. These fans are among the most loyal in the NHL. They're the best.

With a supportive (and affluent) community filling the seats, it was time for the Sharks to take the ice on October 4, 1991, against the Vancouver Canucks.

EVEN SHARKS HAVE GROWING PAINS

Starting their franchise as a considerably isolated team—at least compared to those from the Upper Midwest and northeast regions—the Sharks' first two games were about as short of a distance as they would have to travel the rest of the year, playing the Vancouver Canucks in a "home and away" two-game set. With the team's first game being played on the road, not all Sharks fans in San Jose were privy to the goings on in British Columbia. Rusanowsky explains,

> The first game in the history of the franchise—one of the special memories for me—was a radio-only game in the Bay Area. It was not televised. The

second game was. The reason why the first one wasn't was because they had to pick between the two games. They could either televise the first game in the history of the team on the road and not do the game the next night or do the game the next night at the Cow Palace and return hockey to the Bay Area for the first time since 1976. The first game in the history of the team was very memorable for me because it was my first opportunity to do play-by-play in the NHL, but, also, it was a historic moment, and the only record we have of it in a broadcast sense from a Bay Area perspective is on the radio.

While the Internet and satellite radio/TV were not yet on the scene, the anxious South Bay Patriots and other Sharks fans experienced the irony of living in a place called "Silicon Valley" while their team went dark for the night. The first two contests against Vancouver reflected a majority of the team's showing their inaugural year, as they lost both games before recording the franchise's first-ever win, which came against the Calgary Flames on October 8.

After 80 games, the Sharks had logged only 17 wins, and they finished nearly 30 points behind the Western Conference's second worst team (Toronto). Instead of getting better with age, the team got worse, as, during their second season in the league, the Sharks would go 11–71–2, the most losses ever recorded by a team in a single season in NHL history. In fact, the team had four different occasions where they failed to record a win in the span of at least nine games, including an NHL-record 17 straight losses.

Amid all of this division cellar swimming, the San Jose faithful maintained their fan traditions. Rusanowsky notes,

> The first thing that developed here was the idea of doing the "chomp" whenever the Sharks went on the power play. That happened way back at the Cow Palace the very first year. They were looking for some sort of activity for when the team went on the power play. The people who were doing the game presentation at the time decided to play the theme to *Jaws* at that point, so everyone just started sticking their hands out and chomping them together. The mascot, S. J. Sharkie, is one of the most recognizable characters in all of sports, let alone the NHL, in terms of entertainment. Sharkie was born out of a Zamboni. We had a birthing ceremony out on the ice. The Zamboni came out and there was all this smoke, and out came S. J. Sharkie at the Cow Palace.

As entertaining as S. J. Sharkie has been throughout the years, one night his pregame antics went on just a little too long. Radio play-by-play broadcaster Ken Kal, whose Red Wings had somewhat of a playoff rivalry with the Sharks during their time together in the Western Conference, describes a bizarre memory of the San Jose mascot, saying,

> We were in San Jose one year, and S. J. Sharkie was going to make this grand entrance before the game. He was coming down from the rafters on a rope. He was going to come down, land on the ice, and get the crowd fired up. He comes down, and about 50 feet away from the ice, he gets stuck. He gets tangled up in the rope. So he's hanging there, and it delays the game. He was right above our goaltender, a little bit in front of the net. Scotty Bowman was a little cheesed off because it was delaying the game. They can't get this guy up, so the guy's hanging there, and he's all tied up. They don't know what they're going to do if they try hauling him up there and something happens with the wench, so they start bringing out these wrestling mats and putting them on the ice. Paul Woods and I are describing this on the air, saying, "Don't tell me they're going to cut the rope. The fall's going to kill this guy."
>
> Somebody smart figured out that's not a great idea, so they get the wench fixed and start pulling him up towards the rafters. It was like a Three Stooges movie because every time they pulled down, he was hitting his head on the girder. Two, three times. Bang, bang. I'm going, "This is unbelievable." Paul was joking around while Sharkie was dangling in the air and said something like, "Hook 'em, get a net on him, and throw him in the boat." Finally, they get the guy over onto the catwalk and the game starts. In the first intermission, our producer back at the station calls and says, "ESPN wants your call of what happened there to delay the game." I'm going, "Don't send it. The video says it all."

In the beginning, S. J. Sharkie wasn't the only "character" on the ice. Link Gaetz, a six-foot, 240-pound defenseman from Vancouver, was called up to San Jose from Kansas City for the team's inaugural season. While a car crash that nearly ended his life would cut his season in half, Gaetz certainly left his mark on San Jose Sharks lore for many years to come. Rusanowsky relates,

> Link was one of the best players on the team actually. He was certainly a good passer. He could shoot. He was big and strong, and nobody would mess around when he was on the ice because he was just so feared. The one memory we have of Link is at the Cow Palace when they played the Detroit Red Wings, and he had a legendary battle with Bob Probert. That's something people still talk about. He had a very interesting side to him. He was great around the kids. He would love being around children. They would follow him around, and he was a lovable guy to them, and then, when he was on the ice, he really was a terror. You combine that with

all of his incredible hockey-playing skills and all the stories that go with it, Link was one of the all-timers in that enforcer role. The whole idea of having a line brawl is not something anybody even looks to do anymore. Still, having a hard-checking, rugged player who can be a policemen when somebody tries to take liberties with you is something that hasn't really left the game. Link had 300-plus penalty minutes with the team in 48 games. The Linkster is right up there with really all the all-time enforcers of the game who played for this team.

Even with the enforcement of Gaetz striking fear into opposing players, the team's performance on the ice was in need of an overhaul. Perhaps all that was needed was a change of venue to bring these bottom-feeding Sharks back up to the surface to achieve playoff relevance.

WE'RE GONNA NEED A BIGGER ~~BOAT~~ TANK

In the first season at their new home, the SAP Center, the Sharks brought new meaning to the term *grand entrance*. Rusanowsky elaborates,

> When the arena opened in '93, they had Hollywood special effects people design this shark's head the guys would skate through. It was only supposed to be a temporary thing, but it got so unbelievably popular we just kept and maintained it. It was awesome then. It's awesome now. Even the players talk about how they get chills up and down their spines when they're skating through the shark's head to get onto the ice to the sound of the crowd and the intensity the Sharks fans have.

The intensity was certainly there during the team's first season at the SAP Center, as the Sharks won 22 more and, more importantly, lost 36 fewer games, en route to the their first-ever playoff appearance against the Detroit Red Wings. Two weeks later, the fans in Detroit—as well as the everyone in the NHL—were left in shock, as a team that had only managed 11 victories in 84 games the year before stole four out of seven against the Western Conference's top seed. Rusanowsky adds,

> The first playoff series against the Red Wings, game one was a victory in Detroit, but game seven was one where I almost couldn't believe it was happening. The Red Wings were the best team in the league by far. The Sharks had missed the playoffs the year before by a large margin. They had the greatest single-season turnaround in the history of the league to that point to get into the playoffs. It was a really topsy-turvy year.

San Jose's "Cinderella story" would end in game seven of the following round against the Toronto Maple Leafs, but Sharks fans did not return home unsatisfied. Rusanowsky continues,

> The first couple of years at the Cow Palace, it was like welcoming a new baby into the family almost. Everybody wants to crowd around and see the baby, but they don't expect the baby's going to be able to walk and talk very much. Then we had the brand new building, and it was another honeymoon period. The fact that the Sharks chose to time their history in order to beat Detroit that particular year, that really solidified the franchise in so many ways. Seeing guys like Igor Larionov, Sergei Makarov, Artūrs Irbe, and Jamie Baker be such a huge part of history. It was like a coming out party for the city of San Jose in terms of its place in the major-league sports world and in the major-league city world really.

SCARLET BILLOWS STARTING TO SPREAD

In the 23 seasons since the Sharks moved into the SAP Center, the team has failed to qualify for the postseason only four times. Dating back to the first-round upset in the 1994 playoffs, the Sharks and Red Wings faced off against one another five different times before Detroit switched conferences to start the 2013–2014 season. In 1995, following their first-round upset the previous season, the Red Wings exacted their revenge in the form of a four-game sweep of the Sharks, en route to an appearance in the Stanley Cup Final. The teams took a 12-year furlough from one another and began other rivalries—Detroit with Colorado and San Jose with St. Louis—before resuming their postseason dance in 2007. The Red Wings again came out on top, mounting a deeper playoff run, but it would be the last time Detroit would get the better of the Sharks in the postseason. The two squared off one final time past game 82 in 2011, with the Red Wings overcoming an 0–3 series deficit before finally conceding to the Sharks in game seven. But it was the Western Conference Semifinals of the year before that had Rusanowsky on point for what he considers one of the most memorable games of his career:

> It was a very pressure-filled situation in the Stanley Cup Playoffs. It was round number two in an overtime game against the Detroit Red Wings. The Sharks ended up beating the Red Wings 4–3 on May 4, 2010. It was a quintessential Joe Thornton–Patrick Marleau moment. They came up ice on the turnover. Joe Thornton ended up passing the puck perfectly to Patrick Marleau and Patrick scored the game winner. That was game number three. The Sharks ended up winning the series against the Red Wings in

five games to advance to the Conference Finals. That, to me, was a really magical moment in calling the action of the San Jose Sharks, feeling the emotion and getting the right words out. I got the call right, and it just felt really great.

Where the Sharks left off with Detroit, they picked up with their Southern California counterpart, the Los Angeles Kings. Over a six-year span, San Jose and Los Angeles have faced off four times in the postseason. With the first meeting going in favor of the Sharks, en route to their second straight Conference Finals appearance in 2011, the Kings beat San Jose in back-to-back playoffs (2012–2014), including a 2014 postseason in which Los Angeles overcame a 0–3 deficit as the sixth seed to upset the Sharks, on their way to their second Stanley Cup championship in three years. San Jose currently has the "last laugh" between the two, having ousted the Kings in the opening round of the 2016 playoffs on their way to the team's first-ever trip to the Stanley Cup Final. Needless to say, the rivalry is very much alive between these "Golden State" participants. Rusanowsky notes,

> It falls right into line in that sense with the geographical rivalries other sports have. The biggest one is Los Angeles, and that would be two teams: Anaheim and the L.A. Kings. You hear "Beat L.A." chants the moment the puck is dropped when the Kings are playing. They don't chant that when they play Anaheim, but there certainly is a lot of dislike for the Ducks. It's part of the rivalry between the Northern and Southern California regions. We've got a huge rivalry in California, and there's a lot of pride in how much hockey has grown here.

With team captain Joe Pavelski leading the way, as well as veterans Joel Ward and Paul Martin and playoff heroes Joe Thornton and Patrick Marleau, the Sharks are looking to ship Lord Stanley's Cup north up the California 101, giving Silicon Valley a taste of silver alloy and taking the South Bay Patriot fans on their "third honeymoon."

· 25 ·

St. Louis Blues

$\mathcal{I}$n 1934, with the original Ottawa Senators attempting to stay afloat financially by any means possible, the NHL played the role of strict parent, doling out some tough love and blocking a team merger with the New York Americans, leaving the franchise to fend for itself in a league where every team but Ottawa seemed to be faring well. Eventually, the Americans folded as a team, and the Senators, despite reservations throughout the league, were sold to St. Louis to become the Eagles. With teams dropping like flies due to the financial burdens of the postwar economy and the Great Depression, the league's brightest moment didn't come when they placed the Blues in the Canadian Division rather than the American Division of the NHL.

Rather than traveling 300 miles to play a would-be division rival Chicago Blackhawks team, the Eagles journeyed an extra 500 miles to play the Toronto Maple Leafs and, on just as many occasions, an extra 800 miles to face the Canadiens. The math didn't add up and neither did having a team in the "Gateway to the West," so the Eagles, much like their would-have-been teammates, the New York Americans, folded as a franchise after just one year in St. Louis. Professional hockey at its highest level would not return to the "Show Me State" for another 32 years. With the league's first expansion in 1967 bringing teams as far west as Los Angeles (Kings) and Oakland (Seals), the city of St. Louis was again awarded an NHL franchise, only this time the team's traveling secretary wasn't the most overworked person in professional sports.

VICE PRESIDENTS AND SILVER
MEDALISTS RIGHT OUT THE GATES

Usually when an expansion team comes to town, their results in the stand-ings leave much to be desired, but the St. Louis Blues were a different story during their inaugural 1967–1968 season. Finishing third in the NHL West Division, the Blues, led by captain and eventual New York Islanders Hall of Fame builder Al Arbour, as well as Red Berenson, Gerry Melnyk, and goal-tender Glenn Hall, advanced past Philadelphia and fellow league newcomer the Minnesota North Stars before being swept by the Montreal Canadiens in the Stanley Cup Final. With the exception of a different second-round op-ponent in the Los Angeles Kings, St. Louis' second season in the league must have felt like hockey déjà vu, as the team was again swept by the Montreal Canadiens in the Cup Final.

"Third time's the charm" would not be a phrase used in the springtime of the team's third season in the league, as the Blues, although not facing the Canadiens this time, were again swept in the Stanley Cup Final. Cur-rent Blues TV broadcaster John Kelly, whose father and legendary hockey broadcaster Dan Kelly was in the booth for the Blues one year into their existence, looks back on being in the building the evening the team's 1969–1970 season came to a close, one of the most historic nights in league history:

> I was there the night of the Stanley Cup Final in 1970, when Jacques Plante got hit in the mask in game one and was carted off on a stretcher. He said the mask saved his life. It was a big part of hockey history because, at that point, there were still goalies who, believe it or not, didn't wear masks. He came out of the game, and Glenn Hall came in and played the rest of that series. Glenn Hall was in goal in game four when Bobby Orr scored that historic goal to win the Bruins their Stanley Cup championship in 1970. I was in the arena that night when it happened.

While it's debatable Orr never returned to the ice and just kept "flying" out of St. Louis Arena on the heels of his monumental goal, the "Spirit of St. Louis" grounded itself indefinitely, as the team, to this day, has yet to return to the Stanley Cup Final, let alone hoist their own cup.

While failing to escort the Stanley Cup through the Gateway Arch or along the trail blazed by Lewis and Clark, the Blues certainly made the quick impression on St. Louis fans their predecessors couldn't, making their residence in the "Gateway City" a much longer-lasting one than the Eagles of 1934–1935. Kelly explains,

> Early on in the Blues' existence, the team, in a way, took a city that didn't really have a big tradition with hockey—certainly no tradition with the NHL—by storm. In the early years, it was the place to be. The men wore suits, and the ladies wore dresses. I remember from my early days at the arena whenever the Blues came on the ice, whether it was to start the game or after the first or second period, regardless of the score, the fans got on their feet and gave them a standing ovation. That continues today. Whenever the Blues come on the ice, there's a standing ovation. Also, early on, whenever the Blues would score a goal, all 18,000 fans would sing "When the Saints Go Marching In." Those were some of the early traditions I remember vividly from their first 10 years or so.

The vice president, silver medalist, and first runner-up status of the Blues didn't just apply to their standings in the NHL, but to their place in their hometown as well. Having won 11 World Series championships, with the eighth coming just as the Blues were setting up shop, the St. Louis Cardinals have always dominated the sports landscape in the "Lou"; however, the Blues have given their baseball counterparts a run for their money in the 49 seasons the two have shared mayors. Kelly notes,

> Over the years, the Blues, like the Cardinals, have become part of the fabric of St. Louis. Obviously, the Cardinals have been and always will be number one—this is always going to be a great baseball town—but make no mistake, hockey is a big part of this city. The Blues have had some ups and downs in their existence quite honestly. Every team has some good years and bad years. Certainly the Blues have had more good than bad. They almost left a couple of times when owners ran out of money or wanted to move the team, but there has always been a real die hard core of fans that have supported this team. The loyalty they have shown over the years is tremendous, and whenever they've had a decent to really good team, they almost pack the house every single night. That's a big reason the team is successful and still in St. Louis.

PUTTING THE "BLUES" IN BLUE COLLAR

The *Spirit of St. Louis* was not just a famous plane. Whether it be in the form of Cardinal ushers opening "old" Busch Stadium's gates to championship-starved and fulfilled Red Sox fans without tickets so they could celebrate with their team in 2004, or a simple autographed scorecard given to a young fan by the late Jack Buck, St. Louis extends its hospitality not only via its personnel, but also through the fans. Speaking on the rapport Blues players have with their fans, Kelly comments,

> St. Louis is a blue-collar town by and large, and, over the years, I think the fans have really embraced the blue-collar player, perhaps more than the slick guy who's going to make the fancy passes. I'm talking about people like the Plager brothers back in the early years. The Brian Sutters of the world. Players they have today like T. J. Oshie, who's a hard-working kind of guy who brings it every single night. Maybe that personality of the team is a mirror image of the way the city is. It's blue collar, and they really appreciate their players, especially the guys who dig in the trenches and maybe fight and things like that. The guys the fans have really taken to over the years are those types of players.

Among the first of these blue-collar players in St. Louis Blues history was Bob Gassoff, who, much like the Carlsons, who inspired the Hansons in George Roy Hill's 1977 film *Slap Shot*, had a couple of tough brothers of his own. Columbus Blue Jackets TV play-by-play broadcaster Jeff Rimer, who did pregame and postgame for the Montreal Canadiens during Gassoff's short career with the Blues, describes the "brotherly love" carried out by Bob and his two brothers, Brad and Ken, on the junior syndicate:

> Bob Gassoff was a high draft pick for the St. Louis Blues and had two brothers. The Gassoffs were three tough brothers. I recall one game back in Junior, playing for Calgary, they had to stop the game and turn the lights out because the Gassoffs—all three of them—fought Danny Gare. They were as tough as anybody. There was nobody more feared than Gassoff. He was one tough player.

Tragically, Bob was killed in a motorcycle accident at the age of 24. His number "3" was immediately retired by the team.

NO SHORTAGE OF NICKNAMES HERE

In a town that has branded its most beloved baseball players with such famous nicknames as "Stan the man," the "Machine," and the "Wizard of Oz," the same has been extended to those on the ice. Brett Hull, the Blues' all-time leading goal scorer and son of Bobby "The Golden Jet" Hull, was dubbed the "Golden Brett" as a tribute to both his father and his contribution to the team before going to the Dallas Stars just in time to win his first of two career Stanley Cups. While the "Golden Brett" was skating to the tune of 527 goals in a Blues uniform, he had the support of known league tough guys Kelly Chase and the "Twister," Tony Twist, who, individually and collectively, came to their superstar's aid in 10 of his 11 seasons with St. Louis.

With nearly two-thirds of their combined 3,138 career penalty infraction minutes going to Kelly Chase, the "Twister" was still a noteworthy presence, especially in the handful of seasons during which the two shared the ice in St. Louis. Former NHL defenseman and Florida Panthers radio play-by-play broadcaster Randy Moller, who played against the tandem during his career, describes Twist and Chase, saying, "Everybody had tough guys on their team. Some teams had two, and you don't see that anymore. You had the 'Twister' in St. Louis. With Tony Twist and Kelly Chase, Lord help us all."

THE ST. LOUIS BLUES TODAY

While the Gassoffs, Hulls, Chases, Twists, and Arbours have their place in St. Louis Blues history, the current team is looking to raise that elusive championship banner to the Scottrade Center's rafters. While first-round exits have been the trend three of the past five seasons (2012–2017), the Blues, in 2014, were able to give the defending champion Chicago Blackhawks a brief Cinderella wake-up call to open the postseason. John Kelly recalls,

> Last year's first game of the playoffs against Chicago, the Blues are obviously playing their number-one rival, who were the defending Stanley Cup champions. The Blues had lost their last six games of the regular season and won game one in triple overtime. It was the longest game in Blues history. Alex Steen scored the game-winning goal. As far as games I have broadcast for the Blues, I would say that would have to be number one.

The Blackhawks won four of the next five games to advance, but not without a lesson in "six straight losses in the regular season translates into *nothing* going into the postseason." Gathering 109 points the following season, the Blues took the Western Conference Central Division but once again fell in the opening round, this time to the Minnesota Wild. The team would exact their revenge on Minnesota the following preseason. Not content with a president's trophy for regular-season greatness or the silver medal, runner-up status that defined the team at the onset of its existence, today's Blues, led by Vladimir Tarasenko, Alex Steen, Paul Stastny, and Jay Bouwmeester, carry the franchise torch in the hopes of finally showing the Show Me State a Stanley Cup title.

· 26 ·

Tampa Bay Lightning

$\mathcal{W}$ith baseball's Grapefruit League spring training being held in the area as far back as 1913, one may find it astonishing that the NHL landed in the city of Tampa, Florida, several years before Major League Baseball. Jumping through the hoops necessary to gather the attention of baseball's top brass, Tampa built the Florida Suncoast Dome (Thunderdome/Tropicana Field) in 1990, in the hopes of either getting such teams as the Chicago White Sox, the Seattle Mariners, or the San Francisco Giants to relocate or being awarded a franchise during the league's next expansion. With Miami's H. Wayne Huizenga spoiling the party in 1993 and the Florida Marlins getting the nod for baseball expansion, the Florida Suncoast Dome sat for a year on the shores of St. Petersburg like the wedding cake of a runaway bride.

A year after the Arena League Football's Tampa Bay Storm started paying the building's utility bills through their home-game attendance, the NHL awarded the city of Tampa its second major sports franchise, the Lightning. Considering the tropical shores of the Atlantic aren't as freezable as the ponds of the Upper Midwest and Canada, native Central Floridians required a bit of a tutorial on the traditions of hockey. Tampa Bay Lightning television play-by-play broadcaster Rick Peckham, who came to the team a few years after their inaugural season, retells the legend of the team's first-ever game at Tampa's Expo Hall against the Chicago Blackhawks:

> When they beat the Blackhawks, 7–3, Chris Kontos scored four goals in the first game of the history of the franchise. Phil Esposito was the team president and general manager. He had told the ushers, "Keep an eye on the crowd. We don't want people throwing stuff out on the ice." They forgot about the hat tricks. Some fans from up north, when Kontos scored his third goal, were throwing hats out on the ice, and the ushers were trying to throw these

people out because they didn't understand the tradition. Right from the start, it was crazy, and it's been a crazy experience for a lot of people here who have followed this team from day one. There's still a lot of them out there who at least claim they were at that first game.

After a year of playing in the crowded confines of Expo Hall, the Lightning shot over the Howard Franklin Bridge to set up shop for the next three years in a venue never intended for professional hockey. While neither Expo Hall nor the Florida Suncoast Dome were the most ideal buildings for an average NHL fan's experience, the budding team was able to use them to gather a legion of fans who would continue to support their new "friends." Peckham discusses the team's original stomping grounds, saying,

> The team played its first year at Expo Hall. I was in there once as a Hartford broadcaster and a visitor. Cozy would not describe the confines there. It was really too small. They really only got away with putting the team in there because they had nowhere else to put it at that point. The press box was right over the ice. They had a big tent that was outside the building. It was a party tent where certain fans, based on the tickets they had bought, could go in. Players would go in there. It was a great way for the players to get used to the fans and the sponsors, and that would pay off later when they first made the playoffs in 1996.
>
> At Tropicana Field, they brought that experience in. They got really creative and came up with some great concepts in that building. You could generally call the whole thing "Fan Land," which featured a lot of stuff you now see outside arenas to create an atmosphere before the game. Most of that started from Fan Land. It was just something to entertain fans before games in this vast baseball stadium that they were playing their hockey games in for three seasons. They actually came up with a $99 season ticket for the upper-deck seats. Obviously you wouldn't have the greatest view of the ice, but you would be in the building, and if you checked the attendance figures from those years, they were averaging 22,000 and one time held the indoor record for hockey attendance during the '96 playoffs. It was something like 28,000. They jammed them in there, and the fans went crazy. They really had a great grassroots program at that point, where the players and the fans got to know each other, and they started to enjoy success. Things really exploded at that point, and it was because of that particular experience of the fans of getting to know these guys up close. It really helped to sell the sport here.

THE LIGHTNING'S NEW DOWNTOWN DIGS

Considering the fact that the Florida Suncoast Dome/Tropicana Field is arguably not even suitable for baseball—the sport for which it was built—it was only a matter of time before the team realized it wasn't suitable for hockey either. Peckham describes the unique surroundings of his first year with the team during the 1995–1996 season:

> That was the final year they were at Tropicana Field. They called it the "Thunderdome" because the Rays had not come into existence yet. From the press box area, the rink would start from 30 feet in front of the third-base dugout, so you'd have one team coming out from the dugout. They had the rubberized walkways that would come out on the ice. Behind shortstop, in short left field, would be a long grandstand not unlike what you would see at the Carrier Dome in Syracuse when they set that up for basketball. The other end of the rink was out in short right field. That was where the ice surface was. It went from the third base dugout along the first-base line. Our press box was up in the club section, so it was almost like a football-type press box to call a hockey game. You were way too far from the ice, and, somehow, you got through it.

While $99 season tickets seem appealing for the 22,000-plus in attendance, dugout steps are built for spikes, not blades, and, for broadcasters, a puck is a lot smaller than a football. Something had to give to once again make it a hockey experience for everyone in Tampa. In the fall of 1996, the Lightning took the ice the old-fashioned way in their new home, the (then-named) Ice Palace. With the skip back over the bridge from "St. Pete" to the "Big Guava," the Lightning, being back in the "lightning capital of the world," manifested their team name in a big way. Peckham notes,

> The tesla coils, which go off after goals and when the team comes on for warm-ups, are located in opposite corners of the arena and shoot out lightning bolts that are about 15 to 20 feet in length. That's something that's very unique and obviously unique to the nickname of the team.

The tesla coils aren't the only thing shooting electricity through Amelie Arena these days, as the Lightning, specifically team owner Jeffrey Vinik, have taken great measures to make sure Tampa Bay fans have something to talk about on their tollway-filled drive home. Peckham adds,

> This current ownership group, with Jeff Vinik in charge, has put millions of dollars into this building and has repeatedly enhanced the fan experience. Just our overall game production was really on display this year in the playoffs (2015). These folks had to come up with a different production of videos and music just to make it all work. They put on a whole show inside the building, which I thought was brilliantly done. Compared with other buildings we went to in the playoffs, we heard from fans of other cities, "I wish we had this here in New York" and so forth. Our game production

is second to none. I really think that makes the atmosphere here unique, as well as things like the party deck upstairs. I can't think of more than one or two home games where the weather was so cold and inclement you couldn't go on the upstairs patio outside the arena and enjoy a great view of downtown. Right in the middle of hockey season, you're enjoying a beer outside. That's pretty unique. There's some really unique facets of Amelie Arena and the whole fan experience here.

While Mr. Vinik's Bud Light Party Deck didn't come until after he took over as team owner in 2010, it's unlikely Lightning fans would have been there or anywhere other than in their ticketed seats when the team skated to their first Stanley Cup in the summer of 2004.

THIS TIME, THE LIGHTNING DOUSED THE FLAME

In the 11 seasons prior to the 2003–2004 slate, the Lightning only made the playoffs twice, and in only one of those postseasons did they make it past the first round. The 2003–2004 team, led by their captain and veteran of 21 seasons, Dave Andreychuk, as well as Martin St. Louis, Cory Stillman, Brad Richards, and goaltender Nikolai Khabibulin, finished first in the Southeast Division, with 106 team points. With the Calgary Flames starring in the "Cinderella Story" in the Western Conference playoff bracket, the first two rounds on the Eastern Conference side of things went as planned for the Lightning, as the team only lost once in its first two series against the New York Islanders and the Montreal Canadiens. Peckham, before turning his TV play-by-play duties over to the national broadcasts, was able to call what he considers his most memorable game with the Lightning. Says Peckham,

> The last game I did for that series in Montreal was game three. The Lightning ended up sweeping the Canadiens, but they had to come from behind and had just an almost impossible goal scored by Vinny Lecavalier in the closing moments of regulation, where he reaches between his legs with his hockey stick and tips the shot past José Théodore to tie the game with about 16 seconds to go. Then they go into overtime, and Brad Richards carries the puck behind the net. Théodore overcommits, and Richards sees that and fires it off Theodore into the net for the game-winning goal. It was just such a tremendous atmosphere in the Bell Centre and such a tremendous victory for the Lightning, being able to come from behind in the waning moments of regulation as dramatically and skillfully as they did. Lecavalier with that magical tip and Richards with his play off the goaltender typified what a smart player he was. I'd have to say that was my favorite game in Lightning history for me to broadcast.

The Lightning's first challenge during that 2004 Stanley Cup run came against the Philadelphia Flyers, winner of the Atlantic Division, as the teams went the full seven in an "I win, then you win, then I win" series. Luckily for the Lightning, they had the first, as well as the last, dance in the series and advanced to face the unlikeliest of finals opponents in the Calgary Flames. Coming into the playoffs as the seventh seed, the Flames stormed through the Western Conference's three division champs, the Vancouver Canucks, the Detroit Red Wings, and the San Jose Sharks, stunning the hockey world and bringing the team back to the Cup Final for the first time since winning it all in 1989. Just like in the Lightning's Eastern Conference Finals matchup, the first three games of the Cup Final were a "your turn, my turn" affair, but the Lightning, although losing game three, got a little morale boost courtesy of team center Vincent Lecavalier. Peckham relates,

> The fight Lecavalier had in '04 with Jerome Iginla was pretty significant. He was a pretty good fighter. I don't think a lot of people, unless they remember his early days, would be aware of that. I know from talking with people like Dave Andreychuk, they felt like it was a very significant fight where they knew he was fully engaged in the series. They could really count on him in terms of being there for the other guys. I think they were really fired up by how he took the initiative in that fight. The Lightning that won the cup really wasn't as overly tough team, but certainly with some of the other guys like André Roy and Chris Dingman chipping in, it provided the toughness there.

Tampa Bay won three of the next four games, including a double-overtime, must-win game six in Calgary to force a game seven back home at Amalie Arena, where the Lightning, thanks to two goals by Ruslan Fedotenko, closed out the Flames' improbable run to win the franchise's first and only Stanley Cup. The Lightning paraded the Stanley Cup around a year longer than is customary for league champions, as the team, as well as the rest of the league, was locked out for the entire 2004–2005 season.

THE 2014–2015 LIGHTNING VERSUS
THE HISTORY OF THE LEAGUE

Following their Stanley Cup championship, the closest the team would come to sniffing a Stanley Cup Final appearance was a seven-game Conference Finals loss to the eventual league champion Boston Bruins in 2011; however, in 2014–2015, the Lightning, headed by team captain and leading scorer Steven Stamkos, followed a playoff road taken by no other team in NHL history.

Back when the NHL was just six teams, the playoffs lasted only two rounds. Sure, they were facing two "original six" teams, but that's because there was no one else. In the spring of 2015, the Tampa Bay Lightning faced four of the league's original six, something that had never occurred in playoff history. Peckham describes the team's march through the postseason:

> It was very cool and was a feather in the cap of both the Lightning and a lot of teams that have been in southern and nontraditional markets. The Dallas's, Florida's, Carolina's. The Lightning were carrying the banner for some of these nontraditional places in taking on Detroit, Montreal, and the New York Rangers, and beating all of them and almost beating the Blackhawks. That was very special. Those fans who were able to come down to some games, it opened up a lot of eyes in terms of how intense the interest in the team and hockey is in this area. I think it gets taken for granted by a lot by fans up north. The TV ratings were terrific, even though Tampa Bay, St. Pete, and Clearwater are not that big of a TV market. The numbers were very strong. I think it opened up a lot of eyes around the country and in North America—Canada especially—that hockey in the state of Florida is for real in terms of being a good, solid hockey market.

Another factor bringing the Tampa Bay Lightning to the forefront of NHL viewership—gathering the attention of everyone in Chicago and elsewhere—was found in the palm of practically every hockey fan attending a game. Peckham continues,

> The Lightning, with this current run, benefitted so much through the Internet and the explosion of social media. They didn't have watch parties back in '04. They had wildly successful watch parties for this one. For home games, we're out in the plaza, so we were out there when these 15,000 fans were celebrating, watching the game shown on the side of the parking garage across from the plaza and cheering on the team. You had 22,700-something people inside the building, and you had another 10 to 15,000 outside. It was just tremendous. Everybody's been on board. We expect this is a team that's going to contend for the cup for a number of years, so it's only going to keep growing.

In addition to superstar Steven Stamkos, the Lightning had some interesting players and lines on their 2014–2015 team, including the line nicknamed by team coach Jon Cooper. Tyler Johnson, Ondřej Palát, and Nikita Kucherov, otherwise known as the "triplets," accounted for more than a third of the team's scoring during the 2015 postseason. Coupled with Stamkos, Alex Killorn, and Valtteri Filppula, the "triplets" had their fair share of the blame for the Amelia Arena power bill from April to June, lighting up the tesla coils on a continual basis before yielding to the highly defensive Chicago Blackhawks in the Cup Final. While Tampa Bay came up short against the Blackhawks dynasty, the offense of this Lightning team suggests there may be a few more watch parties in the years to come. Peckham states,

> It's not a team that's built around the trap. It's built around a very explosive, skill-based team, and it's a lot of fun to cover these guys. They are so young, and the contract situation looks pretty strong right now for these guys to be together for a few years. Hopefully, they can keep them together the way Chicago has managed to keep that group of seven together for all of their cups and long playoff runs. Adding it up, it was 20 playoff series in seven years. An average year, you go to the Conference Finals. It's ridiculous. That's what you shoot for, and hopefully this is a start for Tampa Bay.

With a youthful captain, a band of triplets, and an up and coming goal tender like Andrei Vasilevskiy, the Lightning are looking to defy all logic and "strike twice" in the same place.

· 27 ·

Toronto Maple Leafs

$\mathcal{B}$efore there was the NHL, there was the NHA (National Hockey Association) and Eddie Livingstone, and before there was a Maple Leaf in Toronto, there was a "Blueshirt." Livingstone, owner of the NHA's Toronto Blueshirts, was apparently enough of a pain to coexist with on a professional level that those around him went as far as forming a new league just to edge him out, creating the NHL. Although the title of "original" NHL team is worn by the Montreal Canadiens, someone had to step in and dance with the club during the league finals in March 1918.

The Toronto Arenas, consisting mostly of the same Blueshirt players from the NHA, split the NHL Final series, 1–1, with Montreal but took home the NHL's first-ever title by scoring the most goals in the two games. At the time, the NHL wasn't the only league, so winning a Stanley Cup required one more step. The NHL's representing champion then had to face the PCHA's (Pacific Coast Hockey Association) champion to decide who took home the cup. Toronto, fresh off their victory over Montreal, beat the Vancouver Millionaires in a best-of-five series and officially gave the city of Toronto its Stanley Cup title. As glorious as the action was on the ice for Toronto, the proceedings off the ice would make the Arenas' celebration short-lived.

Livingstone, playing the role of vengeful millionaire, sued both the league and the Toronto Arenas franchise, costing the team so much in lawyer fees they had to sell off several of their players. Outmanned, the Arenas finished the 1918–1919 season 5–13 and went on to change their name to the St. Patricks. Seven seasons and another Stanley Cup later, the club, with the threat of being relocated to nearby Philadelphia, was purchased by the recent builder of the New York Rangers, Conn Smythe, who promptly changed the team name to Maple Leafs and set them on a course the likes of which may never be seen again in "Hogtown." Overseeing, managing, and, for a brief period, even coaching Toronto in 35 seasons, Smythe led the charge of the Maple Leafs to the tune of eight Stanley Cup titles, including six during a 10-year period. Even without Smythe running the show, the Leafs won three of the following five league championships. The third of these would be the last, as Toronto, nearly 50 years later, still awaits its return to hockey's summit.

THE HOCKEY CAPITAL OF THE WORLD?

While Montreal was pronounced the birthplace of modern hockey in 2002, referencing a game that took place on March 3, 1875, Toronto has its own arguments for being considered the hockey capital of the world, the first of these being that Toronto is home to the Hockey Hall of Fame. Toronto Maple Leafs radio broadcaster Joe Bowen, who has been with the team since 1982, provides his own argument on the matter:

> I feel Toronto is the center of the hockey universe. It's printed that way in a number of publications. Toronto is the largest, single most important hockey market—certainly in North America—and possibly the world. More kids play hockey in Toronto than anywhere else. More families are involved in the sport than anywhere else, and, to that end, the Maple Leafs have been their team. It's also a situation where there are so many kids involved in the sport, you see jerseys of all kinds of teams. There are a lot of Pittsburgh Penguin fans in Toronto because the kids have gravitated to Sidney Crosby. There are Canadian players who are playing elsewhere, like Steven Stamkos. There are a lot of Steven Stamkos fans in Toronto, and their boy is playing for Tampa Bay. It's an interesting situation how it all works out. Because of the amount of the sport of hockey that's inside the city of Toronto, it really opens up a lot of windows and a lot of doors.

Growing up in Ontario, Bowen's birth predated the team's last Stanley Cup by 16 years, and, some 33 years after his first day on the job, the 1966–1967 banner is the most recent one hanging from the Air Canada Centre's rafters. Considering the team's playoff futility of nearly a half-century, Bowen describes the typical Maple Leaf fan's experience:

> Traditions are a tough thing as far as hockey is concerned. If there's a tradition for the Maple Leafs, I guess it's they haven't won a cup since '67, so the tradition may not be a very good one. The tradition of the Leaf crowd and the Leaf games at home has been kind of a stoic, reactionary crowd more than a proactive crowd. Back in the days of Conn Smythe, you had

to wear a shirt, tie, and a hat like you were dressed up to go to the opera. I think that tradition has carried on to some extent because most of the people who buy tickets for Maple Leaf games are corporations or well-to-do, unlike other areas where you go to a game and bring your family for $100 to get in the door. The tradition is more of a reactionary crowd that is not as boisterous as other areas. It's a crowd that has to be entertained in order to get involved in the actual game itself.

While Mr. Bowen's words conjure up an image of the film *Gladiator* and Russell Crowe throwing swords into the crowd, shouting, "Are you not entertained?" there was no need for such a question during the Maple Leafs' run to the 1993 Clarence Campbell Conference Finals, the most noise they had made since winning it all in 1967.

LIFTING THE ALBATROSS

The New York Yankees had George Steinbrenner, the Oakland Raiders had Al Davis, and the Los Angeles Clippers had Donald Sterling, but perhaps the team owner in major sports who trumps all these figures—as far as villainy goes—was Maple Leafs owner Harold Ballard. Known for his abstinence, both in tax-paying and rule-keeping, Ballard tormented his own players as much as he did the NHL's top brass, making moves that singled out and alienated players and team captains beloved by the fans. The Maple Leafs, under Ballard's ownership, qualified for the postseason almost every year but rarely made it past the first round. Having burned enough bridges to cross Lake Ontario, Ballard passed away in 1990, and the proverbial albatross on the Maple Leafs' back was tossed overboard, ushering in new light and hope for Toronto fans in the form of new team CEO, president, and general manager Cliff Fletcher.

A year after arriving from Calgary, where he had helped lead the Flames to the 1989 Stanley Cup championship, Fletcher made a deal with his former team that likely left Ballard's corpse doing somersaults. Bowen explains,

I've been here since '82. We've gone through some ups and downs like most franchises. When I arrived, Harold Ballard owned the team, and there really wasn't an awful amount of outlook as far as success was concerned. In 1993, Doug Gilmour had been traded to Toronto by the Calgary Flames by Cliff Fletcher's hand, and it was a magical ride with that team.

Scoring 127 points, Doug Gilmour led the team to a 14-win improvement from their previous season, setting a date with the Detroit Red Wings—their original six rival—for the opening round of the 1993 playoffs. Losing the first two games on the road, the Leafs rebounded with three straight wins, putting Detroit on the brink of elimination. A home loss to the Wings in game six set up a decisive game seven, which, fittingly, went into overtime. Regarded as his most memorable game in the Toronto broadcast booth, Bowen recalls the series decider:

> The game in Detroit against the Red Wings in game seven of the opening-round playoff series, it went to overtime, and Nicky (Nikolai) Borschevsky tipped in a shot by Bob Rouse from the point and, because of where I had to sit in the press box at Joe Louis Arena—which was closer to that end of the rink—I could see that it had just ever so slightly been touched by the stick of Borschevsky to deflect it. When you get the opportunity to call an enormous goal like that—an overtime goal—you hope you get it right. I immediately called Nicky Borschevsky, and, as it turns out, it was accurate and the Leafs went on to play 21 playoff games in 42 nights that year.

Unfortunately for the Leafs, their comeback story came to a halt against Wayne Gretzky and the Los Angeles Kings, when Gretzky's hat trick in the Leafs' third game seven of the 1993 playoffs propelled the Kings to their first-ever Stanley Cup Final.

TIE "YOU TOUCH ME, YOU GO ME" DOMI

As much as Harold Ballard enjoyed trading away star players to keep his insolent captains in line, not even he would have dared to issue walking papers to one of the game's all-time most feared players, Tie Domi. Racking up 3,515 penalty infraction minutes (PIM) in his career—good for third most all time—the right winger played 12 of his 16 seasons in front of the Toronto faithful. With three different seasons of more than 300 PIMs, it didn't take a guidance counselor or career fair for Domi to realize his niche in the NHL. Current Winnipeg Jets and former Toronto Maple Leafs radio play-by-play broadcaster Dennis Beyak describes Domi's reputation:

> It didn't matter if you were 6-foot-6, if he felt it was going to change the way the game was going or if somebody was taking advantage of his teammates, he answered the bell. He had the ability to get bigger guys into what we used to call the "spin cycle." He'd get you going around and around, and would start throwing that left hand. Pound for pound, he's probably as tough as anybody in the National Hockey League. Tie was one of those guys who really had an idea of when to do it and when not to do it. The one he got in trouble for was the one with Niedermayer. That got him into hot water.

The incident that landed Domi in "hot water" with Scott Niedermayer occurred in game four of the 2001 Eastern Conference Semifinals against the New Jersey Devils, when Domi elbowed Niedermayer away from the play, bringing the defenseman to the ice and forcing him to be carried out on a stretcher. The right winger was suspended for the remainder of the playoffs and the first eight games of the following season. Niedermayer wasn't the only one in Domi's warpath diring the Ontarian's career, which included scuffles with Bob Probert, Matthew Barnaby, Ken Baumgartner, Craig Berube, Donald Brashear, Patrick Côté, Gord Donnelly, Stu Grimson, Rob Ray, Peter Worrell, and, on the night of March 29, 2001, Philadelphia Flyers fan Chris Falcone.

Making probably every highlight reel in the country's nightly news sportscasts, Falcone got a little more than his price of admission when he leaned over the Wells Fargo Center's penalty-box glass with Domi serving his time inside. Los Angeles Kings Hall of Fame broadcaster Bob Miller recalls,

> What I've seen with Tie is on highlights. He was in the penalty box and squirted the water bottle up at some fan hanging over. The guy was ripping him all night long, and he fell into the penalty box and Tie just started hammering him. A lot of fans are really brave with that glass in front of them.

Falcone received a police citation, and Domi got a refill.

Having played on the same ice as Domi during his career, Florida Panthers radio play-by-play broadcaster Randy Moller notes,

> I played in an era which I think is the toughest era of the NHL as far as toughness. Each team with their tough guy. The Bob Proberts and Joey Kocurs of the Detroit Red Wings. The Daryl Stanleys and Craig Coxes of the Vancouver Canucks. Every team. I played with Gord Donnelly and Jimmy Mann for the Quebec Nordiques. There were some real tough customers. I will say probably pound for pound the scariest, toughest guy I ever played against or with was Chris "Knuckles" Nilan, and number two would be Tie Domi. Tie "You Touch Me, You Go Me" Domi.

Apparently, Domi's presence rubbed off on his teammates, including the goaltenders. Félix Potvin, who defended the crease for Domi during their five seasons together, channeled his "inner Domi" against (who else but) the Philadelphia Flyers on November 10, 1996. Joe Bowen relates,

> We were in Philadelphia a number of years ago, and Ron Hextall was the goaltender for the Flyers. He had a history of being a rather aggressive young man who enjoyed getting into the fisticuffs every once in a while.

There was a bit of a dust up that started down in the Toronto zone, and, all of a sudden, we look over and here comes Ron Hextall roaring down the ice to get at the Leafs goaltender, Félix Potvin. We didn't realize Félix could fight, and I'm pretty sure Ron Hextall didn't either, because when we thought Félix was going to get killed, it turned out to be the other way around. In a really robust goaltender's fight, Félix Potvin put a licking on Ron Hextall. The great thing about the sport of hockey is if you watch it long enough, you're going to see everything, and we've done that.

Just for good measure, Domi, too, dropped his gloves against the Flyers' Scott Daniels during the contest, which was won by Philadelphia, 3–1.

THE TORONTO MAPLE LEAFS TODAY

While the "C" patch-tearing, gondola-destroying former owner lies in his grave and Tie Domi's son Max skates among the ranks in Arizona, quietly hoping Scott Niedermayer doesn't have any revenge-seeking offspring on the ice, the 2015–2016 Maple Leafs began a new era under team-builder and three-time Stanley Cup qualifier Mike Babcock, looking to hoist that cup that has eluded the city for 49 years. Prior to Babcock's second season with the club, the Leafs, with the #1 overall pick in the draft, selected U.S.-born Auston Matthews. Hailing from Scottsdale, Arizona—of all places—Matthews broke the U.S.-born rookie record with 40 goals in his first year with the Leafs; four of which took place during the youngster's premiere against the Ottawa Senators. Coupled with veterans James Van Riemsdyk and Nazem Kadri, Matthews and fellow youngsters William Nylander and Mitch Marner led the Leafs to their first playoff appearance in four seasons. With Babcock behind the bench once again in the postseason, and his former Red Wings missing said postseason for the first time in 26 years, the winds of change certainly seem to be blowing across Lake Ontario and the proverbial yet rhetorical question, "Are you not entertained?" is most assuredly now being answered by a *proactive* and not *reactive* crowd.

· 28 ·

Vancouver Canucks

$\mathcal{F}$or more than 32 years, Montreal and Toronto were the lone Canadian representatives of the NHL. In fact, the last team north of the border to drop from the NHL ranks, the Maroons, hailed from Montreal as well, compacting 5,800 miles of fandom between 300 miles of road. Even when the league doubled in size in 1967, the six new teams were awarded to U.S. cities, making Canada feel like a labor-exhausted mother fading into the background once the delivery-room doors opened to visitors. With yet another U.S. city being granted a team (Buffalo) during the 1970–1971 expansion, Canada finally got its elusive third team when Vancouver was awarded the franchise that would come to be known as the Canucks.

Synonymous with the American "Yankees," the term *Canuck* simply refers to someone born, raised, or living in Canada. Spurring no litigation from offended Canadian natives or bleeding-heart protesters, the Canucks took the ice on October 9, 1970—some 2,100 miles from the nearest maple leaf–bearing neighbor—and lost to another westward, isolated team, the Los Angeles Kings, 3–1. Arriving almost a full decade before Canada's next installment of "West Coast Hockey," the Canucks planted their seed in the beautiful Pacific Northwest.

Tucked away in the corner of the "Great White North," Vancouver, much like any other Canadian NHL franchise post-Montreal or post-Toronto, had to wrangle its regional loyalty from throughout the country. Fighting two and three generations of Canadians bearing the "Habs" or "Leaf" team colors, Vancouver has come into its own in the past 47 years. Canucks TV/radio play-by-play broadcaster John Shorthouse comments,

> It's not a long history, so it's not like the Canadiens and the Maple Leafs, who have fans right across the country. The Canucks have become more

and more popular, and maybe it's just because the people who grew up here have moved away, but you find with each passing year there's more and more support on the road in all the cities and certain ones in particular. You see a lot more Canuck colors as you go around the league and play teams in their buildings.

As far as the Canucks' building, Rogers Arena, goes, there's usually just one color to be found, especially when playing past game 82.

A MISTAKELESS "WHITE OUT"

The Canucks' first deep run in the playoffs took place after the 1981–1982 regular season, more than a decade after the team's inaugural year. During the Conference Finals against the Chicago Blackhawks, team-builder Roger Neilsen made a gesture that would echo throughout the Vancouver community for decades. Shorthouse explains,

> Probably the most famous tradition the Canucks spawned was the waving of the white towels. That stemmed from the 1982 playoffs. There was a Conference Finals game against Chicago, and the Canucks and Roger Neilsen were very unhappy with the officiating at Chicago Stadium. Eventually, Roger Neilsen put a white towel on the end of a stick and surrendered, and then a few of the other players did the same. Tiger Williams was one. They had three or four sticks in the air with white towels on them, and they all got thrown out of the game. The Canucks returned home, and one of the radio stations had a brilliant marketing guy who had the radio station print up 16,000 towels with his radio station's logo on it. When they took the ice for the next game of the series, it was just a sea of white towels waving. Every playoff now, some local company usually prints up all the white towels so the fans can recreate 1982, so that's a tradition that started here and continues each playoff run.

While the white flag was raised in that particular contest, Chicago would eventually be the one surrendering, as the Canucks, led by Thomas Gradin, Stan Smyl, and Ivan Boldirev, won the series, 4–1, before being swept in the Stanley Cup Final by the New York Islanders dynasty of the early 1980s.

FROM RUSSIA WITH LOVE . . . AND TALENT

During the next nine seasons, there was hardly a shortage of white hand towels for hotel stockers in the Vancouver area, as the Canucks failed to make it past the first round in their five playoff appearances. During the 1991–1992 season, the team showed signs of playoff life with the introduction of 20-year-old Pavel Bure. Scoring 34 goals in just three quarters of his rookie season, Bure won the Calder Memorial Trophy and led Vancouver to the second round of the playoffs. With Bure's debut having taken place before his days in the broadcast booth, Shorthouse reflects on the young Russian's presence as follows:

> The Canucks had never had a superstar before. The circumstances were quite unique. It was November and Winnipeg was in town, and Pat Quinn, who was the coach and general manager, wasn't behind the bench because he was in league meetings with his general manager's hat on, so Rick Ley, his assistant, was coaching that night. They had Bure around for a week or two and they hadn't put him in a game yet, and Rick Ley decided to put Bure in the lineup and dress him on the fourth line. It was apparent from the moment that he hit the ice that he was something special. The place was just electric. Over time, he touched the puck and went end to end. People had never seen anything like it before. They knew this was a historic night for the franchise. The playing field had changed because Bure was really the first superstar this franchise ever had.

Two years after his rookie of the year honors, Bure led the league in scoring with 60 goals, but, more importantly, he also led the Canucks as deep into the playoffs as the team had ever gone before losing the seventh and decisive game of the Stanley Cup Final to Mark Messier's New York Rangers. The finals loss sparked riots in Vancouver, prompting the presence of policemen wielding batons and plastic shields. More than 150 unruly Canuck fans were arrested.

CRIME AND PUNISHMENT . . . ON ICE

A year after their game-seven loss and the ensuing riots, the Canucks moved out of their East Vancouver home at Pacific Coliseum and headed downtown to Rogers Arena, the surroundings of which sparked an increase in attendance from Vancouver's more corporate crowd, while the venue still provided friendly, middle-class entertainment. On February 21, 2000, with player enforcement and brawls not yet banished, the Vancouver crowd took in a lopsided victory over the Bruins, as well as one of the most vicious gestures of aggression the game has ever seen. The incident involved Vancouver's Donald Brashear and the Bruins' Marty McSorley, two players who had already fought on numerous occasions throughout the years. Sitting in the broadcast booth, Shorthouse describes the melee:

Maybe what I'm best-known for is calling two of the ugliest incidents in NHL history. One was Marty McSorley slashing Donald Brasher in the head, basically earning himself a lifetime ban from the league. When it happened, I was just aghast and in disbelief as to what I had just witnessed. That came through in my call and my voice. I remember saying, "He slashed him in the *head* Tom!" I just couldn't believe what I had seen.

McSorley would not only be suspended the remaining 23 games of the regular season—and any applicable postseason games—but he would also face charges of assault with a deadly weapon by a Vancouver court. Although he didn't serve any jail time, his career was virtually over, as neither Boston nor any other NHL team picked up the defenseman the following season.

The second of Shorthouse's "ugliest incidents" took place four years down the road, when another noted Canuck tough guy, Todd Bertuzzi, knocked out Colorado's Steve Moore in retaliation for Moore's concussion-inducing hit on Canuck teammate Markus Näslund earlier in the season. Bertuzzi was suspended for the rest of the season, including the postseason, but would return to the league following the 2004–2005 lockout. Shorthouse notes,

> The McSorley incident was much earlier in my career. When people ask the question, I always compare the two calls. In my mind, it's not because one was a Canuck being attacked and the other was a Canuck doing the attacking. To me, it's just a demonstration of more years under my belt. The Bertuzzi incident, many years later, was more of a calm description of what was happening. Everyone knew the history. Steve Moore was a target. The Canucks were losing badly, so it was a perfect opportunity for justice to be served. The puck was at one end of the ice, but we were all watching what was happening at the other end. That was what my play-by-play was describing. The sequence of events that led up to Moore being driven to the ice. It was much more measured and calm, and sort of just a description of the events, as opposed to being completely shocked and not knowing what to say.

Moore was taken off the ice on a stretcher and didn't return, ending his brief career with the Avalanche.

Following the incident, the Canucks, with Markus Näslund and Brendan Morrison picking up the slack for the suspended Bertuzzi, went on to win the division and face an unexpectedly competitive Calgary Flames team in the opening round of the 2004 playoffs. With the series going the distance, the Canucks, down a goal in game seven, had one last memorable moment in their eventful season. Shorthouse recalls,

> In game seven, the Canucks were shorthanded. They were trailing Calgary in the dying seconds and somehow manufactured a shorthanded goal. Matt

Cooke scored, and it was crazy. There was a Canucks jersey thrown on the ice in the sequence of events before. The Canucks pulled the goalie and somehow got the puck up the ice and scored a goal to tie the game and force overtime. There was just bedlam. It was a zoo. Ed Jovanovski was in the penalty box, and he was like a caged animal because he couldn't go anywhere. He was so excited and wanted to be celebrating with his team. He was jumping up and down, and punching the glass in the penalty box because he thought the game was over. They were down a goal, and he took a penalty. Game, set, match. So he's going nuts, but, of course, what we all forgot was when the Canucks started overtime, they were going to be shorthanded.

Calgary promptly came out and scored in the first minute, and it was over. It just completely deflated the building, but the sequence of events— the fans, up in arms, unhappy, knowing the game was over, throwing stuff on the ice—Vancouver somehow goes up and scores. Then to have the balloon pop in the opening seconds of overtime. I won't forget that night very quickly.

The Canucks wouldn't be the only team disposed of by the resurgent Calgary team, as the Flames went all the way to the Cup Final for the first time since the team's championship season in 1989. Although falling in seven games to the Tampa Bay Lightning, Calgary's 2004 playoff run is still regarded as one of the most improbable in NHL history.

BREAK OUT THE BATONS AGAIN

After the brief impromptu Ed Jovanovski display at the Vancouver Zoo, the NHL took a year off. Returning in the fall of 2005, the Canucks, along with Todd Bertuzzi, failed to make the 2006 playoffs; however, thanks mostly to the Sedin brothers, Henrik and Daniel, Vancouver won the division in six of the following seven seasons. Amid this string of playoff appearances was the 2010–2011 season, which again found the Canucks playing for Lord Stanley's Cup, this time as the favorite against the Boston Bruins.

With the first four games being won by the home team, the finals went the distance, and this time Vancouver hosted the decisive game. Much like their "original six" opponent, the New York Rangers of 1994, Boston ended a decades-long cup drought, extending Vancouver's own cupless streak for yet another season. Shorthouse adds, "As disappointing as it was, you can never go beyond the fact that the Stanley Cup was in the building, and it was going to be awarded that night. It's hard to overlook game seven of the Stanley Cup Final."

Corporate setting withstanding, the 2011 Stanley Cup Final, much like 1994, resulted in yet another riot in a place once named a "City of Peace." While the lasting image of the evening is a debatable photo of a man kissing/resuscitating his girlfriend in a riot-littered street just yards from Vancouver's new staple—police again equipped with batons and plastic shields—the city's reputation was once again tarnished by its extreme fandom.

VANCOUVER TODAY

With the fires doused and the kissing couple having long since "outed" themselves as to the circumstances surrounding the image of them lying in the street, the Vancouver Canucks continue to prolong their championshipless history, which now stands at 46+ years; however, with team-builder Willie Desjardins, the Sedin brothers, and import Ryan Miller, the Canucks are looking to "pacify" the West Canadian fan base with a Stanley Cup championship, leaving the streets of downtown Vancouver riot free, at least until *after* the team victory parade.

· 29 ·

Washington Capitals

*W*ith expansion hockey reaching as far south as Atlanta in 1972, the nation's capital "lobbied" for a shot to join the NHL ranks. Two years later, the Washington Capitals were introduced alongside the Kansas City Scouts and took their seat in Landover, Maryland, at the Capital Centre, where they would "room" with the NBA's Washington Bullets for more than two decades. Apparently, any fighting in the D.C. area was taking place off the ice, as the Capitals posted the worst record in NHL history, losing 67 games—including 39 out of 40 on the road—during their inaugural season. In fact, the Washington Redskins, playing in nearly six times fewer games, still had two more wins (10) than their neighbor down the Potomac.

The following season, the Capitals found their only solace in besting their intersport brothers in total wins; however, with only 11 wins, the team had the league's worst record for the second straight year, still finishing 30 points behind the division's second-worst team, the Detroit Red Wings. It took nine regular seasons for the Capitals to finally qualify for the playoffs, but it took 10 for them to win their first playoff game—let alone series—as Washington finally reached the second round, sweeping the Philadelphia Flyers in three games. While the "Caps" lost to the eventual Prince of Wales Conference champion New York Islanders, the team was well into a string of 14 consecutive playoff-qualifying seasons, securing their home amid the Capital Beltway for years to come.

The Capitals took an early vacation at the end of the 1996–1997 regular season to move from their suburban home in Landover and literalize their name, relocating to the nation's capital. While, in other areas of the country, such a move would have incited a huge drop off as far as loyalty and fan attendance are concerned, the Capitals' new home, the (now-named) Verizon

186

Center, proved quite the contrary. Capitals play-by-play TV broadcaster Joe Beninati describes the NHL's version of *Mr. Smith Goes to Washington*:

> I would say there was some concern when the team moved from Lando-
> ver, Maryland, to downtown Washington, D.C., that there would be a
> lessening of the fan base with respect to folks coming in from Baltimore. I
> don't think they were ever worried about them traveling north to Philly or
> New York, but there was a question as to whether or not they would be
> in the seats as much at U.S. Airways compared to Verizon Center. It's very
> important for the Caps franchise to incorporate fans from Baltimore. It's a
> 45-minute to an hour drive, and I know that the organization definitely has
> not cast off or forgotten the fans from the Baltimore region. I know there
> are plenty of them who still make the drive and who are as passionate as
> ever about the Caps.

While the Capitals were moving into the Verizon Center, others, namely the broadcasters themselves, were practically moving out, at least as far as their vantage point was concerned. Beninati explains,

> More than anything, what stands out to me about the difference between
> the two venues is our announce position. At U.S. Airways, we called the
> game from the lower bowl seating area. We were in the 100 sections of the
> rink. We were in a makeshift riser—almost a platform—and the area was
> enveloped with fans. We had a lot more interaction directly with the fans,
> whether positive or negative. We could reach out and touch the people,
> and they could do the same with us. That's what stands out to me the most
> from the time I worked at U.S. Airways Arena. I will never forget some
> of the funny, crazy, odd interactions—mostly with the fans—because they
> were so close. They could communicate, and they could almost cheat their
> way into the booth to see replays. It was really fun and so much different
> than now, where most NHL announce positions are on the moon and kept
> away from fans.
>
> As an announcer, you learn how to rely upon naked eye. You learn
> how to sort of cheat a little to monitor from time to time. There's an art
> form in that, but 90 percent of the time, I'm calling the game naked eye to
> the ice. Still, even up high, you're able to do it. Announcers learn differ-
> ent tells. You're not basing it solely upon a number. Hockey announcers
> are always going to try and concentrate on, "Does a hockey player shoot
> righty or lefty?" I should know every player's shot in the NHL. That way,
> I could never confuse a lefty from a righty. "Does he wear an eye shield or
> not?" "Does he use black tape or white tape on his hockey stick?" There
> are a whole bunch of different tells that allow us to identify players from
> so far away. We watch them so often. We review tapes. We're at so many
> practices. We learn mannerisms, body types, skating strides, and most of us

could call these guys in their practice uniforms with no numbers because we're so familiar with the way they play. Sure, it's nice to be close, and we were really close in Landover. I would say no more than 20 rows off the ice.

During the team's first season in its new building, Beninati could have been broadcasting from the top of the Washington Monument and still would have been able to see that something magical was happening in the D.C. area.

BREAKING IN THE NEW BUILDING

Prior to the 1997–1998 season, the Capitals had only made it past the second round once. With right winger Peter Bondra and veteran journeyman Adam Oates leading the scoring by almost twice that of their teammates, the 1997–1998 Capitals weren't necessarily an offensive machine; however, with the 6-foot-3, 225-pound Olaf Kölzig—better known as "Godzilla"—between the pipes, offense wasn't considered mandatory to win games. Kölzig's .920 save percentage in the regular season was only bested by his .941 save percentage in the playoffs. Although finishing third in their division, the Caps' run to the Stanley Cup Final gained them a new rank in the hearts of Washington fans. Beninati looks back on the Capitals' 1998 postseason:

The Caps went through Boston, Ottawa, and Buffalo to get to Detroit. Sharing that experience with the Capital fans in 1998, it's hard to imagine that building any more vibrant than that, and that is obviously the pre–Alex Ovechkin era. Since Alex has arrived, this place has been hockey mad and incredibly passionate. In 1998, to watch the fan base get rewarded in such a way was tremendous. The Capitals had a very checkered playoff past, to put it kindly. They'd suffered through so many disappointments in the Stanley Cup Playoffs—an unfair amount to be honest—but in 1998, everything was seemingly falling correctly.

The spring of '98 will always be on my most memorable games list. I remember multiple overtime games in the Boston series, just thrilling and incredible swings of emotion in that series. They were really good against Ottawa, and, in particular, Olie (Olaf) Kölzig was marvelous. His nickname of "Godzilla" was never more apparent. He just stomped the competition in that spring. He was off the charts good, and it was a pleasure to help describe what the fans were doing and how the fans were reacting. There was an amazing buildup of enthusiasm in the Conference Finals against Buffalo leading into the arrival to a Stanley Cup Final for the first time in franchise history in 1998. When the Caps took the ice for the first home game in that series, I thought the rafters were coming down. It was that loud.

Washington sports fans get an unfortunate knock but shouldn't when you think about how this city was with the Redskins at the height of their powers, when they were winning Super Bowls. How passionate the fan base was, and the way RFK Stadium shook, there were definite comparisons the way the building was shaking in 1998 throughout that entire spring, and especially so when they arrived at the final. I know the Stanley Cup Final didn't turn out the way they wanted, and they didn't get a chance to celebrate a win, but all the while, I couldn't be more proud of the way Washington hockey fans responded to that great team, and I hope sooner or later, they're going to get another chance to go that far.

While the Caps have yet to win a Stanley Cup Final game, chances are the next time they make the trip, they won't have to face the likes of the "Russian Five" and a roster full of future Hall of Famers.

NOT "SUITED" FOR THE OCCASION

With such nicknames as "Olie the Goalie" and "Godzilla," Olaf Kölzig loved to compete. In fact, when the league was embroiled in a lockout for the 2004–2005 season, Kölzig took a stab at German hockey, playing briefly for the Berlin Polar Bears to tune up for his return to the NHL the following season. At 6-foot-3, the skater was bigger than a lion's share of the men skating alongside him, especially when he was fully suited with pads, but goaltenders aren't generally relegated to the on-ice "business matters" of enforcement and fights. On November 21, 1998, just five months after his team fell in the Stanley Cup Final, Kölzig found himself tangled up with the least likely of opponents. Beninati relates,

> There was an incredible line brawl. Byron Dafoe used to be a goaltender in Washington. Olie Kölzig obviously was a goaltender in Washington. The greatest goalie in the franchise's history. Those two guys happened to be best friends during their time together. They were best men at each other's weddings. There was a time when Washington was playing Boston. Olie was still with the Caps, but Byron was with Boston. There was an old-fashioned 1970s line brawl. All 12 guys on the ice got into it. It was hysterical to eventually watch Olie Kölzig, who was really pissed off by the way the Bruins' Ken Belanger went after Craig Berube, who was the Capitals' tough guy at that time. Dale Hunter was on the ice as well.
>   There was this instance where Hunter was on the ice, Berube was on the ice, and Ken Baumgartner and Belanger for Boston at the time. It got into this heated debate that got into a fracas that turned into a full line brawl. Olie Kölzig, as a goaltender, was a monster. Six-foot-three, 230, and had

a nasty disposition, so much so they nicknamed him "Godzilla." Godzilla comes down from his crease because he didn't like the way things were shaping up at the Boston end. Dafoe was getting involved, which created a six-on-five Olie was not going to stand for. Olie didn't like seeing Baumgartner get involved with Dale Hunter, who was the team's captain. Everybody would come to Dale's aid, even though he was as strong as an ox. So here comes Olie, and they wind up pairing off to the point Olie is going after Boston's toughest guy on the ice at the time, who was either Belanger or Baumgartner, or both. It just so happened Byron is pulling his best man off the pile and getting involved in a goalie brawl with his best buddy. For a while there, Olie is just a volcano of emotion and looked like he was about to throw punches at him. Byron was laughing the whole time.

No punches were actually thrown between the best men, but "Godzilla," much like his cinematic counterpart in the streets of Tokyo, ran rampant through Boston for a night.

CAPITAL GAINS

"Olie the Goalie" wasn't the only Capital who had to wait a year to hit the ice in D.C. Drafted number one overall in 2004, Alex Ovechkin, an 18-year-old Russian left winger, had to wait until the 2005–2006 season to prove his worthiness of being the league's top pick, but once suited up, it wouldn't take him long to make a name for himself. During his 12 seasons in the NHL, Ovechkin has won the Calder Memorial Trophy for rookie of the year, been the league's top goal scorer in six different seasons, been selected three times as the National Hockey League Players' Association's most outstanding player, and taken home the Hart Memorial Trophy for league MVP three times, not to mention having been selected to the All-Star Team in each of those 12 seasons. Outside of Pittsburgh, which is Sidney Crosby's territory, Ovechkin has been considered the league's greatest player for several years running. While Washington fans recognize how fortunate they are to have Ovechkin on their side of the ice, so too does Joe Beninati, who claims,

> I'm truly blessed to have a player like Alex Ovechkin to describe. He challenges your power of description every time you're on the air. I've been lucky enough to see him score four goals in three different games. The one game in particular against Montreal was a "do-it-all" type game. He scores four goals, and he's throwing hits and breaks his nose in the same game. The fourth goal is a game-winner in overtime. Ovechkin's goal in the desert in Arizona his rookie season in 2005–2006, where he's sliding into

the corner on his back and neck, was probably the most incredible goal I will ever have to call.

Having taken home the Maurice "Rocket" Richard Trophy for top goal scorer for four consecutive seasons (2013–2016), chances are Beninati will have a few more shared moments on the air with Alex Ovechkin.

UNLEASHING THE FURY

As if a hat-trick-expectable superstar and a street-fight-seeking goaltender haven't been enough to spark the crowds inside the Verizon Center, it's interesting to note that an actor like Tom Green could finish the job come the third period. Using clips from Green's 2000 film *Road Trip*, as well as clips from such films as *Miracle, Hoosiers, Rudy,* and *Animal House,* the crew in charge of Capitals in-game entertainment finds ways to bring Green's line "Unleash the fury" to life via the 18,000-plus in attendance. Beninati notes,

> Third period of play, up or down in the score—but especially down—they put together a video on the screen at the Verizon Center. It's a montage of clips from movies and such. If you're familiar with the Washington Capitals over the last decade, the building just goes nuts. The decibel level is through the roof, and, at the end of this video montage, when Tom Green asks the fans to "unleash the fury," boy do they ever. I've seen it promote some pretty good responses from the players on the ice. They all know it's happening, and if they're trailing in the game, it pumps some life into them. If they're leading in the game, hopefully it cements the victory.

Despite the team's two straight President's Trophy–worthy seasons (2015–2017), Alexander Ovechkin, thanks mainly to his on-ice nemesis, Sidney Crosby, and his Pittsburgh Penguins, has yet to lead the Capitals past the second round during his tenure as team captain, Washington fans are patiently awaiting the moment when they will be able to "unleash their fury" in the form of a hoisted Stanley Cup prepped to be motorcaded by Capitol Hill, along the Potomac, and down 1600 Pennsylvania Ave, making the league champion's trip to the White House the shortest commute ever.

Winnipeg Jets/Winnipeg Jets "Version 2.0"

*I*n 1979, when the NHL introduced the Canadian province of Manitoba to hockey's biggest stage, the league probably had no idea it would have to do the announcement, press conference, arena groundbreaking, and celebratory parade all over again some 32 years down the road. Coming into the league, along with the Quebec Nordiques, Edmonton Oilers, and Hartford Whalers, via the league merger with the World Hockey Association (WHA), the Winnipeg Jets, already established as a professional team, didn't have the atrocious inaugural season of such teams as the 1974–1975 Washington Capitals or the future expansion 1992–1993 Ottawa Senators; however, during their sophomore campaign, Winnipeg failed to reach double digits in the win column, finishing the season 9–57–14, with their 32 team points being the sixth least in league history with a season schedule of 80 or more games.

The following season (1981–1982), the Jets bounced back with a +24 win differential and finished second in the division before losing to the St. Louis Blues, three games to one, in the opening round of the playoffs. The following six seasons, playoff presence and playoff futility were prevalent themes in "Peg City," as the team, although qualifying to play in the postseason, only advanced past the first round twice (1985 and 1987). After failing to advance to the playoffs for four seasons and four first-round exits later, Keith Tkachuk, Teemu Selänne, and company left "Winterpeg" for the Sonoran Desert in the fall of 1996, to become the (then-named) Phoenix Coyotes, seeming more like a transition from the movie *Star Wars* than a franchise relocation. Coupled with the Nordiques' relocation to Denver, Colorado, the year before and the ensuing Whalers' transfer to Raleigh, North Carolina, the year after, an argument could have been made that WHA stood for "We Had A" team if the Oilers would have followed suit and vacated Edmonton. After their "bi-polar" change of venue, Winnipeg, 15 years later, in the fall of 2011, went the way of Denver and the Minneapolis–St. Paul area in being restored as an NHL-representing city.

AN ATLANTA FAN'S LOSS IS A WINNIPEG FAN'S GAIN

In 2011, with no playoff wins in 11 seasons since coming into the league in 2000, as an expansion team, the Atlanta Thrashers were about to get the "prodigal son" treatment "foster child" style, as the team, finishing third to last in attendance their final season in the Deep South, arrived into the welcoming arms of an NHL-starved city. Winnipeg radio/TV play-by-play broadcaster Dennis Beyak, himself a native Manitoban, describes the fever that quickly spread throughout the Canadian town known for its chilling weather:

> Before the official announcement was made, there was a fairly strong rumor. The story kind of broke that this was going to happen. I happened to be in the city actually. I was on my way to Kelowna, British Columbia, where I spend my summers, and just happened to be in Winnipeg when all that was going down. It wasn't official, but the city was absolutely electric. They were playing hockey in the streets. They were pulling out all their old Winnipeg Jets jerseys and caps from the original team. The city was absolutely wild about the possibility.
>
> I went to Kelowna, and, in the meantime, everything got finalized. I remember watching the news conference on the day that it happened. They were parading in the street. Everything that you could possibly imagine. The support has been very, very good. I grew up about three and a half hours north of Winnipeg in a little place called Winnipegosis. For the most part, I was born and raised in Manitoba. When this opportunity came, 1) to be in on the ground floor, 2) I wasn't doing all the games in Toronto, and 3) the whole coming back to the province, it seemed like at that stage of my career it was coming full circle. It was something special for me, and it's been everything I could have hoped for.

As could be expected, the return to ice in a town that had been deprived of professional hockey for 15 years was one for the ages inside the team's new home at the MTS Centre, for both fans and those in the broadcast booth.

HEY, NHL OPPONENTS. DID YOU MISS US, TOO?

While the team's first preseason game in Winnipeg before the 2011–2012 season, against the Columbus Blue Jackets, was enough to pack the inside of the

MTS Centre, the surreal nature of NHL hockey being back in Manitoba really soaked in on October 9, against a foe from another province, the Montreal Canadiens. Beyak notes,

> When the team came back, just the atmosphere around town and the media publicity that was around that opening game. People were downtown first thing in the morning. It was a beautiful weekend despite the fact it was October. The weather was gorgeous. It was 25 to 30 degrees Celsius, which was pushing the high 80s/low 90s Fahrenheit, and people couldn't believe it. People from national media outlets who were making their first trip to Winnipeg and were expecting winter to have already been here were totally fooled. It was an absolutely gorgeous weekend, and the buzz around the city was incredible. You kind of felt for the players who were actually trying to get ready for a hockey game because none of the questions pertained to the actual "on-ice." It was all about the excitement that was around the city and the building. That game will always stand out as something special, and that will always be the case no matter what happens forward. There's always that old adage, "There's only one first ever game," and that was it.

Although the Jets fell to the Canadiens, 5–1, in front of the sold out MTS Centre crowd, it's safe to say the result on the scoreboard above center ice was hardly the lasting memory for the 15,000-plus onlookers in attendance that night.

Jets fans would have to wait for the next home game to finally get that "W," as Winnipeg edged Pittsburgh, 2–1. While it took only two games to get their first home win, it would take five for the Jets to get one on the road against the Philadelphia Flyers, and with enough scoring to spread across four hockey games no less. Being his second most memorable game to date with Winnipeg Jets "Version 2.0," Beyak revisits the 9–8 affair, saying, "Their first road win in Philadelphia, the Jets were up 5–1 or 6–2 at one time, and the next thing you know, Philadelphia came back and tied it. The Jets went ahead and the Flyers tied it, and the Jets won it by a score of 9–8. That was an absolutely bizarre game."

While the team's regular-season record was a one-slot improvement over the previous year's showing in the Eastern Conference's now-geographically paradoxical Southeast Division, the Jets failed to make the playoffs their first season back, but it's safe to say 82 games was season enough for Winnipeg fans, and anything beyond that would have been gravy on a much-appreciated entrée.

WHILE YOU WERE OUT

With the league makeup changing during their 15-year absence from urban Manitoba, the Jets' days of Shawn Cronin, Mike Hartman, and Gord Donnelly racking up penalty minutes nearing the 300 mark during the team's first campaign in Winnipeg are gone. A new style of hockey has been adopted for this "second tour" to compete with a faster and fuller NHL. Beyak explains,

> The game kind of moved away from enforcing. The closest they've come in the last couple of seasons was Chris Thorburn, but Chris can also play the game. He certainly was more than willing to step in and protect anybody who needed protecting and change the game if he felt it needed changing. More and more, we hear coaches—certainly Paul Maurice—talking about how that part of the game may not be needed on a night-to-night basis. The Jets team wasn't built that way. It was more built on speed, especially now with Paul Maurice here. Intimidation has never really been a big part of that makeup. They use the speed part to their advantage as much as they possibly can because they're big and fast.

Arguably, the fastest people inside the MTS Centre aren't the ones on the ice, but those behind the keyboards at the ticket office, as the team, four days after new owner True North's May 31, 2011, announcement that it had purchased the team, sold out the remaining season-ticket packages within 17 minutes of them becoming available to the public.

NEW ARENA, OLD FRIENDS

Before the original Winnipeg Jets shifted climates to become the Phoenix Coyotes, the team played inside Winnipeg Arena, with more than 300 additional seats than the MTS Centre. Not counted among the seats inside Winnipeg Arena—but a presence nonetheless—was Queen Elizabeth II, or at least her portrait. Measuring 16x23 feet (5x7 meters), a large portrait of the Queen hung from the arena rafters throughout the Jets' residency there and beyond. Beyak recalls, "When I did television for the Edmonton Oilers in the mid-'90s, I actually did some games in the Winnipeg Arena before the team left. No matter where you were in the building, the picture of the Queen, she was looking right at you." The Queen's portrait, subsequent to the team's leaving in 1996 and prior to the arena's demolition in 2006, was stored away in Ontario; however, the piece has since been purchased by the famous railway Canadian National and has made its return to Winnipeg.

While no plans have been made to return Queen Elizabeth II to her "seat" above a sea of Jets fans, attendants inside the MTS Centre already have plenty of familiar faces with whom they can enjoy 60 minutes of hockey. Beyak relates,

> The interesting thing with Winnipeg, at a hockey game, my guess would be probably 60 or 70 percent of the people know each other. Even though it's a big city, it's got a closeness to it. A lot of people who are at the games went to high school together or were employed together at one time, or knew somebody. Whatever the case may be.

While the anthem of the 1980s hair band Cinderella, "Don't Know What You Got 'Till It's Gone" probably wasn't playing throughout the streets of Winnipeg during the NHL's 15-year furlough from the city, the sentiment is ever so present now that the lyrics could be changed to "Don't Know What You Got 'Till You Got It Back." Beyak continues,

> Everybody has their own version as to why the team left, but the bottom line was it wasn't being supported well enough. Nobody wanted to step up and take the losses anymore, so the team moved. I think there's a special feeling when you lose it and get it back, and everybody gets together and says, "We can't let this thing leave again." At the MTS Centre, it's always full. It's a building where, despite the fact there's 15,000 seats, there's not a bad seat in the house. From what I can recollect, it's a much younger and more vocal crowd than what it was in the other rink.

Needless to say, there was no shortage of vocals in the spring of 2015, when the Jets, during the fourth year of their return tour, brought playoff hockey back to Winnipeg for the first time in nearly 20 years.

STILL LOOKING FOR THAT PLAYOFF "W"

Coming into the postseason as the eighth seed, the 2014–2015 Winnipeg Jets got a few extra whiffs of that "second chance" air, as the team faced the number-one seed Anaheim Ducks in the opening round. The Jets, much like their former identity, the Atlanta Thrashers, were unable to muster a playoff win against the Ducks and were swept in the Conference Quarterfinals, sending the 15,000-plus spectators at the MTS Centre home for the summer, still with that grumbling in their tummies for playoff utility rather than futility. While it's a nice break from the cold when hockey's in session, it's arguable that the 2015 summer couldn't have taken longer to pass for Winnipeg fans waiting for their team to make that anticipated playoff push and complete the meal they've been savoring since May 31, 2011.

With speed now the name of the game rather than intimidation, young skaters like Mark Scheifele, Jacob Trouba, and Adam Lowry, as well as the two-headed goaltending threat of Michael Hutchinson and Ondřej Pavelec, have the Jets off to a good start and looking to bring the city to the forefront of the league. While one playoff win has proven elusive, let alone 16, Paul Maurice and the Jets are aiming to keep the MTS Centre's seats filled and the notion of another relocation permanently holstered until the banners hanging from the rafters take up as much space as Queen Elizabeth's portrait.

• *31* •

You Go Away Mad, We'll Just Go Away

*W*hether it be for money, money, or money, the NHL has become no-torious for team relocation. In baseball, the phrase "leave under the cover of night" has been used when a team and the city have been unable to come to an agreement, but a team has rarely—if ever—followed through with such an action. Hockey, on the other hand, has made it not only a substantiated rumor, but also a reality, as franchises have left for greener (green being the color of money) pastures, usually at the request (command) of the team owner. These relocations have left fans standing on the proverbial curb in their now-outdated jerseys, waving somberly as their 41 confirmed date-night reserva-tions ride off into the sunset.

While loyal fans, representing at least 40 percent (at best) of the oc-cupancy inside most arenas, scratch their heads, wondering cluelessly where things went wrong, fans of other, more historic franchises, where lack of at-tendance is not a factor, simply shake both their heads and fists in wonder as the team bus filled with reluctantly departing players pulls away; however, as history shows, money and the promise of seats filled with fans makes the crowd waiting with open arms at the arrival gate an inevitability, beginning the cycle anew.

MINNESOTA NORTH STARS

Although a member of the "second six," the Minnesota North Stars, playing in a land where at least 80 percent of the 10,000 lakes are frozen, managed to find themselves on a plane headed for Dallas in the spring of 1993. Hav-ing the league's worst average attendance from 1988 to 1991, the North Stars rebounded to post numbers nearing the 14,000 mark during the 1992–1993 season, jumping seven slots from the league cellar. But, in the fall of 1993, team owner Norman Green, with his mind made up, went from northern abandoner to southern hero "faster than a sneeze through a screen door."

More than 20 years later, the debate continues about where the team history belongs—Minnesota or Dallas. Current Minnesota Wild radio play-by-play broadcaster Bob Kurtz, who called games for the North Stars during their Minnesota days, offers his take on the debate, saying, "To me, the North Star history belongs in Minnesota. The Dallas Stars are a separate entity. There are retired numbers down in Dallas that people in Dallas have no idea who they even are." Undoubtedly, some Minnesotans could probably tell you not only who the retired numbers belong to, but also the players' waist sizes, favorite foods, and East Coast–West Coast rap preferences.

While in the Upper Midwest for two and a half decades, the North Stars were generally a playoff-worthy squad. Behind star center Bobby Smith, the team advanced to its first Stanley Cup Final in 1981, where it fell to the New York Islanders soon-to-be dynasty. While being a league runner-up is still an accomplishment, it's unlikely anyone who was a hockey fan during the 1980–1981 season remembers the North Stars for any game other than their February 27 matchup at Boston Garden against the Bruins. Kurtz looks back on what was then a record-setting night, stating,

> The North Stars went for years never having won a game in Boston Garden. There was a lot more fighting in hockey then. The North Stars used to be a finesse team, and the Bruins were always more of a rough-and-tumble team. They never had success in the building. I think they went 14 years before they finally won there. There was a big standoff at Boston Garden in 1981. You had Coach Glen Sonmor, who was all set to go to war against the Bruins. We had gone out with them the night before and they said, "If they try anything tomorrow, we're going to go right after them. Not the second time, not the third time, but the first time they do something, we're going to go right after them."
>
> They drop the puck to start the game, and seven seconds into the hockey game, there were brawls all over the place. By the time the first period ended, the benches were just about empty. Glen Sonmor went in and had a pirate's patch. He really played it up to the hilt. He only had one eye to begin with, and he was going around calling for Boston coach Gerry Cheevers's head on a platter. It was good and sort of a "slap-shot entertainment." There was a lot of goofy stuff going on. Boston won the hockey game, but Minnesota won the fight. Brad Maxwell cleaned Stan Jonathan's clock, and there were fights all over the ice.
>
> By the time they got done that night, there were 406 minutes of penalties, which, at the time, had set the National Hockey League record. I don't

know how many people were kicked out of the game. The North Stars ended up needing a police escort around their bus to get out of Boston Garden. The two teams matched up in the playoffs that year. Minnesota went into Boston Garden, won for the first time in 14 years, and swept the Bruins in three straight.

While it wouldn't take another game featuring 400 penalty minutes to propel them there, the North Stars reached the Stanley Cup Final 10 years later, in 1991, thanks to such players as Dave Gagner, Brian Bellows, Brian Propp, and second-year player Mike Modano; however, Minnesota was upended by Mario Lemieux and his Pittsburgh Penguins, winning the first of the team's back-to-back Stanley Cup titles. Modano, the highest-scoring American-born player in NHL history, would finally raise Lord Stanley's Cup in 1999 in a different green-starred uniform.

While Minnesota, referred to by Twins TV play-by-play broadcaster Dick Bremer as having been the "land of vice presidents and Super Bowl runner-ups," has continued to live up to that name in every sport except baseball, the North Star faithful can find some solace in knowing that former team owner Norman Green missed the Stanley Cup train as well by a little less than three years.

HARTFORD WHALERS

Having a roster that includes both "Mr. Hockey" and the "Golden Jet" isn't a bad way to introduce a team to the NHL. The Hartford Whalers, one of four teams added to the league from the World Hockey Association (WHA), entered the league with a 51-year-old Gordie Howe skating the final season of his Hall of Fame career. Bobby Hull, who played opposite Howe for more than a decade, joined his longtime rival in the lineup for nine games, as the two padded their already Hall of Fame–worthy statistics. Adding a goal and an assist in the team's first-round exit from the postseason, Howe ended his career as the NHL's all-time leading scorer. Since Howe's exit from the league, former Edmonton Oilers Wayne Gretzky and Mark Messier, as well as veteran Jaromír Jágr, have surpassed "Mr. Hockey" in career points, but only Gretzky joins Howe as the only two scorers of 800-plus goals in the history of the league.

Beginning his Hall of Fame broadcasting career with the Hartford Whalers, Chuck Kaiton discusses his initiation into the game, relating,

The first game I ever worked was memorable, because, when I was a 25-year-old kid getting the job, my idol, being a Detroit native, was Gordie Howe. Guess who I got to work with in my first broadcast, which was a preseason game against Pittsburgh? I broadcast with Gordie Howe, who sat out that game. He was still with the Whalers at the time. Gordie was my color man. That was a thrill.

Regardless of two of the game's most legendary players suiting up on the same bench, bringing an NHL-level team into the heart of New England meant stepping on the toes of the longest-tenured team south of the "Great White North." Kaiton explains,

> The Boston Bruins didn't even want the Whalers to join the NHL from the WHA days. Reluctantly, the four WHA teams were put in the league. There was always a rivalry because the Whalers' roots were originally in Boston. As time went on and the Whalers became more competitive, we actually had a lot of people who were Bruin fans convert over and become Whaler fans, and we saw a big difference in the crowds. All of a sudden, we had more and more Bruin fans who couldn't get tickets in Boston but would end up coming to the Hartford Civic Center. As the mid- to late '80s moved on, we saw fewer and fewer Bruin fans. It was always a tug of war, especially at the beginning, when the Whalers were joining the NHL.

As far as the rest of the NHL was concerned, this New England rivalry might as well have been for the "north of New York but south of Quebec" division, as neither team, through the Whalers' residency in Connecticut, was putting a Stanley Cup champion on the ice; however, Boston, at the time, was riding their league-record 29 straight playoff appearances, while Hartford had made it past the opening round of the playoffs only once. The Whalers' lone series victory came at the hands of the Quebec Nordiques, setting up a Division Finals showdown with a 20-year-old Patrick Roy and the Montreal Canadiens. Although Hartford lost the series, they made the Canadiens work for it. Kaiton looks back on a seminal moment in Whalers history:

> My most memorable game with the Whalers would probably be game six of the second round of the playoffs back in '86, against the Canadiens. The Whalers were down three games to two, and, in a scoreless game, I remember Kevin Dineen coming down the left side, going right around Larry Robinson, cutting to the net, and scoring a goal against Patrick Roy to win the game, 1–0, to send it to game seven in Montreal, a game they eventually lost. Those mid-'80s Whalers were pretty good, and that was the closest they ever came to going to the Conference Finals that year.

While the franchise's first and only taste of champagne from Lord Stanley's Cup wouldn't come until nearly a decade after traveling down the coast to Carolina, Hartford did play during a "colorful" time for the league and managed to pick up a rival or two along the way. Nashville Predators radio play-by-play broadcaster Pete Weber, who called Buffalo Sabres hockey on the radio, looks back at one of the Whalers' final sendoffs at Hartford Civic Center in the spring of 1997:

> The Sabres and Whalers had two games against each other in a 10-day span. In the first of those, it was kind of like in the movie *Slapshot*, where in just the pregame skate around, all of a sudden a fight started, and it involved Wayne Primeau on the Sabres side and his older brother Keith on the Whalers side. Those guys got going after each other. It really almost seemed like we should have called Richard Dawson there for the *Family Feud*. We weren't on the air when that one happened. Then, 10 days later, our radio station said, "Hey, we could sell advertising should this happen again," and there was a good likelihood of it. So we actually did go on a little bit earlier the next time, and, by God, they did it again. All of a sudden, there's a call coming into our station in Buffalo, and it turns out to be Mrs. Primeau, the mother of the two combatants. She wanted to ask me if I could, during a commercial break, tell her which one of her lovelies actually started that scrap.

Shortly after the "Feud," the Whalers left Boston as the only NHL representative in New England, but as the Carolina Hurricanes they would "one up" the Bruins by winning the Stanley Cup five years sooner. The lone player on the roster for both the Whalers' final season in Hartford and the Carolina Hurricanes' Stanley Cup championship was defenseman Glen Wesley.

QUEBEC NORDIQUES

Like the Hartford Whalers, the Quebec Nordiques came into the league via the WHA merger before the 1979–1980 season. In yet another head-scratcher for abandoned fans, Quebec, although a successful team with a roster chock-full of future Hall of Fame talent the likes of Joe Sakic, Peter Forsberg, and Adam Foote, was forced to relocate to Colorado due to financial hardships suffered by team owner Marcel Aubut. Coupled with the offseason pickups of Montreal goaltender and former Nordique nemesis Patrick Roy, as well as Sandis Ozolinsh, fans in Colorado must have felt like kids who had been handed the keys to brand new Ferraris for their sixteenth birthdays, as the Avalanche took home in just one season what the Nordiques couldn't in 16: Lord Stanley's Cup.

Quebec's arrival in Denver set in motion a rivalry with the Detroit Red Wings many consider to be the greatest in major sports between 1995 and

2002. The Nordiques had their fair share of rivalries during their residency north of the border as well, especially the one with their provincial neighbor, Montreal. Columbus Blue Jackets TV play-by-play broadcaster Jeff Rimer, who began his NHL career with the Canadiens dynasty of the late 1970s, looks back on the "Battle of Quebec" as follows:

> Going back to the old Montreal–Quebec "Battle of Quebec," there were bench-clearing brawls and line brawls. I remember those vividly. It certainly happened on a number of occasions in the playoffs. In fact, it forced the league to have officials visible for pregame warm-up, keeping an eye on what went on, because there were all kinds of animosities between those two. It was some great hockey. One year, Quebec actually beat Montreal in a playoff series, with Dale Hunter, then with Quebec, scoring the game-winning goal on Rick Wamsley. That's certainly a very vivid memory for me. Those Quebec–Montreal games were something to see.

If it were up to officials to regulate the use of amenities in arena bathrooms, they probably would have made a rule for that as well, especially in light of the contest between the Quebec Nordiques and the Hartford Whalers on January 23, 1989. Prefacing what would become known as the "Toilet Bowl," the game between Quebec and Hartford was officiated by Kerry Fraser, who had summoned the wrath of Nordique fans two years prior with his "no goal" call against Alain Côté because of goaltender interference, a goal that would have shifted both the momentum and the series lead to Quebec. Instead, Montreal scored the game-winner and went on to win the series. With Fraser officiating once again in January 1989, a few calls didn't go the way Nordique fans would have liked. Tampa Bay Lightning TV play-by-play broadcaster Rick Peckham, who began his NHL broadcasting career in Hartford, looks back on why his team's goaltender, Peter Sidorkiewicz, labeled this particular contest the "Toilet Bowl":

> Back when the Quebec Nordiques were still in the NHL, they were playing the Hartford Whalers, and they were a pretty good rivalry in the old Adams Division in the mid- and late '80s. We had a regular-season game up in Le Colisée. and Kerry Fraser was the referee. The fans were just going nuts at the penalty calls the Nordiques were getting. The Whalers were getting power play after power play. Some fan ends up going into the men's room and grabs rolls of toilet paper. So he brings them out, and there's a call. The fans are all fired up, and this guy throws a roll of toilet paper on the ice. That just sparked everybody to hit the restrooms and grab all the toilet paper they could. They had all these rolls of toilet paper being thrown out on the ice. They had to stop the game not only to sweep up the ice, but [also] to get control of the crowd. At one point, the Whalers stood to

possibly win the game via forfeit. My partner at the time, Gerry Cheevers, went down and interviewed Kerry Fraser during the delay as to what was going to happen. It was crazy and out of control. A lot of fun and a very unique situation. I can't remember anything else like that ever happening.

It's unlikely that Nordique fans and Fraser were able to make amends before the team moved to Colorado, but the demons of Fraser's officiating would be exercised—at least for the players—via the team's first-ever Stanley Cup title its inaugural year in town.

ATLANTA FLAMES

After hockey was established in Southern California and Northern California in 1967, the league pushed its luck five years later in yet another league expansion by awarding the Deep South city of Atlanta, Georgia, an NHL franchise, the Atlanta Flames. Although reaching the playoffs in six of the eight seasons they were in "A-Town," the Flames never recorded a playoff series win until they were relocated to Calgary, Alberta, Canada, for the 1980–1981 season. In fact, in those six playoff appearances, Atlanta only managed to win a total of two games. While they were only in the "Peach State" for eight seasons, the Flames managed to create a small rivalry with their closest geographical rival—in St. Louis. Hall of Fame play-by-play broadcaster Jiggs McDonald, who called games for the Flames between opening the Los Angeles Kings franchise and calling the New York Islanders during their dynasty of the early 1980s, looks back on one night in particular against the St. Louis Blues:

> There was a situation with a fight on the ice. Steve Durbano was sent one way and an Atlanta player was sent the other way towards the dressing rooms. The referee is at the penalty box assessing penalties when the door to the ice opens from the St. Louis side of things. Out comes Steve Durbano swinging his stick like a tomahawk looking for goaltender Phil Myre and heading right for the net. The crowd is screaming. That's what set that whole rivalry between Atlanta and St. Louis into motion. The benches emptying and the brawl that ensued.

While another release of the proverbial film *Dude, Where's My Owner's Money* caused the Flames to be relocated to Calgary after the 1979–1980 season, the team, within a decade, won not one but four playoff series in 1989, en route to its first and only Stanley Cup title.

ATLANTA THRASHERS

Whether it was during the Bobby Cox years as Atlanta Braves manager or the city hosting the 1996 Summer Olympics, something caused the city of Atlanta to forget about the short-lived history of the Flames the decade before, because the "Big Peach" of the "Peach State" received yet another NHL franchise, the Atlanta Thrashers, in the fall of 1999. While the Flames never won a playoff series in their nine seasons in Atlanta, they still won two more playoff games than their successors. In 11 seasons in Atlanta, the Thrashers qualified for the postseason just once, which followed the team's only Southeast Division title in 2006–2007. Despite having home-ice advantage, the Thrashers lost four straight to the New York Rangers in the Eastern Conference Quarterfinals and did not manage to play past game 82 until 2015, four seasons after once again leaving the city of Atlanta without an NHL franchise. While the city is 0–2 in sports *not* basketball, football, or baseball, Atlanta may just test the phrase "third time's the charm," should the Hawks, Falcons, Bulldogs, or Braves ever bring another championship title to "A-Town."

With the relocation of teams like the Quebec Nordiques and Atlanta Thrashers came the reintroduction of NHL hockey to cities where fans had once been deprived—Winnipeg and Denver—completing hockey relocation's "circle of life." While the NHL has been a league of expansion, as well as relocation, in the past two decades, the flippant nature of commissioners, owners, and even city mayors begs the question asked by all fans: "Which city will be next?"

· 32 ·

The Case of Cookie Cutter versus Old School

ARGUMENT A

I think it's changed for the better. Back when I started in some of those early years, you had certain buildings where the dimensions were not regulation. They didn't have enough room. Chicago Stadium was narrower and shorter than it should have been. Instead of 200x85 feet, the ice was 187x83. Boston Garden was shorter. The same as the Auditorium in Buffalo or the "Aud." Those dimensions were different. What that enabled teams to do was build a team that fit the dimensions of their ice, so if you had a shorter, narrower surface to play on, you wanted bigger players because you wanted to be more physical. That's the way Boston put their team together. It wasn't really fair and probably benefitted the home team more if they got to practice in those buildings because they were more used to those dimensions. Also, in some of those buildings, some of the boards were different into the corners. Home teams would know from practicing there how the puck was going to bounce off of the boards, or if it was going to take a weird bounce in a certain corner. They would be able to take advantage of that, where the visitors weren't up to speed on how the puck was going to act in some of those buildings. I think it's better now where everything is uniform. It's the 200x85, and every team goes in knowing these are the exact dimensions it should be. In hockey, you've got to have the dimensions the same in every arena, and that's what we've come to now.

—Bob Miller, Los Angeles Kings TV play-by-play broadcaster

ARGUMENT B

In the construction of all the new buildings, I believe the one mistake that was made was the insistence you keep every ice surface 200x85 feet. Every football field and basketball court has the same dimensions, and that's okay, but, to me, part of the beauty of hockey in the old days was that going into Boston Garden was different than going into Madison Square Garden, Maple Leaf Gardens, the Montreal Forum, or Chicago Stadium. The corners were shaped a little differently. The Chicago Stadium ice surface was a couple of feet shorter. That was awesome. The corners in Buffalo were different than anywhere else. You had to learn the nuances of different buildings. Now everything is consistent. There's nothing wrong with that, but I think it would have been a little neater to—within certain parameters—have rinks be slightly different from place to place. I think it would have been cooler to have some of the nuances of the old arenas.

—Pat Foley, Chicago Blackhawks TV play-by-play broadcaster

In my opinion, the evolution of hockey has killed the romance of the game. There is such a "cookie cutter" feel to the National Hockey League. The rinks are still different, but you could go from Washington to Pittsburgh to you name it; it's another bowl with different-colored seats. Certainly for what we do as broadcasters, we are farther from the game now than we've ever been. That is the unfortunate part of our trade as broadcasters. People are trying to bring the feel of the game in the NHL right now to where we move farther and farther away from it.

—Dan Dunleavy, Buffalo Sabres TV play-by-play broadcaster

*W*hile this was not a panel discussion and none of the gentlemen knew of other opinions on the matter, a sometimes-silent debate continues about hockey's current state versus that of yesterday. What is better for the game? Uniformity or universality? In a sort of "reverse baseball," team facilities have gone from having unique dimensions in several cases to what followers of America's pastime would label "cookie cutter." Hall of Fame radio broadcaster Jiggs McDonald states, "So many of these new facilities you better look up to see what the name is to remind you of what city you're in because they all seem to look alike." The outside look of the arenas notwithstanding, broadcasters aren't the only ones recessed from the action in today's live hockey experience.

Fans have gone from being on top of the action—in several cases—to being part of an 18,000-person backdrop. The use of monitors in a remote broadcast booth and the installation of a safety net and Plexiglass above the boards (generally as the result of tragic events) have changed the makeup, dynamic, and even the tempo of the game. While the debate concerning nostalgia versus keeping up with the times will likely continue until the proverbial ice melts, some of the greatest edifices the sporting world has ever seen remain in the hearts, minds, and memories of not only the fans, but also the "fans at heart" behind the broadcast microphone.

BOSTON GARDEN

Host to five of the six Bruins Stanley Cup championships, Boston Garden was home to some of the city's greatest players, including Bobby Orr, Phil Esposito, Ray Bourque, and Cam Neely. Standing for almost 70 years, the multiuse facility housed an NBA-record 16 championships won by the Celtics' Oscar Robertson, Bill Russell, Larry Bird, and legendary coach Red Auerbach. With 21 championships between its two tenants, Boston Garden was the standard for indoor professional sports success throughout the latter half of the 20th century. Aside from the talent on the hardwood and ice, the "Garden" certainly distinguished itself from the other arenas at the time, starting with its intimacy.

Boston Garden's 14,448 seating capacity was 1,859 less than that of the next closest "original six" team (Toronto Maple Leafs, Maple Leaf Gardens). Built on a parcel of land that would make Fenway Park feel like an outstretched-legged passenger sitting in first class, its dimensions pushed the small crowd so close to the ice, they might as well have been actual players. Broadcasters were no exception. Columbus Blue Jackets TV play-by-play broadcaster Jeff Rimer explains,

> I had the good fortune of breaking into the NHL as a play-by-play broadcaster when there were a couple of older rinks in the league. Let me tell you, they were a delight to broadcast in. Both in Chicago and in the old Boston Garden, you literally hung over the ice. In Boston in particular, you were in a cage-type situation. You could literally reach out and almost touch the players.

Long-time Rangers radio man and hall of fame NBA broadcaster Marv Albert was definitely no stranger to "The Garden," calling games in the building for two sports over nearly three decades. Albert notes, "I loved doing hockey and NBA at the old Boston Garden. It was the perfect location. You were upstairs on the first balcony but you were over the ice. You saw the game and every aspect of it. It was easily the best and so thrilling to be able to do hockey games from there."

Former Hartford Whalers play-by-play broadcaster Mike Fornes looks back on another of the "perks" of the Garden's intimacy:

> I remember one of the greatest thrills about doing play-by-play for a big game was in knowing that I would have one of the best seats in the house. The old classic buildings like Boston Garden, Chicago Stadium, Maple Leaf Gardens, and even the Capital Centre had fabulous broadcast perspectives. I could hear what was happening on the ice and see the players' faces. I didn't need a lineup card to call the game. I am so grateful I worked in an era when you knew the players by seeing their faces, not looking for numbers. They didn't all wear helmets then, let alone face shields or cages. One night in the Boston Garden, Mark Howe and his famous father were playing for the Whalers against the Bruins. Mark and Marty Howe always called their father "Gordie," like they would call any other player by his name. Mark skated out of the Whalers' zone and hit Gordie with a pass at center ice. Mark went up the boards to the blue line, just below where I was calling the game on TV. He wanted the puck back, and, as he got open, I heard him instinctively call out, "Dad!" and Gordie put it on the tape of Mark's stick. Mark snapped a wrist shot into the top corner of the net. It was priceless. Today, announcers might as well be sitting on the moon. I once had a member of management disagree with my request to keep the broadcast location low in the building instead of moving up to the top of the highest grandstand level. He told me I had a monitor and could call the game while watching the monitor. Totally clueless.

Boston Bruins radio play-by-play broadcaster Dave Goucher, although never having called a Bruins game in the old Garden, did call games there in a different capacity while in college. Having grown up in the Boston area, Goucher describes the Garden experience from a fan's perspective:

> It's hard to replicate what the old Garden was. That was a special place and a unique building. A smaller building. A smaller ice surface. Fans were right on top of you there. In Boston, it's a different atmosphere now. I think there's people who say the old Garden was louder because it was smaller and more crammed. The sight lines were different, and the seats were at a steeper angle to the ice. It was an adjustment, and it took fans a while to adjust to TD Garden. There's still people who tell me how much they miss the old Garden. I do, too, but I also think, in a lot of ways, it had become obsolete. It's 20 years down the road now, and it was time to move on.

Others, like the players themselves, had to "move on" in a physical and not an emotional way in the team's new home at TD Waterhouse Garden, "playing by the rules" with a regulation-size ice surface. Fortunately, for the Bruins, they were eventually able to build the right team for a 200x85 rink and return the Stanley Cup to "Beantown" in 2011, after a nearly 40-year drought, pacifying yet another championship-starved pack of Boston sports fans.

CHICAGO STADIUM

Before Michael Jordan and his Chicago Bulls won their second of two championship "three-peats" and the Chicago Blackhawks once again established themselves as the Western Conference's most formidable team, the two teams shared success in yet another facility on Madison Street. For 65 years, Chicago Stadium was home to the Blackhawks and such players as Tony Esposito, Stan Mikita, and Bobby Hull. Host to three of the Blackhawks' six Stanley Cup championships, as well as the first of the Michael Jordan–led Chicago Bulls three-peats, Chicago Stadium was another sports edifice that offered an intimate setting to its patrons. Chicago Blackhawks Hall of Fame TV play-by-play broadcaster—not to mention lead counsel for "old school" over "cookie cutter"—Pat Foley describes the place he called home for 14 seasons as follows:

> Chicago Stadium was a really special place. We're not going to see anything like that again because of the way the decks were sort of stacked on top of each other. Now, all of the arenas are to some degree a bowl. That building didn't go out. It went up. A seat in the second balcony at the stadium was not very far from the ice surface. Everything was right on top of each other. Because it was a brick building with no acoustics, the sound and atmosphere in there was incredible and unsurpassed, better than anywhere else. When you talked to any of the players that came in there, the mystique was visiting teams were kind of scared by the national anthem and things like that, but the visiting teams couldn't wait to play there because of the atmosphere. Sure they were going to get booed and they were going to get yelled at and all of those things, but they loved coming in there. It was a blast. It was awesome, a great atmosphere. It was second to none.
>
> Now, in saying that, the Blackhawks, in the construction of the United Center, did an incredible job. This building opened in '94. It's over 20 years old and has held up to the test of time. They have consistently worked on it to try to improve different aspects. The atmosphere is still very good and probably as good as anywhere in the NHL currently, but the fact of the matter is the square footage of this place is two and a half times what it was in Chicago Stadium. There's no way you're going to be able to replicate the complete sound and atmosphere of across the street. I remember

they did a hockey night in Canada in one of the playoff series in the '90s. Somebody brought in a noise meter to do a sound test as the anthem was going on. The meter reading was that of a jet engine. Literally, it felt like the walls were shaking even though they weren't. Because of the size and square footage of that building, it's something you're never going to be able to replicate.

While goaltenders like Glenn Hall and Tony Esposito graced Chicago Stadium for years, they weren't the only ones "manning the pipes." With the world's largest theater pipe organ situated among its faculties, Chicago Stadium rarely offered any break in the action for fans. Long-time New York Rangers radio play-by-play voice Marv Albert explains, "At the old Chicago Stadium, Bobby Hull would be coming down the wing on one side and then Stan Mikita would be surging across the blue line. The fans were cheering wildly, and it was a raucous atmosphere. At breaks in the play, there was a crowd favorite by the name of Al Melgard playing the organ. He would pound away at it, and the broadcast booth was actually shaking, which was, at times, a little concerning but it was well built so we were all fine." Melgard served as the Chicago Stadium "phantom" for over four decades, retiring in 1974 at the age of 85.

While the Blackhawks and Bulls have been able to "replicate" the number of championships won in the old building—and in a much shorter period of time—the smaller, narrower rink of Chicago Stadium, as well as the skaters placed strategically within it, have faded into the 3,000 extra seats surrounding the ice of its United Center successor.

BUFFALO MEMORIAL AUDITORIUM (THE "AUD")

Although never having hosted multiple Stanley Cup championships—or any for that matter—Buffalo Memorial Auditorium, better known as the "Aud," was home to the Buffalo Sabres for 27 years. Home of the unforgettable "French Connection"—the line of Gilbert Perreault, René Robert, and Richard Martin—the Aud saw its fair share of postseason hockey, especially during the mid-1970s, when the team made its first of two Stanley Cup Final appearances in the team's 46-year history. Like Chicago Stadium and Boston Garden, the Aud's structure lent itself to nonuniform playing dimensions, which was allowed by the league so long as the seating capacity was increased by as much as 50 percent. With the cement dry and the windows already hung, an expansion of that magnitude, like the one carried out in Chicago Stadium, would have to go up rather than out. Current Sabres TV play-by-play broadcaster Dan

Dunleavy, who never broadcast in Buffalo Memorial Auditorium, describes a fan's experience inside the building:

> I saw Buffalo play the Montreal Canadiens, which was a great rivalry at the Aud. One of many, but it was a good one. I remember the steepness of the seats, hanging right over the game, very similar to my first time at Maple Leaf Gardens when I was a little kid, walking out and just seeing that bowl lit and just remembering how much bigger it looked on TV. Then you walk in, and, all of a sudden, you are right on top of the game. That was a really neat feeling about the Aud. I don't remember much about the concessions or anything like that. I'd just get into that bowl and didn't want to leave. It's similar to Yankee Stadium. You just remember how steep those seats were.

While visitor Brett Hull's controversial Stanley Cup–clinching goal took place at the team's current home at First Niagara Center, the Aud was certainly home to innumerable memorable moments, many of which will never be forgotten, but, with the help of the team's first-ever Stanley Cup championship, will hopefully be repeated.

MONTREAL FORUM

Home to more championship banners than any other indoor sporting facility, the Montreal Forum, thanks to its resident Canadiens, was host to some of the greatest hockey teams ever assembled, including three verifiable dynasties. With players like Jean Béliveau, Jacques Plante, Guy Lafleur, and Maurice "Rocket" Richard, the Canadiens won 22 Stanley Cup championships in their former home, setting the league standard as high as the antenna on Montreal's CIBC Tower. Home (although temporarily) to a Montreal Maroons team that itself won two Stanley Cup championships, the Forum had its swan song during the 1995–1996 season; however, instead of closing its doors to end the regular season or postseason, the Forum hosted its final game on March 11, 1996, passing the torch (literally) to its successor, the Molson Centre, with 10 regular-season games yet to be played. In the booth as the visiting broadcaster on March 11, former Dallas Stars TV play-by-play voice Mike Fornes describes the Forum's farewell:

> I had the pleasure and honor of announcing the very last game in the Montreal Forum. That was a pretty neat thing. All the history, legend, and culture of hockey in Quebec was there that night because it was the last time they were ever going to play a game at the Forum. That was quite a

thing because the coach was Bob Gainey, who had so many great years. He had won five Stanley Cups with the Montreal Canadiens and had won the Selke Trophy. He was so revered in that city, and here he was coaching for Dallas. Fittingly, the Canadiens won the game. There was just so much tradition and glory in that building that night because the Canadiens were able to draw on all those ghosts of the past. It was so fun to be there and be a part of that. Just seeing all that was happening and being able to take it all in. Everything that was the old Montreal Forum.

Though not being present for the Forum's swan song, former New York Rangers radio play-by-play broadcaster Marv Albert still had his fair share of experiences at "Le Forum de Montréal." The hall of fame broadcaster notes, "I got a kick out of doing the games at the Forum in Montreal because of the storied history there. It was chilling. As a kid, I grew up listening to everything and watching everything, playing ball in the schoolyards, playing street hockey, and, at times, doing play by play in my own head, so these places are like cathedrals to me."

Although the Canadiens have yet to hoist a Stanley Cup championship banner into the rafters of their current home at the Bell Centre, the team went to great lengths to recreate the Forum experience for everyone involved. Buffalo Sabres TV play-by-play broadcaster (and assistant counsel to the defendant in the case of *Cookie Cutter v. Old School*) Dan Dunleavy notes,

> In my opinion, the best place to broadcast a game in the NHL—because of the way their gondola is set up—is Montreal. You would hang right over the top of the game. You feel the game. When I call a game, I don't sit down. I stand up. I literally hang over the rail to get as close to the game as I can, and, in Montreal, once you're looking over the ledge, you're right on top of the game. It's a gondola that's built right around the whole circumference of the ice surface, which is really cool. Everywhere else you go, you're standing up in the stands for crying out loud. In the back row calling the game. You couldn't feel farther away from the game.

MAPLE LEAF GARDENS

While the Toronto Maple Leafs don't make a habit of "retiring" the numbers of great players—say, players like George Armstrong, Tim Horton, Mats Sundin, and Börje Salming—the proof of their mastery on the ice is stitched into the 13 banners that once hung from the rafters at Maple Leaf Gardens. Standing for 69 seasons, Maple Leaf Gardens was home to two Toronto NHL dynasties in the 1940s and 1960s. While the craft of such players as Ted Kennedy,

Doug Gilmour, and Wendel Clark developed and flourished on the Maple Leaf Gardens' ice, the ingenuity of broadcasters like Foster Hewitt took place high above it, revolutionizing the way hockey games are called. Columbus Blue Jackets TV play-by-play broadcaster Jeff Rimer, who worked with the Montreal Canadiens during a rivalrous time with the Maple Leafs, discusses the innovation brought about by Mr. Hewitt:

> They tried to emulate and duplicate the old Maple Leaf Gardens as best as they could with the Air Canada Centre, hanging in the gondola, where Foster Hewitt made it certainly a famous spot being the first and greatest broadcaster. Foster had the gondola in the old Maple Leaf Gardens, and that was really great. Those old buildings were a delight to broadcast in. As it turns out with a lot of these newer buildings, the TV broadcast booths are up higher and a little farther away from the play.

Hewitt's original gondola was ordered to be dismantled and incinerated by the villainous owner of the Maple Leafs, Harold Ballard. Sitting in the same "seat" (but not the same gondola) as both Foster and his son, Bill Hewitt, radio/TV play-by-play broadcaster Joe Bowen describes his vantage point while calling Toronto Maple Leafs hockey:

> I got to do games in the Forum, Boston Garden, Chicago Stadium, and Maple Leaf Gardens. Those were the first buildings—if you will—of the original six teams. Obviously, the new buildings—the amenities, the sight lines—everything is so much better. Private boxes for corporate people. It's much better. As a broadcaster, I miss the old buildings because we were so much closer to the ice, and our job was a whole lot easier. In Canada, at least, they have thought about broadcasters because they have built gondolas from the back of the building out over the ice so our sight lines are much better. In the United States, it's an afterthought. It's "stick those guys in the back and let them do as best as they can."
>
> When you go to a mausoleum like in Dallas, the United Center in Chicago, or in Washington, you are a long, long way from the ice, trying to do a job that dictates you cannot do it off a monitor. You need to do it by visual, seeing the puck and who might get it next. It makes our job a lot more difficult because of that. We did a game the other night in the All Star Game in Columbus on radio, and they decided it would be a great idea if they came out wearing black sweaters with black numbers and just a little outline. Let me tell you, for an hour of hockey, it was damn near impossible to tell who had the puck on the black team. They don't think a lot of times—designing sweaters and everything else—that there's a guy upstairs who may be talking to a couple of million people. You put him in the worst seat and provide him with the worst sight line in the house, and you're asking him to do his job. That's pretty tough.

While the Maple Leafs continue their Stanley Cup drought, which is approaching the half-century mark, Maple Leaf Gardens, still standing some 16 years after its replacement, will continue on as Toronto's standard for success until a 14th Stanley Cup banner passes the gondola on its way to being hung high above the Air Canada Centre's ice.

NASSAU VETERANS MEMORIAL COLISEUM

Once referred to as "Fort Never Lose," Nassau Veterans Memorial Coliseum is one of the most recent arenas to close its doors to NHL crowds. Opened in 1972, Nassau has housed eight different teams of several sports, including indoor soccer, basketball, and, of course, hockey. The New York Islanders came into the league during the 1972–1973 expansion and took only eight seasons to create an NHL dynasty. Thanks to team-builder Al Arbour and players like Mike Bossy, Clark Gillies, Bryan Trottier, and Billy Smith, the Islanders were able to win four straight Stanley Cup titles in the early 1980s, before passing the dynasty torch to the Edmonton Oilers. Having broadcast a good portion of his Hall of Fame career from inside the Coliseum's booth, former Islanders radio play-by-play voice Jiggs McDonald reflects on the suburban sports mecca, saying,

> I don't think there was a better arena to watch a hockey game in than Nassau Coliseum, and that's because of the degree of the angle of seating. You were right on top of the ice no matter where you sat in the building. Yes, it was outdated. At the end, it was probably in comparison to the other arenas that were new in 1972. It was maybe a little outdated even when it opened. It had a lack of elevators, lack of luxury suites, and the dressing rooms were small. For the majority of the players—if not all—it was like your old hometown arena. Small dressing rooms, great atmosphere, loud, rocking. You could drive to the games. It wasn't right downtown anywhere. It had a parking lot. You could be in and out of there. You could leave home, and, in some cases, you could be 20 minutes [to a] half hour to the building and 20 minutes [to a] half hour home after the game. Fans were probably spoiled in that respect. It was a hockey arena. There was no question. It was loud. The concourse level was narrow and often jammed. I didn't get to the concourse between periods, but the one thing you heard was how narrow and congested it was trying to get a hot dog or a beer. The sight lines and the atmosphere were just phenomenal. It wasn't a cookie cutter. It was just a good old-time hockey rink.

As a "good old-time hockey rink," the entertainment value of Nassau Coliseum didn't extend to just the fans. Rangers radio voice Dave Maloney, who also played 11 seasons with the team, describes his experience at the Coliseum as a visiting player, saying,

> I loved playing in the Coliseum. The fans were right on top of you. There seemed to be an equal representation of Ranger and Islander fans. The intimacy of the Nassau Coliseum was neat and the Islanders were a team that was skilled. They played hard, and there were all kinds of things that add up to be very exciting and very intense. We were probably better as a team in the early '80's under Herb Brooks, but we could never beat the Islanders, but, of course, they beat everybody else. It was an exciting time. It was a legitimate rivalry, and it was enhanced as both teams were a little bit better.

As Maloney's playing career was enveloped by the team's 54-season cup-less drought, the former defenseman was reminded who the better team was every time he glanced up to the Coliseum rafters to see a fresher championship banner dangling with each new year.

Former New York Islanders radio voice, Howie Rose, who is perhaps better known for his play-by-play calls with the New York Mets, was in the booth on April 25, 2015, when the Islanders played what would be their final game in the Coliseum. Looking back on his road to becoming a broadcaster, Rose describes Nassau's key role:

> It meant a great deal to me when I was going to college. My college career coincided with the arrival of the Islanders. My freshman year of college was the Islanders' first in the NHL. As I went through my time with the college radio station at Queens College, WQMC, I was able to gain accreditation to the Coliseum for select Islanders games. I would bring my tape recorder and practice play-by-play and then do interviews after the game and treat it as though I were a regular NHL announcer. It was over 40 years ago now. I look at that experience as having been central towards my achieving the goal of becoming a play-by-play broadcaster in the National Hockey League. In that respect—from that very narrow perspective—that building has meant a great deal to me.
>
> I think to see, through attrition, the Coliseum become this sort of fabled old barn so many of the others—Boston Garden, Montreal Forum, etc.— had become over the years was kind of ironic because no one ever considered it more than a slab of cement and a bunch of seats to begin with. As all those older buildings disappeared, suddenly there was the Coliseum, with its low ceiling and the ability to really hold in the noise. It became unique. It never was unique before. It was unique largely through attrition. I'll miss all of it. Our broadcast location was probably the best in the league. They make it very difficult for us to broadcast games now. The new buildings put all the broadcast locations way up and far back. Really, the hardest part of the job is identifying the players. It's gotten very tiresome. The whole pro-

cess of trying to do a game the way you used to do it when you're having trouble just seeing who the hell has the puck because of where they make us do these games has really made me kind of weary of the whole thing.

Rose's—and the Islanders'—new home in Brooklyn, the Barclays Center, although not providing the easy commute, parking, and intimacy of its predecessor, still hopes to house the team's return to championship glory.

THE OLYMPIA

While Joe Louis Arena stood as one of the oldest arenas in the NHL before closing its doors following the 2016–2017 season, the "Joe" is not the original home of the Detroit Red Wings. Built in 1927, the Olympia housed some of this original-six team's all-time greatest players, including Ted Lindsay, Alex Delvecchio, and Sid Abel, but none were as quintessential to the Red Wings—or perhaps hockey in general—than number 9, "Mr. Hockey," Gordie Howe. Being a part of four of the team's seven Stanley Cups won inside the Olympia, Howe left as the game's all-time leading scorer after 26 seasons in the league. With 25 of those being played in a Detroit Red Wings uniform, he easily proved his longevity, even to current team radio play-by-play broadcaster Ken Kal, who recalls,

> I saw Gordie Howe late in his career. I was only 12 years old when I saw my first game at Olympia, a matinee game against the Oakland Seals. It was January 25, 1969. Gordie actually scored a goal in that game. I had never seen him live. I had always seen him on television, but I remember watching him. He was a right-handed shot, but there were also times in the game where if he was on the left side, he'd shoot left-handed, and he didn't miss a beat. He was such an amazing player even at that age, and I could only imagine what he was like in his prime.

By the time Howe returned to the NHL as a Hartford Whaler in 1979, his former team had already pulled up stakes and moved into their current home at Joe Louis Arena, a name that may have been better suited for its predecessor. Kal continues,

> The old stadiums like Madison Square Garden—the old one, not the new one—Chicago, Boston, Detroit were all built for boxing basically in the '20s and '30s. It turned out when they put a hockey rink in there that the sight lines were unbelievable just because of the way it was built. Back then, hockey was kind of like a secondary sport that was put into the boxing arena, and it became intimate.

The Olympia's intimacy continued long after the building hosted its final game in 1979. Philadelphia Flyers lead radio play-by-play voice Tim Saunders, who grew up in Detroit, describes the Olympia's presence in his life, saying,

> I grew up in Olympia Stadium. As a kid, I probably went to 35–40 games a year. I grew up spending more time at Olympia Stadium than I did school and I had the grades to prove it. That place was a shrine. It was such a special place. It was a sad time to see that building go, especially after they let it sit there decaying for as long as they did. The weekend before they were finally going to take a wrecking ball to it, I was coming home from college and I decided to drive by to see it one last time. A lot of people had turned out who had the same impulse. The building was boarded up, but I noticed that people had pulled the boards away and were actually going in. There was no electricity, and it had been decaying for a couple of years so it was in awful, terrible shape, but it was one of the strangest, coolest feelings to be in that building again. This was before they realized they could sell all the seats and stuff in the building. People were coming out of there with anything they could carry, so I quickly went home, got a tool box, came back, and took out six chairs that I still have today. It was scary and sad, but it was a cool memory before they finally took the building down.

CALGARY "STAMPEDE" CORRAL

While the width and length of the ice surface certainly had an effect on how the game was played in "old school" hockey arenas, other factors came into effect as well. The Calgary Corral, more commonly referred to as the "Stampede" Corral, was an interim home for the Calgary Flames as they moved from Atlanta to start the 1980–1981 NHL season. Although only in the building for three years before moving to the team's current home at Scotiabank Saddledome, the Stampede Corral proved itself a nemesis to visiting teams because of both its features and the imported product on the ice. Former Calgary Flames radio broadcaster and Hall of Famer Peter Maher explains,

> In the Corral, where the Flames played their first three seasons, it was kind of a unique situation in many, many ways. When you looked at the dimensions of the Corral, I believe they had the highest boards of any in the NHL then and since. The team coming in from Atlanta, being a large-sized team, they worked that to their advantage, especially in the very first season in '80–'81, when the Flames lost only five games in the Corral all season. I think it was quite intimidating in three ways. The size of the players, the height of the boards, and the crowd in that building seemed to be right on top of you. The visiting teams had a lot of difficulty comprehending

those factors. The Flames had a great regular season in their home building and wound up winning two playoff series before losing out in the league semifinals.

Considering that the team boasted a winning record during its time in the Corral, many contested moving the team to the Scotiabank Saddledome; however, with almost 12,000 more seats and lower ticket prices, the debate was quickly quashed, especially among season ticket-holders paying premium prices and the team owner. The Flames won their first and only Stanley Cup title in 1989 at the Saddledome, and came dangerously close again in 2004.

ST. LOUIS ARENA (THE "CHECKERDOME")

Generally, the transition from "old school" to "cookie cutter" has come with an increased seating capacity. But such was not the case for the St. Louis Blues. The team's old home, St. Louis Arena, otherwise known as the "Checkerdome," had 740 more seats than its successor, the Scottrade Center. While the Blues have failed to secure a Stanley Cup championship, the team came closest in the Checkerdome early in the franchise's history.

Thanks to players like Red Berenson, Al Arbour, and Frank St. Marseille, the Blues came in as runner-up their first three seasons in the league. Present for practically all of the team's initial success, legendary play-by-play broadcaster Dan Kelly had a plus-one for most of the games he chronicled from the booth, his son John. Going from a spectator at St. Louis Arena to TV play-by-play broadcaster inside the team's new home at the Scottrade Center, John Kelly compares the transition from one to the other:

> It really is like night and day. It would be like living in a house that was 100 years old and then buying a brand new one. It's really hard to compare. The arena was so distinct. It had such great charm. The seats would feel like the fans were more on top of you at the old arena. The slope of the seats was a lot greater than it is in the current arena. Some of the seats were partially obstructed. Early in the history of the Blues, they didn't have any air conditioning, so when it would come to be playoff time, it was 80 degrees outside, and it was really warm in that building.
>
> The Blues, with the crowd and the fans singing and the organist, it was a very intimidating place to play. It was a distinct home-ice advantage for the Blues. To go into Scottrade, it's a wonderful arena, but, quite honestly, it's a lot like 25 other arenas of the NHL, except the fact that it's the Blues' arena. The downside is you don't have the unique feel and looks. Some of the arenas had smaller ice surfaces. There's really no comparison between

St. Louis Arena, Chicago Stadium, Boston Garden, the Forum, and all these new arenas. In the old days with the old arenas, the home teams had a bigger advantage than they do today because of a lot of those reasons.

While most, if not all, of the 740-seat differential between the two buildings is distributed throughout the Scottrade Center's luxury boxes and suites, the one factor that could pull the team's new home out from the shadow of its old one would be a first-ever Stanley Cup championship. Stay tuned.

CIVIC ARENA (THE "IGLOO")

Built in 1961, Civic Arena, also known as the "Igloo," was the first sports venue to feature a retractable roof, beating Toronto's (then named) Skydome by nearly three decades. The Igloo was home to the Pittsburgh Penguins for more than four decades, housing three Stanley Cup champions and witnessing the birth of the hall of fame worthy careers of Penguin superstars Mario Lemieux, Jaromír Jágr, and Sidney Crosby. A pioneer of architectural technology, Civic Arena definitely had no shortage of defining characteristics. Penguins TV play-by-play voice Paul Steigerwald explains,

> The thing that stands out the most is it had a modern feel to it forever because of its roof. The fact that the roof opened. It was the first building of its kind in that regard. It had a different look to it. It was a dome. No other building in the league looked quite like The Igloo inside. Because it was originally a building of only about 10,000 seats, when they remodeled it a couple of times, they had to jam the balconies in there and create new seating that made for some pretty cool looks. The two balconies at either end were steep and good seats. When you sat, you were looking down at the ice. In order to put those balconies in, they had to pile drive down into the ground to support them and the steel structures. The building took on a different look and became a more intimate building as they added more seats.

Having been with the team almost since their coming to Pittsburgh, Hall of Fame play-by-play voice of the Penguins Mike Lange describes the team's former venue:

> The arena itself was such a unique place. It was built like an igloo. It was the first retractable dome where they started to make buildings like that. The difference in the uniqueness of it was really a focal point, too. As it was, Civic Arena was never built for hockey. It was built to be a show place for cultural events, and it turned out to be a big centerpiece for the

Penguins' success in the NHL. When it first opened up, it was a gigantic place for the opera and the symphony.

This original intention for the Penguins' home of more than 30 years gave fans an auditory experience perhaps not shared in any of hockey's other venues. Paul Steigerwald continues, "The Igloo's roof was different. The other old arenas like Chicago Stadium and Maple Leaf Gardens had a different kind of ceiling where the crowd really echoed and reverberated in the building, whereas that building was created for the Civic Life Opera. It was more acoustically created for music, so it didn't have that echoing and reverberating kind of sound some buildings do. Fans figured out a way to make it loud when the Penguins won the Cup in '91 and '92. It was unique unto itself because of the shape of the building and the whole concept of it."

CONTINENTAL AIRLINES ARENA (THE "MEADOWLANDS")

While the argument regarding the pros and cons of new versus old arenas continues, some tend to forget what's on the *outside*. Located in the Meadowlands of East Rutherford, New Jersey, Continental Airlines Arena, home to three New Jersey Devils Stanley Cup championship teams, is a world apart from the team's new home at Prudential Center in the city of Newark.

Former Devils play-by-play broadcaster Gary Thorne describes the Devils' original home and setting, saying,

> The fact that it was at the Meadowlands made it a part of a sports complex, which I think fed into helping the Devils grow as a franchise. They got connected to the Jets, the Giants, and the NBA. They were part of a larger sports milieu that was going on at the time, and I think that helped the Devils establish themselves. It was a pretty good fan building. It was fan friendly, and people liked it. When there were big games being played there, there was a lot of noise. It was over in an area where the Devils were trying to propagate a real fan base in New Jersey. It had a lot going for it. It was a good building to play in. It certainly wasn't an old barn in any sense of the word like Chicago Stadium or the old building in St. Louis, but it still was a place where the fans felt this was really a home. This is where the team belonged and where they belonged as fans of the club. It was a positive for the Devils and establishing themselves.

A lot of the establishment of the Devils didn't just take place on a parcel of land in East Rutherford. The relocated team also faced the task of winning so many rooted New York Rangers fans of the area as well. New York radio play-by-play voice Kenny Albert, who was in the New York/New Jersey area amidst this change, notes, "For Rangers versus Devils games at the Meadowlands, I always felt like whichever team scored in those games, you'd have 60% of the fans cheering. Any Devils fan who was born any time before 1975 or before the Devils came in '82 were probably a Rangers fan first. Then they switched their allegiances—especially New Jersey residents—when the Devils came. You probably don't have as many crossover fans now, but back then, you really did because of all the folks in New Jersey who had been Rangers fans and switched their allegiances over."

After the switching of allegiances and raising of three Stanley Cup championship banners to their Continental Airlines Arena rafters, the Devils eventually moved into their new digs to start the 2007–2008 season. The results on the scoreboard didn't change much, but the fan experience did. New Jersey Devils TV play-by-play broadcaster Steve Cangialosi describes both the loss and gain of fans resulting from the team's move:

> The entire experience changed for a lot of people who have supported the team for a very long time. The aspect of tailgating was taken away from those warm-weather games where some fans would be out in the parking lot in the Meadowlands. In Newark, the team moved into a gorgeous, state-of-the-art facility, but it was in the inner city, which meant the dynamic of the whole experience would change. It was met with resistance clearly by some fans in that first season of '07–'08 because—let's face it—some people are creatures of habit. Many people, for 20 some odd years, would get into the habit.
>
> They had the routine down. You put the key in the ignition with the car in the driveway at 6:15 and you had the whole route to the old Meadowlands arena mapped out. You did that for years and years, and, suddenly, the team is moving into a more complicated patch of real estate, which is what Newark is. It's New Jersey's largest city. There are some who easily adapted to taking the train. It is a hub for mass transit in New Jersey. For some, it was a wonderful thing. For instance, the scattered Devil fans across the Hudson River suddenly had easy access to the rink to root on their team just by hopping on an NJ Transit or PATH train. It made it so much easier.

Being comparatively younger, especially to the Chicago Stadiums and Boston Gardens of the past, Continental Airlines Arena didn't have the "right-on-top-of-the-ice" feel of the older NHL venues. In fact, the transition, unlike the ones experienced by practically every other NHL team moving into a new arena, involved going to a smaller—not bigger—facility, making the inside adjustment a positive one for fans. Cangialosi continues,

The sight lines at Prudential Center far outweigh what you had at the Meadowlands. It's smaller, more intimate, and, just in terms of amenities, it beats the Meadowlands on levels too numerous to mention. I believe there was only one Devils game that sold out that last season at the Meadowlands, and it was a second-round playoff game against the Ottawa Senators. The arena was enormous. That was an issue. When you moved into the more confined setting of the Prudential Center, it just created so much more of a bona fide, intimidating atmosphere that really helped the experience. The one thing about Prudential Center that I think is probably the best aspect of the arena that nobody talks about is the lighting. It's a great place to call a game. It's a superb place to watch a game. I've been in every rink in the NHL that's existed since 2006, and, between the sight lines and the lighting in that arena, it's really second to none.

With the loss of all-time winningest goaltender Martin Brodeur to retirement, the Devils, a rebuilding team, are looking to put their suburban fan base back on that PATH train and through the Prudential Center doors in time for what would be the team's fourth Stanley Cup championship.

REXALL PLACE

The oldest nonrenovated arena in the NHL at the time of its closure, Rexall Place, home of the Edmonton Oilers for 35-plus years, gave way to Rogers Place to begin the 2016–2017 season. Host to five Stanley Cup championship–winning teams that included the likes of Wayne Gretzky, Mark Messier, Grant Fuhr, Jari Kurri, Glenn Anderson, and Randy Gregg, Rexall Place saw so much success that the sign outside Edmonton read, "City of Champions." Today, with the sign changed and the team more than 26 years removed from its last Stanley Cup, perhaps the most lasting impression of Rexall Place was the one left on the team personnel *not* taking the ice. Oilers TV play-by-play broadcaster Kevin Quinn describes his experience calling games inside Rexall Place:

> The thing I like about Rexall Place, from my perspective, is the press box is a ring as opposed to being at the back of the arena. You're not at the back and you're over the rink and ice surface more than other places, like New Jersey, where you're right at the back. The modern facilities now have the writers in front and the broadcasters in back, in kind of a tiered setup. Rexall has press boxes where you can walk all the way around, and it's just the press box. The writers are on one side and the broadcasters are on another. The scouts, all the visiting GM's, and player personnel are all in this ring. You've got to walk upstairs, and you're sort of above the action that

way. You're over the ice and the fans are at the back. It's a multipurpose facility, so it's not like the old "Aud" or Boston Garden, or some of those rinks where you have a real steep grade and the fans are more on top of the action. I would say the slope of the seats is about standard.

Capable of seating 1,500 more fans than its predecessor, the Edmonton Oilers are seeking to raise a Stanley Cup banner into the heights of Rogers Place, inspiring the city of Edmonton to change that welcome sign back to its previous greeting.

JOE LOUIS ARENA

While its 38 seasons hosting the Red Wings are 14 fewer than its Olympia predecessor, Joe Louis Arena hosted more playoff action than many venues with twice its tenure. Housing all 25 consecutive playoff appearances for the Detroit Red Wings from 1990–1991 thru 2015–2016 (third most all time), Joe Louis Arena saw the birth of the hall of fame careers of Steve Yzerman, Sergei Fedorov, and Nicklas Lidström, as well as the death of the team's 42 year cupless drought in 1997. Raising four championship banners to add to the team's seven from the Olympia, the Red Wings, with its "Russian Five," "Stevie Y's," and "Datsyukian" goal scoring, set a new tone for offense in the NHL and were able to establish the team's first dynasty since "The Production Line" days of Gordie Howe, Ted Lindsay, and Sid Abel.

Though the end of Joe Louis Arena would coincide with that of the Red Wings' 25 year playoff streak, the team, fans, and even the broadcasters have something to take with them transitioning into the team's new home of Little Caesars Arena. Red Wings TV play-by-play broadcaster Ken Daniels, notes,

> When people ask, 'What are you going to take from The Joe?' I say, 'Nothing but memories.' The people you meet. The walk you take through the north gate, down towards the zamboni, and then up the elevator. The people you meet along the way. Eugene in the elevator. Georgette upstairs. I think about that walk often. I always used to see the old footage of Foster Hewitt walking through Maple Leaf Gardens amongst the crowd. You'd just get lost in that crowd and there's Foster who stood out. He could have been the prime minister of Canada at the time because of his popularity there. It was so cool to see Foster Hewitt do that walk and he did that walk so many nights. I think of the walk I have taken so many times. Just going up there, getting off on the fourth floor, and walking down one flight to the press box. I've done that walk close to 1,000 times. I'll miss that and those moments, but I'll find a new walk in the new building.

THE VERDICT

While the debate seems quite one-sided—at least from the broadcaster's point of view—the bottom line is and will always be the one marked "net income" on the yearly tax return. Broadcasters may miss being able to see the players' numbers, players may miss the overwhelming home-ice advantage created by hometown fans, and fans may miss being able to practically touch the players, but the game has indeed changed, becoming less "old school" and more "cookie cutter."

With the 2015–2017 Pittsburgh Penguins becoming the first back-to-back Stanley Cup champions since the 1996–1998 Detroit Red Wings, the NHL's parity has truly been demonstrated over the past two plus decades. Eighth seeds are upsetting one seeds in the playoffs more frequently, and overcoming an 0–3 series deficit has gone from an impossibility to a feasible outcome. With an increased league size prompting the fear of a more watered-down, one-sided playoff atmosphere, the competition has instead become fiercer. The discussion may continue for years to come concerning nostalgia versus forward thinking; however, consecutive sellout streaks, full corporate boxes, and quarterly earning reports void of red ink will always trump the "glory days" mentality, making the "reverse baseball" trend one that will remain in place until all the old arenas have been replaced or torn down.

· 33 ·

A Hockey Séance from the Booth

*A*lthough the game of hockey predates the introduction of radio and television broadcasts, hockey and broadcasting have been together for nearly a century. Beginning with the incomparable Foster Hewitt, radio broadcasts for the sport go back as far as 1923. The fast-paced nature of the game doesn't allow for much "wiggle room" or many "liberties" when it comes to calling a game and leaving a signature; however, many of the greatest voices in the game's history have left an indelible mark on not only the fans, but also the broadcasters who, once fans themselves, caught the broadcasting bug.

From the boards and ice of a hockey arena to the Bermuda grass and crushed clay of a baseball diamond, the play-by-play broadcasters of yesterday, while passed on from this world, still reside in the hearts and memories of those they left behind. With voices so impressionable they kindled the fire that became the career of most every play-by-play broadcaster in the sport of hockey, these icons and their calls linger inside the arenas long after the "on-air" light outside their booth went dim for the last time.

DAN KELLY

Being defined by two separate eras of his career, Patrick Daniel Kelly called the game both at the national level and for the St. Louis Blues a year into their introduction to the league. Aside from his duties broadcasting *Hockey Night in Canada*, Kelly announced some of the most historic moments of the Stanley Cup Finals, including Bobby Orr's historic "flying goal" to clinch the title in overtime for the Boston Bruins in 1970. Calling the game with the assistance of media juggernaut KMOX out of St. Louis, Kelly's voice reached throughout the United States and into Canada. The Kelly broadcasting torch has gone from Dan to two of his sons, John and Daniel. Following in the steps of his father, John is lead TV play-by-play broadcaster for the St. Louis Blues.

I grew up in St. Louis. Dan Kelly was the guy I would listen to every night. There was something special about this guy's voice. It was smooth. He gave a solid description of the play-by-play. He knew where the puck was, and he made it exciting at the proper times. In hockey, you've got to have a certain time element where the inflection comes in. You've got to know when the guy's getting ready to take a shot, maybe when he's ready to score a big goal in the game and be ready for that moment. I listened to Dan Kelly every night. I've got tapes of him. I just thought he was the best hockey announcer, and there's been a lot of them. Even going back to the '50s and '60s. The great ones from Montreal and Toronto, but there was something special about him. Maybe it was because I was a Blues fan. I said, "You know what? That's the guy I want to be like. Hopefully, I can have a broadcast voice like that."

I actually went to broadcast school in St. Louis and got to meet him one time. He was an instructor for one day at the school I was going to. You can imagine that was a big thrill. I used to go to a lot of Blues home games growing up in South St. Louis and bring my radio with me to listen to the games. It was just something unique about this guy. The voice quality was clear. I knew what was going on. He made it exciting.

—Steve Carroll, Anaheim Ducks
radio play-by-play broadcaster

I will certainly give huge thanks to the great Dan Kelly, who was kind of a hero of mine as a young guy trying to learn the business. When I got into the NHL, I became really good friends with him. He took me under his wing. I would annually try to set up a dinner with him because back then, we weren't chartering. We would play a game, stay in the city, and then leave the next morning. I would make sure every year to go out to dinner with Dan Kelly at least once. One time, we were in St. Louis, and I told him, "Next week, you and I are going out to dinner." He said, "Great. We'll go out after the game." So the next week comes, the game ends, and I see Dan after and he's with his wife, the beautiful Fran. I said, "Dan, don't worry about it. I'll see you next time," and he says, "No way. We're going and you're coming with us." So we go out to dinner, and as the night goes on, I realize it's actually their anniversary. I'm thinking, "Holy crap.

He brought her to Chicago for their anniversary. What am I doing here?" Dan was a really special guy and incredibly helpful.

—Pat Foley, Chicago Blackhawks
TV play-by-play broadcaster

When I had gotten older into my late teens/early 20s, when I got into broadcasting, probably the guy I listened to the most was a guy by the name of Dan Kelly, who is in the Hockey Hall of Fame and who [has] also passed away. Dan Kelly was the guy I listened to a lot, and I really thought, "That's the way you should broadcast a hockey game." He was kind of the guy I really modeled myself after in a lot of ways and had a great impact on me.

—Dean Brown, Ottawa Senators
radio play-by-play broadcaster

The one guy who really jumped out to me was Dan Kelly. He was the broadcaster for the Blues, but he was also often the broadcaster for national games. I just loved his goal call and his enthusiasm. When he would call a game, you could be in another room, and, when you would hear his voice, you were drawn to it because he just had that enthusiasm. I just loved his style. Dan Kelly was the guy I was drawn to the most as a kid and would have loved to have followed in his footsteps.

As it turns out, in the American Hockey League, I was doing games up in Utica, and his son John was in the league as well. It was fun to work with him. As far as hockey goes, Dan Kelly was the person I was influenced most by. In my mind, the announcer's job is to not get in the way of the game. It's to enhance either the viewing or listening of the game, and I think Dan Kelly did that to the utmost. All those games seemed more exciting when he was calling them. I think the best thing you can say about an announcer is that he doesn't get in the way of the game, and he makes it even more exciting. Some guys start to make it more exciting and get in the way of it. Then there are others who don't do it justice or don't convey the excitement of the game at all, so you've got to find that happy medium and hopefully deliver it.

—Jim Jackson, Philadelphia Flyers
TV play-by-play broadcaster

I remember Dan Kelly would do Sunday afternoon hockey games. I was in public school and just remember listening to his calls. I thought he was great. I loved the way he called the game. It brought me into the game and carried me along. Immediately after some of my buddies and I would watch the game, we had a pool and the water was still frozen, so we'd go out and play on that afterward. We'd say, "There's an instant rink. Let's go." We used to go out there Sunday afternoons. There would be two of us. We'd go up and down, and I would do the play-by-play. I wasn't trying to imitate Dan Kelly, because I couldn't. I remember calling the game was also part of our playing the game. I remember playing hockey in the hallway in college, and I would always be the guy calling it. For whatever reason, I always loved doing that. Dan Kelly would have to be my favorite.

—Kevin Quinn, Edmonton Oilers
TV play-by-play broadcaster

Dan Kelly was a longtime national voice in Canada for CBC. *Hockey Night in Canada.* He was another guy I would listen to because we could get a KMOX signal in northwest Indiana. It was really from Dan Kelly I became a Blues fan for a while in the early to mid-'70s. Just a great voice. Very distinct. He could call a game as well as anyone. Just a great person. I met him later on in life, and he couldn't have been nicer.

—Matt McConnell, Arizona Coyotes
TV play-by-play broadcaster

Dan Kelly, the longtime voice of the Blues, would do the Sunday afternoon games on CBS. The Blues games were on KMOX. I grew up in Dayton, Ohio, and we could very easily pick up KMOX at night. I did not become a hockey fan until I was in high school. I saw a game between the Bruins and the Maple Leafs. They had about three fights. It was a 6–4 game. There were all these goals. Bobby Orr was dominating the game, and Derek Sanderson got into a fight and I thought, "Wow. This is a crazy game. I kinda like this," so I started tuning in every Sunday afternoon.

We'd have to watch the NHL games on a station out of Cincinnati, so it came in kind of snowy, but Kelly was doing the game. I just started listening to games so I could hear Dan do the St. Louis Blues. I knew at that point I wanted to become a sportscaster, and as I got more and more interested in hockey, I really focused on becoming a hockey announcer. No question he was my biggest influence. When you consider when he was doing the CBS games, it was after the first expansion, and there was an explosion of interest in the country in hockey. So many more people were drawn to the sport, and that was right when he was at the height of his popularity. The Blues were a very good team, and, obviously, he kept going with that into the '80s before he died. I think the timing of his career and what a strong voice he was combined to make him be the dominant voice of that era. It was just the right time in terms of being able to influence people like me and some of the other guys.

—Rick Peckham, Tampa Bay Lightning
TV play-by-play broadcaster

I remember watching his games as a kid in Ottawa, Ontario, when he was doing *Hockey Night in Canada*. As a young Canadian, it was the thing to do on a Saturday night. For someone to have their dad on the show, it was amazing. I was only eight years old when he came to St. Louis, and our family didn't know a lot about St. Louis. I had never been there. I had never been to the States. He became a huge hit in St. Louis, along with the Blues. I never really thought he was that big a deal until, one day, they asked my dad to come to school with me and speak to our class. Every single kid in the school wanted his autograph. I was blown away. I'm thinking, "He's my dad. What's the big deal," but, the more I was around him—whether at the grocery store or in the arena—people would constantly ask him for his autograph or pictures. He was beloved.

When I got to be older, I realized I wasn't going to be an athlete. I was certainly a huge sports fan. I played hockey, but I knew I wasn't going to make it in that part of the business, so why not try broadcasting? He was a big help to me obviously. He would listen to my tapes, support me, and critique my games. He was and always will be my broadcasting hero. I was so fortunate to have someone like that. It's a huge advantage, not just how to broadcast and get tips on how to announce a game or use different phrases or how excited to get but just how to conduct yourself around other broadcasters. I would go to practices and into the press room with him before a game. I would be with the owner at dinner after the game, and I saw how he conducted himself and how he treated people; whether they were the owner of the restaurant or the bus boy. I learned as much about that as I did about broadcasting from him.

I've had a lot of fans tell me over the years I sound more and more like him every year. Any kind of comparison like that, to me, is a huge compliment. My dad was known for saying, "He shoots, he scores," and other broadcasters have used that. As a matter of fact, the first-ever broadcaster of hockey, Foster Hewitt, is the one who came up with that phrase. My dad had other phrases he would use. He would say, "Shooting" when the player had the puck or "The glide." When I was younger, he told me to try to come up with different phrases and catchphrases. I have done that, but, at times, when I'm broadcasting a game, I'll use one of those he used. I won't do it a lot, but I'll do it in a way that I want the fans to know I'm still Dan Kelly's son. If I think this is a great way to call a certain play or situation, I'll pull one of those out of my hat and use it. I think it's cool that I can do that. I think the fans of St. Louis appreciate it, and it probably brings back memories of my dad.

—John Kelly, St. Louis Blues TV play-by-play broadcaster

DANNY GALLIVAN

Broadcasting a record 16 Stanley Cup championships, former Montreal Canadiens play-by-play broadcaster Danny Gallivan announced the game of hockey for more than three decades. Calling games for three dynasties, Gallivan covered such beloved all-time Montreal players as Jean Béliveau, Maurice "Rocket" Richard, Guy Lafleur, Jacques Lemaire, and Larry Robinson. Devout to the "old school" ways of calling a hockey game, he insisted on holding a microphone in his hand while doing a broadcast, even with his producer-mandated headset on and the microphone unplugged and "dead." Known mainly as the voice of the Canadiens, Gallivan also worked on *Hockey Night in Canada* for 32 years, beginning in 1952. He was a recipient of the Foster Hewitt Memorial Award.

> A big influence was Danny Gallivan. I'm from New Brunswick, and that's in the east and pretty much Montreal Canadiens territory. I was never a Canadiens fan. I was a Toronto Maple Leafs fan, but there were more Canadiens games on television and even aired on the radio in the area I was, so I got to listen to Danny quite frequently. He was from the Maritime provinces, as I was. Eventually, I would get to meet him. Interestingly, I sent him a tape recording of one of my games. In fact, I think it was reel to reel in those days of the '70s. He wrote back with some comments, and then, later that year, at a minor hockey banquet in my hometown, he was the featured speaker. During his speech, he said, "There's a guy in this room you fans all know well, but he's too talented of a broadcaster to be staying in your city for that much longer." What was interesting was three months after he made that comment, I became a broadcaster for the Toronto Maple Leafs.
>
> —Peter Maher, former Calgary Flames
> radio play-by-play broadcaster

The way Danny Gallivan would describe the way the Canadiens would "carry the puck up the ice," it was as if he was just floating along right beside them.

—Dan Dunleavy, Buffalo Sabres
TV play-by-play broadcaster

I was always a big hockey fan and I would listen to it on my powerful radio that picked up stations from Canada. I would turn on and listen to Foster Hewitt, who was the long-time voice of the Toronto Maple Leafs and Danny Gallivan, who was a long-time Montreal Canadiens announcer. I got to know Danny very well when I was doing the Rangers. He was so kind to me and just great to talk to.

—Marv Albert, former New York Rangers
radio play-by-play broadcaster

I got a chance to listen to Danny Gallivan on a regular basis once I became a professional myself. I admired so much how he could turn a phrase and how he'd capture the excitement of those glorious teams in Montreal.

—Mike "Doc" Emrick, NBC national TV and former
New Jersey Devils TV play-by-play broadcaster

I always felt and still feel Danny Gallivan was the best broadcaster I'd ever heard. He is still at that pinnacle up there. The rest of us are floundering around at the back end, just trying to hold our own. I think Bill and Foster Hewitt and Danny Gallivan would have been the guys who influenced me and made me want to get into broadcasting after it became apparent I wasn't going to actually play in the league.

—Joe Bowen, Toronto Maple Leafs TV/
radio play-by-play broadcaster

When it comes to Montreal, for me, the position is something to be held with a lot of humble respect for the past because the men who sat in the chair before were Danny Gallivan and Dick Irvin. For me, Foster Hewitt started the job, and Danny Gallivan brought life to it. Danny Gallivan was so important to what we do nowadays and, of course, to the Montreal Canadiens and the fan base. I'm honored. There's not a day that goes by I don't feel privileged to be able to do the job of calling the Montreal Canadiens because I look back to Danny Gallivan and Dick Irvin, and what they brought to the job and the legacy of the team. The most special part of it is the ability to be able to do the same job they did for so many years and with the same team. I think that's what I've always brought to it from day one, that understanding and respect for who was there before. I'm just very fortunate enough to be able to live my dream out now and call the games. That's really the one key thing for me when I think of doing the Montreal Canadiens, is to honor the legacy of Danny Gallivan and Dick Irvin.

—John Bartlett, Montreal Canadiens
radio play-by-play broadcaster

LLOYD PETTIT

Working in four different capacities in three sports in Chicago, broadcaster Lloyd Pettit left his biggest mark on hockey and the Blackhawks. Pettit called the Blackhawks during a time when the team was most famous for players Bobby Hull and Stan Mikita. Pettit left the Blackhawks in 1976, but not the game, as he and his wife purchased the Milwaukee Admirals of the International Hockey League. Although not having called a Stanley Cup championship–winning team during his time with the Blackhawks, Pettit remains a beloved figure in both the "Windy City" and the hearts of many of today's broadcasters.

I knew early on if I couldn't be a professional athlete, I thought I'd love to be out at the ballpark, stadium, or arena every night doing a broadcast. Playing little league baseball, I'd do the play-by-play of the game in my head. I grew up in Chicago, so I listened to the Chicago announcers, Jack Brickhouse and Bob Elson. Lloyd Pettit was a very exciting hockey announcer. He's in the Hockey Hall of Fame. He was the announcer during those really great years of the Blackhawks with Bobby Hull and Stan Mikita. I would listen to him before I started doing hockey, but, after I started, I would listen to him just to hear how he described certain plays and certain things that happened in the game.

Chicago Stadium, in those days, was a tremendously exciting arena in which to broadcast. As far as hockey goes, I would say it was Lloyd Pettit from Chicago who I listened to the most. I didn't necessarily try to pattern myself after him, but I did take from him the energy and enthusiasm you can put into a broadcast and have the audience really excited about it and almost feel like they're in the arena.

—Bob Miller, Los Angeles Kings
TV play-by-play broadcaster

No question. I think my interest in hockey came from a curiosity one night in the basement of our family's house in Gary, Indiana. My dad had a Blackhawks game on. I remember it was in black and white. I sat down and watched, and I had no idea what was going on. I liked what I saw and started watching more games with my dad, and, through that, I started listening to the Blackhawks on the radio. Without a doubt, the biggest influence to me was really two people: Lloyd Pettit and Dan Kelly.

Lloyd Pettit, who was the longtime voice of the Chicago Blackhawks, was a huge inspiration for me. He was a guy who called the game with such great description you could close your eyes. I'd be laying in bed with WMAQ, listening to Lloyd Pettit and the Blackhawks on Sunday night. I knew exactly where the puck was at all times. He was that good. His signature call was "shot and a goal." He was the biggest influence for me to get that interested in the sport of hockey and then later on in broadcasting.

—Matt McConnell, Arizona Coyotes
TV play-by-play broadcaster

I thought both Lloyd Pettit in Chicago and Dan Kelly in St. Louis had a command of the game that I admired. They didn't shout or scream. You could understand the words they were saying. They let you know they were excited about what was happening, but they were always understandable. That was something I worked really hard to incorporate into my broadcasts. To me, it was very similar to the tone and tempo of a baseball announcer. I thought they were so in control of what they were saying. Then, when it was appropriate, they could get highly excitable. They were always understandable, and that's something that is lacking in many of the accounts you hear today.

—Mike Fornes, former Dallas Stars
TV play-by-play broadcaster

Lloyd Pettit is the guy I grew up listening to as a kid. He was very nice to me as a young broadcaster. I actually interviewed him a couple of times as a young guy, and he was supportive, helpful. In fact, at one point, I was working in Grand Rapids. We used to play the Milwaukee Admirals, which he owned. I asked for an interview between periods, and he said, "Sure. I'll come up." I do the interview with him between periods, and, at the end of it, I'm thanking him and he says, "By the way, I was listening to you the last five minutes of that period. You didn't know I was here, but I heard you. You keep it up, you're going to be in the NHL someday." Believe me, I saved that tape. It really meant a lot having a guy like that say something like that. Lloyd Pettit was a big part of my inspiration.

—Pat Foley, Chicago Blackhawks
TV play-by-play broadcaster

FOSTER AND BILL HEWITT

Coining hockey's most famous phrase, "He shoots, he scores," Foster Hewitt was not only the original voice of the Toronto Maple Leafs, but also arguably the first voice of hockey itself. Son of William A. Hewitt, a sports journalist in Toronto, Foster was on the reporting side of the game at a considerably young age. Once calling a game in a box with no ventilation at ice level and nearly suffocating, he sought to improve the environment of broadcasting and, in doing so, revolutionized the craft in more ways than one. Using an upright telephone on March 22, 1923, Foster made the first radio broadcast of a hockey game. His innovation would forever affect the game from a broadcasting standpoint, as the concept of his "brain child," the broadcast gondola, has been carried over into several of today's hockey arenas, including Toronto's Air Canada Centre, the home of his Maple Leafs. A third-generation member of the family journalistic lineage, Foster's son Bill called Maple Leafs games alongside him until his return to the radio. Bill continued to broadcast for the Maple Leafs on television until his retirement. Not only receiving the award, but also having it named after him, Foster Hewitt, and Bill, are recognized in the Hockey Hall of Fame for their broadcasting contributions.

> Foster Hewitt was the voice of hockey in Canada when I was growing up. He was the voice of the Toronto Maple Leafs. Growing up in Sudbury, Ontario, we would get *Hockey Night in Canada* on Saturday nights, and Foster and Bill Hewitt were the two voices. I was a Leaf fan, and Foster and Bill, of course, were my favorites.

—Joe Bowen, Toronto Maple Leafs
TV/radio play-by-play broadcaster

> Danny Gallivan, who was the voice of the Montreal Canadiens, and Foster Hewitt, the voice of the Leafs, were essentially the voices of hockey in Canada when 90% of the country on

Saturday night was listening to one of those two. Gallivan, to me, was a more dramatic call. Perhaps more representative of the French with the flair. Foster Hewitt was a little more conservative. I remember Foster Hewitt's game beat of the Canada/Russia series in '72 when Paul Henderson scored late for Canada to win. "Henderson scores, Henderson scores" was Foster Hewitt's call. For many of those of my generation, they would be the voices of hockey in Canada.

—Dave Maloney, New York Rangers
radio play-by-play broadcaster

I wanted to be a hockey broadcaster, obviously. I grew up in Toronto, and I was a die-hard Leafs fan. I was a rink rat who used to hang around Maple Leaf Gardens. I'd go down there for junior games and on Saturday mornings with the six-team NHL in the early '60s. I would hang out, and I knew exactly where the players would take the subway in downtown Toronto. I would wait for players to come up the stairs, walk with them, and they would sneak me into Maple Leaf Gardens Saturday mornings. I'd get to watch the morning skate. A couple of players—Bobby Hull, Gordie Howe—were great to talk to. I wanted to be a hockey player. I was obviously never good enough to be a player, so the next best thing was to be a broadcaster. I knew in high school that's what I was going to do.

Foster and, later on, his son Bill Hewitt were the guys I listened to growing up. Of course, there's the Foster Hewitt Award now that's won by many of the top NHL broadcasters. Foster owned CKFH in Toronto, which is now The Fan 590, the first Canadian all-sports station. In those days, the games would start at 7:00, 7:30, and *Hockey Night in Canada* wouldn't come on the air until 8 o'clock. I was perched in front of the TV.

Frank Mahovlich was my favorite player growing up. My dad would always say to me, "How's Frank gonna help you get a job when you finish your education." He passed away when I was 14, and I kind of wish he would have still been around because he could have gotten the thrill I had. I never got to go to an NHL game as a young kid. We could never get the tickets and my family couldn't afford it, but I went to a lot of the junior games and hung around the rink. That certainly formulated my plans for my future.

—Jeff Rimer, Columbus Blue Jackets
TV play-by-play broadcaster

BOB WILSON

Working with the team for nearly three decades, Bob Wilson served as the voice of the Boston Bruins until the mid-1990s. Shortly after Wilson's start with the team, the Bruins left their station, WHDH, for WBZ. Wilson worked temporarily at KMOX, out of St. Louis, in 1970, which just so happened to be the year of #4 Bobby Orr's "flying goal" to defeat the St. Louis Blues for the Stanley Cup title. Wilson would eventually return to Boston Bruins hockey on the radio after another beloved voice of the team, Fred Cusick, switched from the airwaves to television. The second time around for Wilson, as well as "#4," the broadcaster called the team's 1972 Stanley Cup championship against the New York Rangers. Success was in large supply for Boston during the 1971–1972 season, as the team went a record 33 consecutive games without being defeated. With an NHL lockout looming, Wilson retired from the game following the 1993–1994 campaign.

> Having always loved and played sports as a kid—hockey and baseball, in particular—once I became a teenager and started listening to sportscasters, one of the benefits of living in upstate New York was I could get a lot of the major-market stations at night in the winter and listen to WBZ in Boston. I would listen to Bob Wilson, who passed away last season. He was one guy I enjoyed listening to. Even though I wasn't aware of it, he probably influenced the way I started out calling hockey games.
>
> —Nick Nickson, Los Angeles Kings
> radio play-by-play broadcaster

> I think one of the best voices ever in the game was Bob Wilson, who did the radio games for the Bruins. He was just spectacular. You talk about "The Voice of God" sort of presentation, that was Bob. He knew the game. A great radio voice. Just a tremendous broadcaster to listen to.
>
> —Gary Thorne, former New Jersey Devils
> TV play-by-play broadcaster

> Bob Wilson did the Bruins on radio for over 25 years. For me, he'll always be the voice of the Bruins, I'm just the guy who currently has the job. Unfortunately, he passed away just over a year ago. He was the reason I wanted to become an announcer. He had this phenomenal, deep, baritone voice. He was in control, he

wasn't somebody who yelled and screamed for three hours every night. He used his voice to let you know the urgency of the certain situation in a game. When a big moment was there, Bob was ready for it. There were peaks and valleys in his voice. He's the best I've ever heard at it, just phenomenal talent, and in the Hockey Hall of Fame for a reason. I still have people who send me CDs of his work. To this day, I still pop them in and just marvel at how good he was. And to me personally, he was unbelievable, no ego, no attitude, just always willing to listen and help. I still carry in my work bag a handwritten note he sent me after listening to one of my old cassette tapes. He didn't have to do that, but he did.

—Dave Goucher, Boston Bruins
radio play-by-play broadcaster

GENE HART

The original voice of the Flyers, Gene Hart broadcast for Philadelphia for nearly 30 years. Calling games during the era of the "Broad Street Bullies," Hart's voice was well tested with every fight, line brawl, and penalty assessment. He is best known in the Philadelphia community for his call of the team's first-ever Stanley Cup championship at the end of the 1973–1974 season. Hart would get another chance to broadcast during a championship run the following season, for the second of the team's back-to-back titles. Calling games until the end of the 1994–1995 season, he was inducted into the Hockey Hall of Fame two years later, only to return to the booth in a minor-league capacity for the affiliate Philadelphia Phantoms.

Gene Hart, for many years, was the broadcaster in Philadelphia. Gene believed in laughing a lot and having a good time, but also paying attention to business. I think the blend of those two parts of it—doing a solid job of broadcasting, but also realizing this is fun for people—that would have been the influence Gene would have had.

—Mike "Doc" Emrick, NBC national TV and former
Philadelphia Flyers TV play-by-play broadcaster

MEL ALLEN

Arguably one of the greatest baseball voices in the history of the game, Mel Allen called games for the New York Yankees from 1939 to 1964. Present for 21 American League pennant–clinching seasons, as well as 15 of a major sports–record 27 World Series championship seasons, Allen worked with and influenced many of today's greatest and longest-tenured play-by-play broadcasters, including Vin Scully. While inspiring many of today's baseball voices to join the booth overlooking the diamond, he did the same for those wanting to join the one overlooking the ice.

> I live in a house where there's a TV in virtually every room. You go out and you can watch games on your phone. I'm sitting in a restaurant, and I'm watching hockey games on my phone. So, everywhere you go, there's some form of TV. You go into a restaurant, a bar, or my yogurt shop, and they have a giant TV with games on. When I was a kid, we had one small black-and-white TV in the house, and at times, if a tube had blown, it stayed unfixed for a while. So I turned on the radio a lot. In the '50s when I grew up, you had the announcer teams doing TV and then going over to call the game on radio. The voice that always stood out to me was the voice of the New York Yankees. That was Mel Allen.
>
> I loved him because he had this great excitement in his voice and his delivery. Any ball that was hit hard, any play that was above average or required something special—whether it was the outfielder chasing it down, a run scoring, or a great throw—whatever it was, he had so much excitement in his voice. I loved to listen to him. I tried to emulate that as a kid. Out on the street, growing up in Brooklyn, I would play games with my friends. We would play stickball games or any other kind of game that involved scoring runs. I would announce those games. We played a one-on-one stickball game, and I would announce the pitch, the swing, the hits, and all the plays. Mel Allen was the inspiration for me. I played sports right through college, and then, when I reached the end of my sports career graduating college, the next best thing for me was to become an announcer, and the inspiration for that was growing up listening to Mel Allen and his calls.

> —Sam Rosen, New York Rangers
> TV play-by-play broadcaster

BILL KING

Calling every major professional sport except hockey, Bill King has been referred to in broadcasting circles as the "Renaissance Man of the Mic." Broadcasting championships for the Oakland/Los Angeles Raiders, Oakland A's, and Golden

State Warriors, King electrified the Bay Area audience with his personality and famous call, "Holy Toledo." Although never having called a hockey game, King was the voice of inspiration for one of the game's greatest broadcasting legends, Mike Lange.

> Nobody influenced me to want to be an NHL or hockey broadcaster. I was born in Sacramento, California, so I didn't grow up with hockey. I grew up with baseball, football, and basketball. Actually, hockey turned out to be an afterthought. In college, I did some games, sent some tapes, and, lo and behold, I ended up in hockey. That is not where I thought I was going to be headed, but it obviously did turn out that way.
>
> The gentleman who actually made me want to take a grasp and say, "I really want to do this" was Bill King, the longtime broadcaster for the San Francisco Warriors of the NBA, the Oakland Raiders, and the Oakland A's. He really turned my head. There are other names in the Bay Area—baseball guys—including Vin Scully, Russ Hodges, and Lon Simmons. Those were the guys who had some influence on me, but Bill King probably would be the most definitive person I could relate to who I wanted to be like. Just listening to the games. We would go and sit in a bar and just listen to Bill King work. Whether it was the Raiders or the Warriors, we would think we were so cool, and we would be riveted just listening to him.
>
> —Mike Lange, Pittsburgh Penguins
> TV play-by-play broadcaster

BOB PRINCE

Known as "Gunner," Bob Prince was the voice of the Pittsburgh Pirates for nearly 30 years. Broadcasting some of the most legendary moments in team history, including Bill Mazeroski's game seven walk-off home run against the New York Yankees in the 1960 World Series. Calling games alongside his partner, Jim Woods, known as "Possum," Prince broadcast for the team until 1975, when he was fired by the Pirates, a decision that did not sit well with Pirates fans or the team itself. Before returning to baseball for a brief stint in the 1980s, he attempted to do hockey play-by-play for the Pittsburgh Penguins but was found to be better suited as an interviewer. Closing out his career in the town for which he showed love for most of his life, Prince continues to be one of Pittsburgh's biggest names some 30 years after his death.

Growing up, I listened to Bob Prince doing baseball. He had so much personality, and his style was so exciting. I was a big Pirates fan. I loved Roberto Clemente and Bob Prince brought Clemente to life. I watched a lot of ball games on television, but I also heard the radio in Pittsburgh so much back in those days. If you were sitting outside in the summer, you could hear six different porches with the Pirates game on. Cars were going by, and you could hear Bob Prince's voice coming out of them. He was just ubiquitous in the summer time in Pittsburgh. I loved hearing his voice and I loved hearing the way he called the games. Mike Lange has kind of carried on the tradition of Bob Prince in Pittsburgh with his sayings, but "The Gunner" was the original. He was a guy who made the games colorful. He was like a master of ceremonies through the games. With baseball having so much down time, you need a personality to bring it to life, and he certainly did that better than anybody. He was the most influential guy in my life in terms of sportscasting.

—Paul Steigerwald, Pittsburgh Penguins
TV play-by-play broadcaster

The first radio station to hire me was KDKA Radio, and KDKA Radio goes probably even farther than KMOX. They'd go to 37 states and Canada. That was a powerful thing to be on. When I started, television wasn't the thing. If you had 10 games broadcast TV-wise, you had a lot in the mid-'70s and early '80s, all the way until satellite revolutionized everything. Radio was the dominant force. The most recognizable figure I've ever been with in my life was Bob Prince. He did two years of TV on the Penguins side in the late '70s, and every place we'd go on the road, people would shout his name at the airport. This guy wasn't on television. He was radio. They'd yell out, "Hey, Gunner." Our whole team would walk by, and they wouldn't even know who in the hell they were. Bob Prince they knew. That's how big those guys were.

—Mike Lange, Pittsburgh Penguins
TV play-by-play broadcaster

BOB CHASE

Who says you have to be in the NHL to influence other NHL broadcasters? Bob Chase, having broadcast the game of hockey just two fewer years than Vin Scully has called the sport of baseball, called the game of hockey into his 90s.

The voice behind the East Coast Hockey League's Fort Wayne Komets since 1963, Chase saw many of today's broadcasters when they were still "paying their dues" at the minor-league level. Staying with the team for more than six decades, Chase called more than 500 playoff games and was the biggest inspiration for Mike "Doc" Emrick, arguably the game's most recognizable voice.

> The guy I grew up listening to and is still working to this day is Bob Chase. He will turn 90 in January [2016]. I grew up about 40 miles from Fort Wayne. In 1953, I was seven years old, and a hockey team arrived in Fort Wayne. Shortly thereafter, Bob wound up becoming the announcer for the team. He was a mentor of mine in the early years, when I would sit in the corner of the Coliseum in Fort Wayne in an empty section and record the game for myself. He was very helpful in not only helping me catch the bug by listening to his broadcasts and caring about the team as a fan, but also to believe I could actually make a living at doing this. The fact that he's still living [2015] and still broadcasting gives us all hope.
>
> —Mike "Doc" Emrick, NBC national TV and former
> New Jersey Devils TV play-by-play broadcaster

While their gondolas have been incinerated, their arenas imploded, or their booths simply renovated to keep up with the changing times of the game, the former voices of hockey live on in the calls of their successors. Although they may not be on top or directly in front of the action the way the broadcasters of yesterday were during their time in the booth, box, or gondola, today's play-by-play voices summon the spirit, enthusiasm, and personality of those who have gone before them, hoping to one day leave their own mark as they themselves pass the torch and become voices of the past.

• 34 •

Living Legends

$\mathcal{N}$ot every play-by-play broadcaster uses each and every breath—including their last—to call the game they love. Oftentimes, health, priorities, or unceremonious firings at the hands of a power-wielding general manager, team president, or owner may cause a legendary broadcaster to put down the headset one final time before the proverbial third-period clock winds down on their life. Other times, the Hall of Fame accolades have already been won, the "broadcast footprints" have already been cast in the sand, and the bronze statue has already been forged and is just waiting for the "final call" before gracing the entrance to the arena, but the broadcasters still continue well into their "twilight years." Perhaps waiting for that elusive Stanley Cup–winning call, clinging to the hope of christening the next Wayne Gretzky into the league, or simply just refusing to step down from their post, these voices continue to preside over the airwaves.

BOB COLE

Successor to such voices as Dan Kelly, Danny Gallivan, and Foster Hewitt for the continuously running *Hockey Night in Canada*, Bob Cole has been calling the game for more than six decades. During his career, Cole has not only broadcast *Hockey Night in Canada*, but he has also called at least one game for the Canadian broadcast of the Stanley Cup Final for nearly 30 years. Not to be excluded from his native Canada's triumphs on a global level, he also called the game during which the Canadian Men's Hockey Team won the Olympic gold medal in 2002.

I always loved the way Bob Cole would call a game. The way he could bring you out of your seat. He still does to this day, and he's in his 80s. He's kind of the Vin Scully of hockey broadcasting.

—Dean Brown, Ottawa Senators
radio play-by-play broadcaster

Bob Cole, Danny Gallivan, and Ted Darling would be the top three broadcasting influences for me. The energy in the moment that Bob Cole could bring when he was in the prime of his game.

—Dan Dunleavy, Buffalo Sabres
TV play-by-play broadcaster

BRUCE MARTYN

The voice behind the production line of "Mr. Hockey," Gordie Howe, Bruce Martyn broadcast Detroit Red Wings hockey for more than three decades. Getting a head start broadcasting college and pro football in the Michigan area, as well as Detroit Pistons basketball, Martyn missed the "championship boat" of Howe, Ted Lindsay, and Sid Abel; however, he ended up working alongside Abel in the booth for a good portion of his career. Missing yet another Red Wings championship—this time following the tail end of his career—Martyn returned to the booth during the 1997 Stanley Cup Final to call one period of action in the series-clincher for Detroit. He was enshrined in the Hockey Hall of Fame in 1991, four years before his "official" retirement.

I grew up in Detroit, and I am old enough to go back to when I was a kid, the National Hockey League only had six teams, and one of them was the Detroit Red Wings. They were huge, and I was a big Red Wing and Tiger fan who always wanted to get into broadcasting. The Tigers, of course, had the legendary Ernie Harwell, who I met on several occasions. He was very, very kind and then became a colleague later when I was doing the Red Sox and Twins, and Ernie was still doing the Tigers. The two hockey broadcasters were Bruce Martyn and Bud Lynch.

Bud has passed on, and Bruce was tremendous. He was my first National Hockey League partner. I got into the game a strange way. Sid Abel, who was a Hall of Famer, was the color man for the Detroit Red Wings. He was doing a father–daughter skate with his granddaughter, and Sid went to jump on the ice, but he had forgotten to take his skate guards off, so he slipped, fell, and broke his hip. I wound up having to fill in for the remainder of the '76–'77 season. My first partner in the National Hockey League and my mentor at the time was Bruce Martyn, who went on to be in the National Hockey League Hall of Fame. Bruce was terrific.

—Bob Kurtz, Minnesota Wild
radio play-by-play broadcaster

I grew up in Detroit. I think every broadcaster is a product of, in some ways, the guys he grew up listening to. Whether you do it intentionally or not, I think you incorporate the guy you listened to into your own style and call. That guy for me was the Red Wing's Bruce Martyn. He was the guy I grew up listening to. Network guys have to play it down the middle and be as objective as possible, but as a fan, especially as a young fan growing up, I always gravitated to the guys that were homers—or at least were obviously pulling for my team. I want to hear a guy that's as passionate about my team as I am and he was the guy that was the soundtrack of my childhood. I was a radio sportscaster for about 10 years after college, until I realized I had to get out of broadcasting to become a hockey broadcaster. I started sending tapes around the country to every minor league team I could find. I ended up in Tulsa, Oklahoma in the Central Hockey League. I was doing PR, sales, and broadcasting in Tulsa. If we had games on back-to-back nights, I'd go back to the office after the game to start working on notes for the next night. It was then I discovered that late at night I could get WJR (the Red Wing's Station) in my office in Tulsa. I had moved away and had been working, so I hadn't really heard Bruce Martyn for a couple of years at that point. I had called games for a while, but listening to Bruce again, I was shocked to hear where all my phrasing came from without having ever recognized it. It was a surreal experience because the way I said things and my inflection all came directly from Bruce Martyn. I think we are a product of the guys we grew up listening to, and, in my case, for hockey, it was Bruce Martyn.

—Tim Saunders, Philadelphia Flyers
radio play-by-play broadcaster

Bruce Martyn was a Red Wings announcer for 32 years. As a kid growing up, to me, the way he described the game, he was the best. He was the guy who I emulated and who really got me interested in the game. I really enjoyed listening to him. What's interesting is out of the 32 years Bruce Martyn called the Red Wings, a lot of those years, they weren't very good. In the late '60s and '70s, and even in the early '80s, he never called a Stanley

Cup championship. In 1997, we go up three games to none, and I invited him back into the booth. It's amazing how things work out. I had him call the second period of game four against the Flyers, and, wouldn't you know it, he called Darren McCarty's cup-winning goal.

The Wings won that Stanley Cup. First time in 42 years, but he's the one who called that beautiful goal by McCarty that proved to be the cup-winning goal. It was great for me. First of all, I was honored to be able to work a game with Bruce Martyn, who was my hero and idol growing up. Secondly, for me personally, after all those years with bad teams and everything, for him to call the cup-winning goal just meant a lot. It meant everything to me, and I know it meant a lot to him, too. It's just amazing how life is and how things happen for a reason. It was a great night. To me, game four against Philadelphia, to be able to work with Bruce Martyn and see him call the cup-winning goal, as a broadcaster, that was my all-time greatest memory.

—Ken Kal, Detroit Red Wings
radio play-by-play broadcaster

JIM ROBSON

The original voice of the Vancouver Canucks, Jim Robson is a great example of what would probably be referred to in football as "iron-man broadcasting." Christening the airwaves for the Canucks, Robson worked without a color commentator during his broadcasts and performed pregame, postgame, and intermission segments. Calling the Canucks to game seven of the 1994 Stanley Cup Final against the New York Rangers, he later switched over to television play-by-play broadcasting for five years to close out his career, passing the broadcasting torch to John Shorthouse.

Jim Robson, the original voice of the Canucks, is the only reason I'm doing this. The reason is simple. The Canucks came into the league in 1970, and they went to the Final in '82, but that was a fluke. Basically for the first 25 or 30 years of their existence, they were just the laughing stock of the league. Year in and year out, with rare exceptions, they were just a sad-sack hockey team. Never competitive. Never threatening to do anything special, but, in our minds—and in my mind, in particular—the one thing we could lay claim to was the best hockey broadcaster on the planet, and that was Jim Robson.

I decided early on, when it became clear I wasn't a very good skater, rather than dream of playing for the Canucks, I would dream of doing what he did, and that's all I've wanted to do since I was eight or nine years old. I have tapes dating back to then to prove it. I'm not the only one. There are kids from my era who had probably the same dream and went through the same imaginations I did in terms of doing mock broadcasts and calling games off the TV. I just happen to be the lucky one who weaseled his way into the job.

—John Shorthouse, Vancouver Canucks
TV/radio play-by-play broadcaster

DICK IRVIN JR.

Doing color commentary for the legendary Danny Gallivan for a good portion of his career, Dick Irvin Jr. is a man ingrained in the Montreal Canadiens' DNA. Irvin's father played for and coached several of the franchise's Stanley Cup championship–winning teams. Irvin Jr. worked with Danny Gallivan on *Hockey Night in Canada* until Gallivan's retirement after the 1983–1984 season. Irvin Jr. continued to work on *Hockey Night in Canada* for another 15 seasons and left as the longest-tenured member of the program in 1999. He still works the annual *Hockey Day in Canada* broadcasts.

I grew up in Canada, watching and listening to *Hockey Night in Canada*. Thirty percent of the time it was Danny Gallivan and Dick Irvin. They were the voices of *Hockey Night in Canada*, whether we got the Toronto Maple Leafs or the Montreal Canadiens. That's what I grew up with, sitting with my father and my family. I never met Danny Gallivan, but I met and still know Dick Irvin. He's still alive, and I'm honored to be considered a friend of his. What a legend in the game. He's done it all.

—Randy Moller, Florida Panthers
radio play-by-play broadcaster

BOB MILLER

Having waited nearly 40 years to see his team's first-ever Stanley Cup championship–winning season, Bob Miller, the TV voice of the Los Angeles Kings, is a true ambassador for the sports community in Southern California, which is known for its long-tenured broadcasters. During his interview, Miller noted, "With Vin (Scully) 66 years with the Dodgers, I'm in my 42nd with the Kings, and Chick (Hearn) was around 40, 41 with the Lakers, if a 10-year-old kid said, 'Someday, I want to be an announcer for one of those teams,' he'd be about ready to retire now and the job has never come open." Miller graced his colleagues with his warm personality and gracious nature throughout his Hall of Fame career.

> I've been here in Anaheim since '99. Since day one of being in Anaheim, Bob and I have visited before many of our Ducks–Kings matchups, whether it be in Los Angeles or Anaheim. We've joked around and talked hockey. That a Hall of Fame broadcaster would take the time to drop by to talk with me is very special. He's a class guy.
>
> —Steve Carroll, Anaheim Ducks
> radio play-by-play broadcaster

> As a broadcaster, he has been my mentor. I was doing color with him. He was doing play-by-play. He taught me how to prepare to do the play-by-play. I have modeled a lot of the things I do after Bob. This thing about being a sportscaster in Southern California, I guess people can't just hold their jobs. Bob's been there since '73. Vin Scully, since the Dodgers moved in '58. Chick Hearn was there from '61 and another 40-plus years until he unfortunately passed away. When I came to Los Angeles to work, I was 27 years old, and I was very fortunate to have people like that around from whom I could learn so much as to how to prepare and how to approach the job.
>
> —Pete Weber, Nashville Predators
> radio play-by-play broadcaster

MIKE LANGE

Calling games for the Pittsburgh Penguins since 1974, Mike Lange is one of the most unique personalities to sit behind a broadcast microphone in major sports. Known for such catchphrases as "Slap me silly, Sidney," "Smile like a butcher's dog," and "Elvis has just left the building," Lange has seen four Stanley Cup championships in Pittsburgh with the likes of Ron Francis, Evgeni Malkin, and arguably three of the game's biggest stars ever, Jaromír Jágr, Sidney Crosby, and Mario Lemieux. With talented, offensive players a constant in the "Steel City," Lange answers the broadcasting call, providing fans with just as much excitement after the goal as before and during.

> When we moved to Pittsburgh when I was a sophomore, we listened to Mike all the time. Mike is a Hall of Famer. When I went to Pittsburgh from Anaheim in '96, Mike was doing the TV and I was doing the radio, and it was an unbelievable thrill to be able to be one of the guys with Mike. He's given me outstanding advice in life and broadcasting. He's just a great guy and somebody who I stay in contact with to this day. He is the most recognizable piece of the Penguins besides Mario Lemieux. He's been around forever. Just a great person and a great broadcaster. He has so much history and so much knowledge.
>
> —Matt McConnell, Arizona Coyotes
> TV play-by-play broadcaster

MIKE "DOC" EMRICK AND GARY THORNE

The first voice of the Devils after their move to New Jersey, Mike "Doc" Emrick is best known for his work on national telecasts, including the NHL All-Star Game, the Conference Finals, and the Stanley Cup Final. Having worked with both the Devils and the Philadelphia Flyers for a number of years prior to his national broadcasting duties, Emrick had the good fortune of calling three Stanley Cup–winning teams in New Jersey. Broadcasting for the Olympics as well, he has become the hockey voice of NBC. Gary Thorne was the Devils broadcaster during one of Emrick's stints in Philadelphia. Known mainly for his work in baseball—mostly with the New York Mets and Baltimore Orioles—Thorne, as well as Emrick, called many of the national postseason telecasts, including the Stanley Cup Final, for more than 10 years. With ESPN and Fox switching duties during the 1995 Cup Final, Emrick was able to call that season's cup-clincher.

> I owe Mike Emrick and Gary Thorne a tremendous amount of credit because they were kind enough to critique me constructively when I was a puppy in this business at 22, 23 years old. They were kind enough to listen to my tapes from my college radio days and my time in the American Hockey League and tell me what it was I was doing correctly and what I could do to improve. Both of them were very generous with their time and wrote letters back to me. At that time, there was no e-mail.

It was all typewritten or handwritten letters or phone conversations. Those two were and still are broadcasting heroes to me. I think it's so cool that 20, 25 years into my career I can still call them colleagues. They were incredibly helpful to me, way more than they know when I was growing up in the business.

—Joe Beninati, Washington Capitals
TV play-by-play broadcaster

Doc was a colleague of mine for five years at MSG, and the value of watching him work at his craft is immeasurable. The thing I try to take most from him is not necessarily his approach to the profession—which is extraordinary—but his approach to people. It carries over on the air. When he does a game, his love for the people in the game just seeps out of every broadcast. You hear it. You feel it. And it's all genuine. I can only attempt to bring the same things to the table. Someone once told me, "You don't want to be the guy who follows a legend," but that's the case anyway, and I don't mind. If you ever get caught up in thinking about those things you're probably not taking the best approach to the job. I don't try to recreate a Doc Emrick call. It would be silly to do so, and people would see through that anyway. I've tried to put my own stamp on how to call a game, and you can only hope fans enjoy it.

—Steve Cangialosi, New Jersey Devils
TV play-by-play broadcaster

MARV ALBERT

Arguably the most recognizable voice in sports, Marv Albert, most commonly known as the "Czar," has called games in the NBA, the NHL, the NFL, the NCAA, and MLB, as well as horse racing, boxing, and even tennis, throughout his broadcasting career, which dates back as far as 1965. While national telecasts have become his most recent seat, Albert is best known for his work in the "Big Apple," calling games for the New York Knicks, New York Rangers, and New Jersey Nets. Calling the Rangers' first Stanley Cup title in 54 years in 1994, he eventually passed the broadcasting torch on, at least at the local level, to his son Kenny, who works both Knicks and Rangers games.

I remember when I was 7, 8 years old, I was supposed to be in my room going to sleep. My late father, who was a New York

City firefighter for a long, long time, loved the New York Rangers. He knew that I was a huge hockey fan at that age. I'm supposed to be asleep, but I'm listening to the game, and I'm hearing Marv Albert, whether it be on radio or on TV. Marv's calls resonate, whether it be in football, basketball, or hockey. I'll never forget those times when I'd be pretending to sleep, I'd hear Marv call a goal or a basket in hoops and come out to try and watch a replay, hear Marv describe the goal on radio, or ask my dad who scored. Those memories, to me, are just fabulous. There was always a part of me when I was 7, 8 years old that knew all the stats and all the players' names. It was because I spent so much time listening to the great broadcasters in New York when I was growing up. Marv has to be one of those guys who influenced me.

—Joe Beninati, Washington Capitals
TV play-by-play broadcaster

I can't say that I grew up idolizing certain announcers because to me it's always been about the broadcast "team." Marv Albert was terrific calling Rangers games on the radio, but I was always more appreciative of the on-air relationship with his color man, Sal Messina. They would needle each other and play off of each other perfectly. I think there are great examples of that throughout sports television. Curt Gowdy and Al Derogatis doing football on NBC. (Bob) Costas and (Tony) Kubek calling baseball. There is no tangible explanation for why it sounds right, it just does. The thing that I want most is to be that guy who makes it work as a team, because let's face it—unless you're Vin Scully, you're not doing this alone.

—Steve Cangialosi, New Jersey Devils
TV play-by-play broadcaster

The number one broadcasting influence for me was Marv Albert. Marv did the Knicks and the Rangers. When he would say, "The Rangers skate from the 7th avenue end to the 8th avenue end of the Garden," he gave you that description on the radio and painted the picture. It was just incredible. I would always love Marv's play by play with a touch of humor with his color man, no matter who it was. He still continues that to this day. Whoever his partner is, he has a little fun with him.

—Steve Goldstein, Florida Panthers
TV play-by-play broadcaster

My biggest broadcast inspiration was Marv Albert. I knew I wanted to be a broadcaster from about age 12 or so, and Marv was the central figure. I became the president of his fan club when I was 13, and he wrote the foreword to my book. He was the biggest influence on my career. He ended up bringing me into Madison Square Garden to work as his backup with the New York Rangers, so I was lucky enough to be there in '94 when they won the cup. Marv and I actually shared the play-by-play of the final game, when he did two periods and I did one. It was the confluence of any number of different dreams that I had as a kid, so I would certainly say Marv would be my overall broadcast idol, even to this day.

—Howie Rose, New York Islanders
radio play-by-play broadcaster

BOB LAMEY

Known as the "voice of the Indianapolis Colts" for the past three decades, Bob Lamey is a staple in the Indiana broadcasting community. Calling games for the NBA's Pacers as well, Lamey, formerly referred to as "Hockey Bob," broadcast minor-league hockey for the International Hockey League's Indianapolis Checkers, the Eastern Hockey League's Charlotte Checkers, and the World Hockey Association's Indianapolis Racers. Although not having called an actual hockey game for more than 30 years, his influence carries over to today's NHL play-by-play broadcasters.

At about 10 years old, I knew I wanted to be a broadcaster. We would play sports in the street or play basketball in the driveway, and I was always calling the game. In the early 1970s, my parents moved to Indianapolis, and they had a brand new hockey team called the Indianapolis Racers. There was a broadcaster there named Bob Lamey. He is still the Indianapolis Colts' announcer. He was the most exciting broadcaster I had ever heard or have ever heard since. He would make your hair stand up on your head. Every goal was so exciting. Every fight was like a heavyweight championship. He was just absolutely exciting and thrilling.

I remember listening to him as a kid, and then, after the game, my father and I would race out to the car and listen to the postgame show. I listened to every game with a radio under my pillow. I just wanted to be him. I remember listening to him doing those Racer games and going, "That's what I want to do when I get older." Through all the ups and downs of going through minor-league hockey, baseball, and other sports, I just kept thinking of him and how I wanted to do it and said, "I'm just gonna keep going until I get the job," and I finally did. It was the thrill of a lifetime. I still listen to the Colts games. He still is the most exciting broadcaster I've ever heard in my life.

—Michael Haynes, Colorado Avalanche
TV play-by-play broadcaster

While their Foster Hewitt Awards have started collecting dust long before any plans have surfaced to hang up their headsets for good, the voices of these walking landmarks of the sport continue to boom in our ears. Like they say, "Slow and steady wins the marathon."

Epilogue

Winding down the Third Period

*A*nother 26 hours, 37 minutes, and 15 seconds worth of material from 62 interviews conducted with 42 broadcasters later and I've got another book . . . well . . . "in the books." I'll tell you one thing: When you talk with 42 different people about one general subject, you're going to get different perspectives, and this book is a representation of that. One thing I was able to do differently in this book—as opposed to *The Voices of Baseball: The Game's Greatest Broadcasters Reflect on America's Pastime*—was to focus less on the teams' venues. Quite the opposite of baseball, the trend of today's hockey arena construction has been toward more "cookie cutter" facilities, so my questions regarding most memorable experiences had to extend beyond the home broadcast booth, and it's a good thing they did.

As far as the four major sports go, none is more evenly matched than hockey. Where else do you see the eighth seed oust the first seed in the opening round of the playoffs with such frequency? Four times in the history of the four major sports has a team overcome an 0–3 deficit in a best-of-seven series to advance in the playoffs, and three of those have been in hockey (1942 Maple Leafs, 2010 Flyers, 2014 Kings). Listing the teams that have managed a comeback after falling behind three games to one would require an entire chapter. With this overwhelming parity, magic is bound to occur on someone else's ice and not just your own. Losing side and winning side, two of the broadcasters I interviewed had the same most memorable game—Steve Cangialosi of the New Jersey Devils and Randy Moller of the Florida Panthers—who both fondly recall game seven of the 2012 Eastern Conference Quarterfinal. How great is that? One's (Cangialosi) ecstasy was another's (Moller) agony. Yet, both are able to look back at the game for the sheer thrill, winning or losing.

Concerning the biggest thrills for me as an interviewer, I don't think anything can compare to speaking to four different broadcasters about the Red Wings–Avalanche rivalry of the mid-1990s and early 2000s. With five Stanley Cup championships, four playoff series, and countless penalty minutes between the two during a comparatively brief amount of time, I don't feel I'm too far off in saying that was the greatest rivalry in sports by a "country mile," and I was able to get a perspective from both sides of this "blood feud." Even John Kelly, who now broadcasts for his late father's St. Louis Blues, looks back on that rivalry as one of the craziest things he's ever witnessed in hockey. Looking at the YouTube videos of the brawls described in my interviews with Mr. Kelly, as well as those with Ken Kal and Ken Daniels of the Red Wings and Michael Haynes of the Colorado Avalanche, I can see their words and memories come to life, taking me back to those days watching the heated Conference Finals between the two teams. Once one knocked the other out of the postseason, the cup was as good as theirs. What a remarkable rivalry.

I conducted one interview in person, and who better to do it with than Hall of Famer Bob Miller. We sat in the MGM Grand Garden Arena's seats during the Kings' morning skate for a preseason exhibition game against the Avalanche. Bob and I talked enforcers, a subject I had not intended to include in this book, but a friend of mine suggested I add it because of its unquestionable presence in a prior era. Hearing Mr. Miller discuss such players as Tie Domi, Dave "Tiger" Williams, and Broad Street Bully Dave "The Hammer" Schultz, I kept thinking to myself, "What a jewel to the game this gentleman is and still gracious enough to spend a half-hour with me while at work." The enforcer element became a must-have once I started hearing the stories of line brawls, bounties, and fan-involved donnybrooks. Nowadays, sports outlets like ESPN and Fox Sports are hesitant to show teams climbing into the stands to execute justice on an unruly fan, but that wasn't always the case. There was a day when stations would seek out such spectacles. With two blood brothers on opposite teams going at it on the ice the way Keith and Wayne Primeau did one night, how could you not love this game?

Baseball is by far my favorite sport, but I will not hesitate to say that hockey is the most exciting to watch, and the game's broadcasters add to the excitement. It was such a thrill for me to talk with the New York Rangers' Hall of Fame voices Sam Rosen and Marv Albert about the Rangers hoisting their first Stanley Cup in 54 years. Not even the Maple Leafs' current drought has been going on that long. I told Mr. Rosen how much he sounds like the New York Yankees' John Sterling, a broadcaster with whom I had the pleasure of speaking for my baseball book. Mr. Rosen chuckled and replied, "A lot of it comes from our love and enthusiasm for what we do." And how lucky is the city of Pittsburgh to not only have a player as exciting as Sidney Crosby, but also a legend like Mike Lange, with such signature goal calls as "Slap me silly, Sidney" or "He beat him like a rented mule."

Mike Lange, Sam Rosen, Marv Albert, and Bob Miller weren't the only Hall of Famers I had the fortune of interviewing. Pat Foley, Nick Nickson, Chuck Kaiton, and retirees Ken "Jiggs" McDonald and Peter Maher also appear in this book, but my proverbial "Vin Scully" in terms of diligence and effort was Mike "Doc" Emrick. In the baseball book, it took continual inquiries to the Los Angeles Dodgers PR staff to finally get through to Mr. Scully, not because he wasn't willing to speak with me, but because they didn't want to impose on him during the season. For this book, I tried for months to get through to Mr. Emrick, using his colleagues with whom I already had the pleasure of speaking. Then, one day, I got an e-mail from "Doc." The delay in hearing back from him wasn't due to an unwillingness to speak with me. It was simply a matter of timing. Thanks to my favorite interviewee, Ken Kal, striking up a conversation with Doc during the morning skate of what would be a national broadcast on TV for Doc and a radio broadcast for Ken, the introductory seed was planted, and Hall of Fame member number 10 was soon to be on the slate. What an incredible addition to the already-amazing chapter on the New Jersey Devils (largely thanks to Steve Cangialosi and Gary Thorne sharing their experiences).

Being a Red Wings fan, I was able to, thanks to Mr. Emrick, better appreciate the joy experienced by Devils fans when the team hoisted their first Stanley Cup in 1995, even though I was embittered about it 20 years ago. Much like the circumstances surrounding the baseball book, that happened quite a bit. Regardless of which team you follow, how can you not appreciate a team going from losing an NHL-record 71 games in one season to ousting the number-one seed in the playoffs the following year? Again, being a Red Wings fan, I was still able to soak in San Jose Sharks broadcaster Dan Rusanowsky's enthusiasm and love for his team and gain some form of closure. If there's anything these two books have taught me, it's that one person's loss is another's gain. From the Lightning's Rick Peckham to the Ducks' Steve Carroll, I was able to see just how much besting a team as good as the conference-leading Red Wings in the first round meant to not only the team, but also the home city, even if the season didn't end with a Stanley Cup.

While the number of Stanley Cup championship rings among the broadcasters interviewed continues to rise with each passing postseason, even long-suffering, cupless voices like Joe Bowen, Pete Weber, Bob Kurtz, and Joe Beninati had more than enough of their love for the game to share. With the evolution of the game—including the elimination of ties, line brawls, and nonregulation skating surfaces—broadcasters have had to adapt. With line changes taking place before all of the skaters have even had a chance to handle the puck, the ability of these broadcasters to keep up with the action without missing a beat is uncanny. Considering the fact that people like Jiggs McDonald and Marv Albert were calling the game when there were only 12 teams in the league, one can only imagine the continual adjustments that have been made with the NHL more than doubling in size, and that's just the change in personnel. Now take into account the recessed broadcast booths, the constantly changing uniforms, and the fluctuating pace of the game. Fewer enforcers and "team tough guys" often translates into greater speed among the skaters, and it requires skill and experience to keep up with the action, while calling names many times consisting of at least four syllables.

Say what you will about the 1–0 decisions after nearly three hours of viewership, no one can refute the amount of action that takes place during three 20-minute periods and how refreshing that proverbial "glass of water" must be for these gentlemen once their "on-air" light goes dim. If that can be said after just one contest, imagine the indelible mark these voices will have left on the game once their light stays dim and the next generation of Mike Langes, Bob Millers, Jiggs McDonalds, Marv Alberts, Gary Thornes, and Sam Rosens take the reins and try to keep lit that broadcasting fire kindled so long ago by Foster Hewitt until they themselves put that proverbial *and* literal headset down for the final time. Stay tuned.

Bibliography

"INTRODUCTION: THE *OTHER* "MIRACLE ON ICE"

www.hockey-reference.com/teams/EDM/
www.nyidynasty.freeservers.com
www.hockey-reference.com/teams/EDM/1982_games.html
www.hockey-reference.com/players/g/gretzwa01.html

"ANAHEIM DUCKS"

www.contently.com/strategist/2015/03/19/the-mighty-ducks-the-story-behind-the-
    nhl-team-that-doubled-as-an-all-time-great-marketing-stunt/
www.sportsecyclopedia.com/nhl/anaheim/mducks.html
www.hockey-reference.com/teams/ANA
www.hockey-reference.com/players/g/gigueje01.html
www.hockey-reference.com/players/s/selante01.html
www.hockey-reference.com/players/k/kariypa01.html
www.hockey-reference.com/teams/NJD/2003.html
www.ducks.nhl.com/club/gamelog.htm?season=20022--3&gametype=3
www.hockey-reference.com/coaches/boudsbr01c.html
www.ducks.nhl.com/club/statshtm?season=20062007

"ARIZONA COYOTES"

www.sportsecyclopedia.com/nhl/phxaz/coyotes.html
www.hockey-reference.com/teams/PHX/

www.hockey-reference.com/teams/PHX/2012.html
www.hockeydb.com/nhl-attendance/att_graph?tmi=7450
www.hockey-reference.com/players/g/gretzwa01.html
www.hockeydb.com/nhl-attendance/att-graph_season.php?/id=NHL1927&sid
    =2007

"BOSTON BRUINS"

www.sportsecyclopedia.com/nhl/boston/bruins.html
www.hockey-reference.com/players/r/ratelje01.html
www.hockey-reference.com/players/o/orrbo01.html
www.hockey-reference.com/players/e/esposph01.html
www.hockey-reference.com/players/o/oreilte01.html
www.nytimes.com/2009/12/23/sports/hockey/23brawl.html?pagewanted=all&_r=0
www.statshockey.homestead.com/alltimepenminutes.html
www.hockey-reference.com/teams/BOS/2011.html
www.hockey-reference.com/teams/BOS/2016.html

"BUFFALO SABRES"

www.pro-football-reference.com/teams/buf/
www.weather.com/sports-recreation/ski/news/20-coldest-large-cities-america-2014
    0107#/12
www.hockey-reference.com/teams/BUF/
www.ballparks.phanfare.com/2414430
www.hockeydb.com/stte/buffalo-bisons-5049.html
www.sabresalumni.com/page.cshtml/4
www.hockey-reference.com/teams/BUF/leaders_career.html
www.hockey-reference.com/teams/BUF/1996.html
www.espn.go.com/nhl/story/_/id/8496678/buffalo-sabres-unveil-statue-honor-
    french-connection
www.hockey-reference.com/teams/BUF/1993.html
www.hockey-reference.com/players/h/hasekdo01.html
www.hockey-reference.com/players/h/hullbr01.html
www.sportsecyclopedia.com/nhl/buffalo/sabres.html
www.hockey-reference.com/teams/BUF/1999.html
www.hockey-reference.com/teams/BUF/leaders_career.html
www.nhl.com/stats/player
www.hockey-reference.com/teams/BUF/2015.html
www.sabres.nhl.com/club/page.htm?id=67958

"CALGARY FLAMES"

www.hockey-reference.com/teams/CGY/1989.html
www.hockey-reference.com/teams/EDM/
www.rauzulustreet.com/hockey/nhlhistory/nhlhistory.html
www.sportsecyclopedia.com/nhl/atlflames/aflames.html
www.hockey-reference.com/teams/CGY/1989_games.html
www.hockeynut.com/0304/playoffs2004/boxscores/vancgy7.html
www.hockey-reference.com/teams/CGY/2015.html
www.hockey-reference.com/teams/CGY/
www.hockeydb.com/nhl/attendance/att_graph_season.php

"CAROLINA HURRICANES"

www.hockeydb.com/nhl-attendance/att_graph_season.php?/id=NHL1927&
    sid=2000
www.sportsecyclopedia.com/nhl/carolina/hurricanes.html
www.hockey-reference.com/teams/CAR/
www.hockey-reference.com/players/h/howego01.html
www.rauzulustreet.com/hockey/nhlhistory/nhlhistory.html
www.hockey-reference.com/players/f/francro01.html
www.hockey-reference.com/players/s/staaler01.html
www.sportsespn.go.com/nhl/playoffs2006/news/story?id=2492068

"CHICAGO BLACKHAWKS"

www.proicehockey.about.com/od/hockeyfaqsandtrivia/f/most_goals_game.htm
www.chicagonow.com/blogs/chicago_sports_mob/2010/05/chicago-blackhawks-
    all-time-leading-goal-scorers.html
www.sportsecyclopedia.com/nhl/chicagoblackhawks.html
www.hockey-reference.com/players/m/mikitst01.html
www.hockey-reference.com/players/h/hullbo01.html
www.espn.go.com/nhl/story/_/id/7552171/nhl-examining-chicago-blackhawks-
    detroit-red-wings-rivalry-espn-magazine
www.hockey-reference.com/teams/CHI/

"COLORADO AVALANCHE"

www.hockey-reference.com/players/b/bourqra01.html
www.sportsecyclopedia.com/nhl/colnj/nhlrockies.html

www.hockey-reference.com/teams/COL/
www.hockey-reference.com/teams/COL/1996.html
www.hockey-reference.com/teams/QUE/1995.html
www.hockey-reference.com/players/r/roypa01.html
www.quanthockey.com/nhl/records/nhl-goalies-all-time-playoff-wins-leaders.html
www.hockey-reference.com/leaders/wins_goalie_career.html
www.bleacherreport.com/articles/1613684-ranking-the-most-dominant-regular-season-campaigns-in-nhl-history
www.hockey-reference.com/teams/DET/1996_games.html
www.redwingsnhl.com/club/news.htm?id=519458
www.hockey-reference.com/boxscores/199804010DET.html
www.hockeyfights.com/fights/5473
www.avalanche.nhl.com/club/stats.htm
www.nhl.com/ice/player.htm?id=8471262
www.avalanche.nhl.com/club/roster.htm

"COLUMBUS BLUE JACKETS"

www.foxsports.com/nhl/boxscore?id=10096
www.sportsecyclopedia.com/nhl/cbj/jackets.html
www.hockey-reference.com/teams/CBJ/
www.hockey-reference.com/teams/CBJ/2014.html
www.hockey-reference.com/teams/2014_games.html
www.hockey-reference.com/teams/CBJ/2009.html
www.usatoday30.usatoday.com/sports/scores/00/100281/100281374.htm
www.hockey-reference.com/boxscores/200010070CBJ.html

"DALLAS STARS"

www.exploratorium.edu/hockey/ice1.html
www.sportsecyclopedia.com/nhl/dallas/dalstars.html
www.mlive.com/redwings/index.ssf/2014/06/former_detroit_red_wings_cente.html
www.hockey-reference.com/leagues/NHL_1994.html
www.hockey-reference.com/teams/DAL/
www.hockey-reference.com/teams/DAL/2000_games.html
www.hockey-reference.com/players/m/modanmi01.html

"DETROIT RED WINGS"

www.historicdetroit.org/building/olympic_stadium/
www.hockey-reference.com/coaches/bowmasc99c.html

www.hockey-reference.com/teams/DET/
www.redwings.nhl.com/club/page.htm?id=43759
www.infobarrel.com/oldest_NHL_Arenas
www.quanthockey.com/hockey-stats/cn/profile.php?player=2573
www.washingtonpost.com/archive/lifestyle/1998/06/11/the-octopus-on-the-ice/
www.hockeyfeed.com/videos/bruise-brothers-video/
www.history.vintagemnhockey.com
www.hockey-reference.com/players/y/yzermst01.html
www.hockey-reference.com/playoffs/1997-detroit-red-wings-vs-philadelphia-flyers-
stanley-cup-final.html
www.redwings.nhl.com/club/page.htm?id=44034
www.hockey-reference.com/teams/BOS/
www.redwings.nhl.com/club/news.htm?id=731873
www.hockey-reference.com/teams/DET/2015.html
www.dropyourgloves.com/stat/players.aspx?league=1&season=2008&team=6
www.hockeydb.com/ihdb/stats/leagues/seasons/teams/0000342002.html
www.sports.espn.go.com/nhl/playoffs/2009/news?id=4133702
http://www.hockey-reference.com/players/f/fedorse01.html
http://www.hockey-reference.com/teams/DET/1996.html

"EDMONTON OILERS"

www.hockeydb.com/ihdb/stats/leagues/seasons/teams/0001711979.html
www.hockeydb.com/ihdb/stats/leagues/seasons/teams/0001721979.html
www.rauzulusstreet.com/hockey/nhlhistory/nhlhistory.html
www.hockey-reference.com/players/g/gretzwa01.html
www.hhof.com/htmltimecapsule/dyntmoil.shtml
www.hockey-reference.com/players/m/messima01.html
www.thepostgame.com/blog/throwback/201508/throwback-edmonton-oilers-
trade-eight-time-mvp-wayne-gretzky-los-angeles-kings
www.statshockey.homestead.com/nhlrecords.html
www.hockey-reference.com/teams/EDM/2006_games.html

"FLORIDA PANTHERS"

www.sportsecyclopedia.com/nhl/florida/flapanthers.html
www.hockey-reference.com/teams/FLA/
www.panthers.nhl.com/club/page.htm?id-61432
www.espn.go.com/nhl/attendance/_/year/2015
www.espn.go.com/nhl/attendance
www.hockey-reference.com/players/w/worrepe01.html
www.nhlplayoffsbracket.com/2012/

www.hockeydb.xom/ihdb/stats/pdisplay.php?pid=662
www.hockey-reference.com/boxscores/201204260FLA.html
www.hockey-reference.com/players/z/zedniri01.html
www.espn.go.com/nhl/history/leaders

"LOS ANGELES KINGS"

www.onthisdayinsports.blogspot.com/2013/03/march-11-1979-randy-holt-of-la-kings-is.html
www.hockey-reference.com/teams/LAK/
www.hockey-reference.com/players/w/williti01.html
www.hockey-reference.com/players/h/holtra01.html
www.quanthockey.com/nhl/records/nhl-players-all-time-penalty-minutes-leaders.html
www.thepostgame.com/blog/throwback/201508/throwback-edmonton-oilers-trade-eight-time-mvp-wayne-gretzky-los-angeles-kings
www.mayorsmanor.com/2012/05/1993-looking-back-at-the-la-kings-vs-toronto-maple-leafs/
www.mynewsla.com/sports/2015/10/07/kings-to-face-sharks-in-wednesday-season-opener-amid-changes/
www.quanthockey.com/nhl/records/nhl-players-all-time-assists-leaders.html
www.hockey-reference.com/players/g/gretzwa01.html
www.hockey-reference.com/boxscores/199305290TOR.html

"MINNESOTA WILD"

www.hockey-reference.com/teams/MIN/2015.html
www.hockey-reference.com/teams/MIN/2003.html
www.hockeywilderness.com/2013/9/6/4700306/goosebumps-re-living-the-wild-v-stars-first-match-up
www.mprnews.org/story/2007/12/17/hockeyusa
www.history.vintageminhockey.com/page/show/788323-timeline-of-minnesota-hockey-history-1883-1980
www.sportingcharts.com/articles/nhl/detailed-history-of-nhl-expansion-and-realignment.aspx
www.hockey-reference.com/teams/MIN/

"MONTREAL CANADIENS"

www.habs.com/montreal-canadiens-history/montreal-canadiens-hockey-hall-of-fame/
www.ourhistory.canadiens.com/greatest-moment/Stanley-Cup-No-1#timeline/

www.michmarkers.com/startup.asp?startpage=50690.htm
www.thepeoplehistory.com/icehockeyhistory.html
www.sportsecyclopedia.com/nhl/montreal/canadiens.html
www.hockey-reference.com/teams/MTL/
www.whof.com/htmlTimeCapsule/dyntmmon.shtml
www.hockey-reference.com/players/n/nilanch01.html
www.quanthockey.com/nhl/records/nhl-players-all-time-penalty-minutes-leaders
    .html
www.hockey-reference.com/coaches/bowmasc99c.html
www.quanthockey.com/nhl/records/most-wins-in-one-season-by-nhl-goalies.html
www.quanthockey.com/nhl/teams/montreal-canadiens-goalies-career-nhl-stats.html
www.allhabs.net/the-mario-tremblay-vs-patrick-roy-saga-who-is-to-blame/
www.hockey-reference.com/players/r/roypa01.html
www.quanthockey.com/nhl/records/nhl-goalies-all-time-playoff-wins-leaders.html

"NASHVILLE PREDATORS"

www.hockey-reference.com/players/r/rinnepe01.html
www.hovkey-reference.com/teams/NSH/
www.hockeydb.com/ihdb/stats/leagues/seasons/teams/0014121999.html
www.thehockeynews.com/blog/former-predator-patrick-cote-gets-30-months-in-
    prison-for-bank-heists/
www.hockey-reference.com/teams/NSH/2011_games.html

"NEW JERSEY DEVILS"

www.sportsecyclopedia.com/nhl/colnj/nhlrockies.html
www.sportsecyclopedia.com/nhl/kansascity/kcscouts.html
www.quanthockey.com/nhl/records/nhl-goalies-all-time-wins-leaders.html
www.hockey-reference.com/players/b/brodema01.html
www.hockey-reference.com/boxscores/199405270NYR.html
www.hockey-reference.com/teams/MDA/2003.html
www.sportsecyclopedia.com/nhl/nj/njdevils.html

"NEW YORK ISLANDERS"

www.lighthousehockey.com/2015/4/9/8351387/nassau-coliseum-history-before-
    new-york-islanders
www.nydailynews.com/sports/hockey/rangers/rangers-islanders-rivalry-article-1.160
    1683

www.sbnation.com/nhl/2014/8/26/6005021/new-york-americans-history-nhl-
   hockey-rangers
www.hockey-reference.com/teams/EDM/1983.html
www.nhl.com/ice/page.htm?id=31167
www.sportsecyclopedia.com/nhl/nyi/nyislanders.html
www.hockey-reference.com/teams/NYI/1980.html
www.nyidynasty.freeservers.com/1981-82/index.html
www.islanders.nhl.com/club/news.htm?id=465041

"NEW YORK RANGERS"

www.hockey-reference.com/teams/NYR/
www.sbnation.com/nhl/2014/8/26/6005021/new-york-americans-history-nhl-
   hockey-rangers
www.nytimes.com/2009/12/23/sports/hockey/23brawl.html?pagewanted=all
www.hockey-reference.com/teams/NYR/1994.html
www.nhl.com/ice/page.htm?id=31167
www.hockey-reference.com/players/m/messima01.html
www.hockey-reference.com/teams/NYR/2015.html
www.espn.go.com/nhl/history/leaders

"OTTAWA SENATORS"

www.sportsecyclopedia.com/nhl/ott/originalsens.html
www.hhof.com/htmlTimeCapsule/dyntmott.shtml
www.onthisdayinsports.blogspot.com/2013/02/february-26-1981-minnesota-north-
   stars_26.html
www.hockey-reference.com/teams/OTT/
www.scores.espngo.com/nhl/boxscore?gameid=240305015

"PHILADELPHIA FLYERS"

www.sportsecyclopedia.com/nhl/philly/flyers.html
www.hockey.ballparks.com/NHL/PhiladelphiaFlyers/old.index.html
www.rauzulustreet.com/hockey/nhlhistory.html
www.quakers.flyershistory.net
www.hockey-reference.com/teams/PHI/
www.hockey-reference.com/teams/PHI/1974.html

www.thehockeynews.com/blog/an-oral-history-of-the-broad-street-bully-era-phila-
  delphia-flyers/
www.quanthockey.com/nhl/records/most-penalty-minutes-in-one-season-by-nhl-
  players.html
www.hfboards.hockeysfuture.com/showthreadphp?t=514081
www.flyershistory.com/cgi-bin/hm.cgi?011hm
www.sportsecyclopedia.com/nhl/philly/flyers.html
www.espn.go.com/nhl/recap?gameid=240305015
www.nytimes.com/2010/05/15/sports/hockey/15flyers.html?_r=0
www.puckreport.com/2009/04/nhl-playoff-comebacks-trailing-3-0.html
www.hockey-reference.com/players/l/lindrer01.html

"PITTSBURGH PENGUINS"

www.hockey-reference.com/players/l/lemiema01.html
www.greatesthockeylegends.com/2006/09/mario-lemieux.html
www.espn.go.com/nhl/history/leaders
www.sportsecyclopedia.com/nhl/pittsburgh/penguins.html
www.hockey-reference.com/teams/PIT/
www.hockey-reference.com/players/j/jagrja01.html
www.hockey-reference.com/players/c/crosbsi01.html

"SAN JOSE SHARKS"

www.hockey-reference.com/teams/SJS/
www.sportsecyclopedia.com/nhl/sanjose/Sharks.shtml
www.hockey-reference.com/teams/SJS/1993_games.html
www.sharkspage.com/?page_id-116
www.hockey-reference.com/teams/SJS/2016.html
www.hockeydb.com/ihdb/stats/pdisplay.php?pid=1802

"ST. LOUIS BLUES"

www.rauzulustreet.com/hockey/nhlhistory/nhlhistory.html
www.sportsecyclopedia.com/nhl/ott/originalsens.html
www.hockey-reference.com/teams/STL/
www.hockey-reference.com/players/h/hullbr01.html
www.baseball-reference.com/teams/STL/

"TAMPA BAY LIGHTNING"

www.bethethunder.com/club-level-renovations-0
www.sportsecyclopedia.com/nhl/tampa/lightning.html
www.tampabay.com/sports/hockey/lightning/lightnings-triplets-line-a-unique-blend-on-off-ice/2225521
www.hockey-reference.com/teams/TBL/2015.html
www.hockey-reference.com/teams/TBL/
www.springtrainingonline.com/features/history-1.htm

"TORONTO MAPLE LEAFS"

www.hockey-reference.com/teams/TOR/
www.sportsecyclopedia.com/nhl/tml/leafs.html
www.legendsofhockey.net/legendsofhockey/jsp/legendsMember.jsp?mem=b1
www.proicehockey.about.com/od/stanleycupbunker/a/stanley-cuplist.htm
www.hockey-reference.com/teams/TOR/1993.html
www.fiveminutesforfighting.com/2012/09/a-history-of-world-ballards-villainy.html
www.abcnews.go.com/sports/story?id=99747&page=1
www.quanthockey.com/nhl/records/nhl-players-all-time-penalty-minutes-leaders.html
www.hockey-reference.com/players/d/domiti01.html
www.cbc.ca/sports/hockey/domi-suspended-for-playoffs-1.277856

"VANCOUVER CANUCKS"

www.hockey-reference.com/teams/VAN/
www.rauzulustreet.com/hockey/nhlhistory/nhlhistory.html
www.hockey-reference.com/players/b/burepa01.html
www.bc.ctvnewsca/1994-vancouver-riots-shadow-stanley-cup-final-1-657030
www.proicehockey.about.com/cs/history/a/nhl_suspensions.htm
www.spectorshockey.net/the-legacy-of-the-bertuzzi-moore-incident/
www.today.com/id/43461996/ns/today-today_news/t/vancouver-kissing-couple-reveal-secret-viral-photo/#.vfwfQLQVYqd

"WASHINGTON CAPITALS"

www.sportsecyclopedia.com/nhl/washington/capitals.html
www.hockey-reference.com/teams/WSH/
www.bleacherreport.com/articles/788978-nhl-history-the-10-worst-teams-in-nhl-history

www.hockey-reference.com/teams/WSH/1998.html
www.hockeyfights.com/fights/387
www.hockey-reference.com/teams/BOS/1999.html
www.hockeydb.com/ihdb/stats/pdisplay.php?pid=2774
www.hockey-reference.com/teams/WSH/1999.html
www.hockey-reference.com/players/o/ovechal01.html

"WINNIPEG JETS/WINNIPEG JETS 'VERSION 2.0'"

www.hockey-reference.com/teams/PHX/
www.cbc.ca/news/canada/manitoba/queen-portrait-that-hung-in-old-winnipeg-jets-arena-coming-home-1.2973613
www.hockey-reference.com/teams/WPG/
www.hockey-reference.com/teams/WPG/2012_games.html
www.hockeydb.com/nhl-attendance/att_graph_season.php?lid=NHL1927&sid=2011
www.rauzulustreet.com/hockey/nhlhistory/nhlhistory.html

"*YOU* GO AWAY MAD, WE'LL JUST GO AWAY"

www.hockey-reference.com/players/h/hullbo01.html
www.quanthockey.com/nhl/records/nhl-players-all-time-points-leaders.html
www.hockwey-reference.com/players/h/howego01.html
www.hockey-reference.com/teams/CAR/2006.html
www.onthisdayinsports.blogspot.com/2013/02/february-26-1981-minnesota-north-stars_26.html
www.hockey-reference.com/teams/DAL/
www.sportsecyclopedia.com/nhl/quebec/nordiques.html
www.hockey-reference.com/teams/QUE/1995.html
www.articles.courant.com/1992-10-18/sports/0000111039_1_le-colisee-toilet-paper-quebec
www.ourhistory.canadiens.com/opponent/Quebec-Nordiques
www.sportsecyclopedia.com/nhl/atlflames/aflames.html
www.hockey-reference.com/teams/WPG/
www.hockey-reference.com/teams/ATL/2007.html

"THE CASE OF COOKIE CUTTER VERSUS OLD SCHOOL"

www.hockey.ballparks.com/NHL/BostonBruins/oldindex.htm
www.basketball.ballparks.com/NBA/BostonCeltics/oldindex.htm
www.hockey.ballparks.com/NHL/ChicagoBlackhawks/oldindex.htm
www.basketball.ballparks.com/NBA/ChicagoBulls/oldindex.htm

www.hockey.ballparks.com/NHL/BuffaloSabres/oldindex.htm
www.hockey.ballparks.com/NHL/MontrealCanadiens/oldindex.htm
www.hockey.ballparks.com/NH:/TorontoMapleLeafs/
www.lakingsinsider.com/2012/11/19/there-used-to-be-an-arena-maple-leaf-gardens/
www.hockey.ballparks.com/NHL/NewYorkIslanders/
www.hockey-reference.com/players/h/howego01.html
www.hockey.ballparks.com/NHL/DetroitRedWings/oldindex.htm
www.quanthockey.com/nhl/records/nhl-players-all-time-points-leaders.html
www.hockey.ballparks.com/NHL/CalgaryFlames/oldindex.htm
www.hockey.ballparks.com/NHL/St.LouisBlues/oldindex.htm
www.hockey-reference.com/teams/STL/
www.hockey.ballparks.com/NHL/PittsburghPenguins/
www.sportsecyclopedia.com/nhl/nj/njdevils.html
www.basketball.ballparks.com/NBA/NewJerseyNets/
www.hockey.ballparks.com/NHL/EdmontonOilers/
www.hockey.ballparks.com/NHL/EdmontonOilers/newindex.htm

"A SÉANCE FROM THE BOOTH"

https://www.hhof.com/html/leg_broadcasters.shtml
www.habslegends.blogspot.com/2010/08/danny-gallivan.html
https://jabartlett.wordpress.com/2010/06/07/here-come-the-hawks/
https://canadainthe20sand30s.wikispaces.com/Foster-Hewitt+and+Hockey+Night+in+Canada
www.icehockey.wikia.com/wiki/Bob_Wilson_/hockey_announcer/

Index

About the Author

Kirk McKnight is an American author specializing in interview-based sports books ranging from the Zamboni-swept ice of hockey to the diamonds of baseball. A 2002 graduate of Brigham Young University's Marriott School of Business Management, he studied screenwriting as a postgraduate at the University of Nevada Las Vegas but subsequently transitioned his writing from fiction to nonfiction, with an emphasis on collegiate and professional sports. McKnight currently resides in Las Vegas, Nevada, with his wife, Collette, and daughter, Adaira.